DARE
TO BELIEVE

———————✳———————

Jean-Marie Cardinal
Lustiger

DARE
TO BELIEVE

✳

Addresses, Sermons, Interviews
·1981–1984·

Translated by Nelly Marans
and Maurice Couve de Murville

CROSSROAD · NEW YORK

1986
The Crossroad Publishing Company
370 Lexington Avenue, New York, N.Y. 10017

Originally published as *Osez croire: Articles, conférences, sermons,
interviews, 1981–1984* © Editions du Centurion, 1985
English translation by Nelly Marans copyright © 1986 by The Crossroad Publishing Company
Translation "Well, If I Must . . ." © 1986 by Maurice Couve de Murville

Library of Congress Cataloging in Publication Data

Lustiger, Jean-Marie, 1926–
Dare to believe.

Translation of: Osez croire.
1. Catholic Church—Doctrines. I. Title.
BX1755.L9713 1986   230′.2   86-4591
ISBN 0-8245-0778-9

Contents

Preface

Have you ever collected butterflies? If so, you may understand what I feel like in submitting these words for publication.

For the most part, these pages contain spoken words which were improvised under God's eye and were born from a continuous dialogue with men and women of all creeds, believers and nonbelievers alike. These words of mine, captured in the net of a tape recorder and then set down on paper, are like the butterflies pinned down in my collection as a child.

These words used to live. Sometimes they faltered. Often they stumbled. And here they are now, immobile and fixed in print. These words have become the book which you, the reader unknown to me, now hold in your hands. Between us how shall we recapture the sound of the voice? How shall we give birth to silence by an exchange of glances? How transcribe what can barely be uttered?

It is you who will make these words live now. What I said to a few individuals or to crowds of people matters less to me now than what you will say to yourself as you go through these pages quickly or pause here and there at your leisure. I only spoke to carry out the mission I had received. The Spirit of God to whom I tried to submit my spirit will whisper to your spirit as you speak to yourself. If I have allowed my words to be held fast like butterflies, it is because I hope that you will allow them to live again in yourself.

There is another secret I want to share with you readers whom I do not know. It is that I am happy to write to you. Among you are men and women whose thoughts and experiences are close to mine, even if your convictions are different, even if your discovery of God has taken another route. I know as I finish these lines that I am writing to brothers and sisters for whom I am waiting and who are waiting for me and with whom God has arranged for me a secret rendezvous.

Yes, I am happy to meet with you, thanks to these pages, you whom I shall not see perhaps until we recognize one another in the Jerusalem on high.

JEAN-MARIE CARDINAL LUSTIGER

Paris
Holy Week, 1986

THE
ARCHBISHOP
OF PARIS

The Role of the Bishop

*Y*ou *yourself were a priest in Paris. Before you officially came back as archbishop, you stressed your wish to celebrate the litugy and to preach. Was this not a way to protect yourself beforehand from the administrative work that is also part of your duties?*

No. When I said, "I want to celebrate," I wanted to recall to mind the bishop's role. The specific role of the bishop is within the context of the sacramentally gathered church.

When the church meets to celebrate the Eucharist and the sacraments, what she really is becomes visible. Of course the eucharistic celebration is not an object to be exhibited; it is not put in a show-case in order to be seen by others. But the church is not truly herself if she is not a church celebrating the Eucharist of Christ.

Christians can be perceived as a group of some kind, be it social or ideological, a movement, a party, a union, the followers of a philosophical school. But the only real image Christians can give of themselves is that of the church gathered in order to celebrate the Eucharist, of the church receiving its existence from Christ who is present and active.

To say that I want to celebrate means that if I do not bring about this sacramental gathering of the church, where one can see Christ forming her and giving her existence, I am a C.E.O., a party leader, a prime minister, or a professor, but not a bishop. In order for me to witness to the word, to proclaim the Gospel, to fulfill my mission

Interview by Patrice Canette and Henri Caro in *Le Pèlerin* [Catholic weekly], 10 May 1981.

3

as bishop sent by Christ to a people, this church must first be gathered; I was going to say that she has to exist in the flesh. Otherwise I'm just a solitary individual. But the Christian is always rooted in the church.

The apostle and the martyr might seem to be solitaries. This is only an appearance. Even if they are isolated, they are the representatives of the ecclesial communion. This is so true that in the past people used the bodily relics of martyrs for the eucharistic table. And the martyr himself or herself becomes a sign, a sacrament, of the whole church.

The bishop is not an isolated individual speaking on his own behalf. He is the surety, the sign that it is Christ himself who gathers his church, forms her, creates her unity. The church is not a club of friends who are in agreement and meet around a table. She does not exist because there is a crowd coming to listen to Father So-and-so, who is particularly eloquent. She is the assembly of those who believe that Christ gave them unity, and the ministry of the bishop lies in ceaselessly reminding believers that Christ is the head of a church that is constantly rent from within because she is made up of sinners.

This is why the ministry of the bishop, my ministry, is a ministry of gathering for the celebration of the Eucharist and the celebration of pardon, of reconciliation with God and reconciliation among brothers.

You are the archbishop of Paris. This title gives you a special responsibility with respect to the universal church—because you are a bishop and because you are in Paris.

The internal problems of French Catholicism prevent us at times from understanding the image that people have about us in foreign countries, especially in the Third World. The missionary drive throughout the world certainly owes much to France, historically speaking. France is seen as the symbol of the Christian country in the Western world. It might be that we are ill at ease with such an image because we perceive that things are not all that simple.

If we are faithful to our history as a creative Catholic nation, we have duties. First of all, we must be humble and not be deluded by the image reflected in the eyes of outsiders. One does not always live up to the level of one's own history. The churches of Africa, for instance, blame us for not being faithful to what we taught them and for remaining prisoners of our internal problems. We must not think that the universal church is contained in France and has to function like the church of France.

Moreover, we have to receive from others. We must have a good knowledge of the spiritual experience of other churches, of the Third World but also of Western and Eastern Europe, in order to return to our own fruitfulness. As a bishop I must bear, together with other bishops and the pope, the burden of all the churches. I am quite aware that the spiritual destiny of Paris is not determined in Paris but in solidarity with the whole Christian West. And the destiny of the West is determined in solidarity with that of the churches on other continents.

As a bishop I am in solidarity with the universal church and I must see to it that the diocese of Paris remains open to the call of the universal church. At the same time, I have to witness in my diocese to what is lived in the universal church, and secure the communion of a local church with the universal church.

The Tasks of a Parish
in the Years to Come

You should have been the ones to answer your own question about "the task of a parish today." Given the demands of faith and of the church, what can you really accomplish in this parish, within the present circumstances, taking into account your spiritual past, the priests with whom you work? . . . For my part, I will take a more general point of view.

The parish can be the focus of the most relevant innovation

How should we ask the question? You know that the concept of the parish is a very ancient one; it is linked to the whole of Christian history since this is the form of Christian community that has existed in our country down the centuries. Conversely, especially for younger generations, the parish conjures up something that is weighed down by age, laden with nobility and tradition, and therefore unlikely to renew and readjust itself. In a world where things move very fast, one can wonder whether the parish as it used to be can still function as it must. The parish of old was defined by its territory; one belonged to such and such a parish because one lived at such and such an address. This is clearly not the case anymore. But I will not go any further in this type of reflection. I prefer to define aims rather than limits: What must we do to help the formation of a Christian community?

Lecture at Saint-Ferdinand des Ternes, Paris, 30 September 1981.

Whatever we call a "parish" exists, after all, within the context of the strange and enormous world of Paris, the place where the existence of the church becomes visible and where new and significant forms of Christian existence can come into being. Not in spite of the difficulties of Paris, but because of them and also because of its riches. These places, these parishes, can and must be the centers where the life of the church is able to radiate with the greatest intensity. If nothing else, they should be foci of the most relevant and strongest responses to the needs of our time.

Not "what do people want" but "what does God ask"

Parishes have the merit of being, in an urban context, the visible sign of the church, hence a rallying point. Christians who belong to them have to prove to themselves that parishes are more than historical monuments. This visible and social sign will depend, in its workings and effectiveness, on what you will do with it. Far from being a foregone conclusion, these places of Christianity's emergence in the urban context, which I symbolize (as do most French people) with a spire; their force of impact and of innovation, their presence will be thrust totally into your hands. Your parish is a Christian community, a living form which must come to light today in such a way that the church of Christ will be able to carry on its mission.

Presenting the problem in such a way, I go against a certain vision of things to which we are only too used as consumers. Those among you who are familiar with the problems of urbanism know quite well the term "public facility" (for example, schools, stores, swimming pools, that is, places of service available to the public). In the same vein, there should be a church to meet the religious needs of people. The parish would be the facility capable of meeting the multiple demands of a certain potential public. One could say that a church makes a go of it if, like a department store, it has a sufficient inventory and is open for the satisfaction of existing needs.

I do not want to venture further in this direction, since the church, the parish, is not a facility available to whoever wants to use it. First of all, there is a responsibility that Christ gave you by asking you to be the church. The parish exists if it is a Christian community, not a facility in the hands of some people taking care of market demands. In its way, the parish is somebody; it is a subject of initiative, an articulate and living body responding to its vocation and accomplishing what God asks it to do.

The fundamental question is therefore: What do you do with this parish and what do you do with the call of God to his church?

How do you respond to this mission that God himself has given you, since he gave you the grace of being baptized and like unto Christ? The fundamental resource that is given you to face this mission is the Holy Spirit: this is the only capital of the church, her only resource. We can do without all the rest. The problem is no longer what is the purpose of the parish? but what is the vocation to which you are called, and what tasks have to bring you together. In a city like Paris, with so many diversified relationships, some which are kept, others which can't be, isn't it a challenge for us to want people to be aware that they form together the body of Christ and to be able to identify their common God-given mission?

This is your challenge. It is our task, under the power of God, with the strength of the Holy Spirit, to discover the forms that Christian existence must have in the society in which we live, with its flaws, its weaknesses, and also its riches.

Our very first task: the Eucharist

As people enter a church, vague, different, and strangers to one another, how can they form a body in such a manner that they could say: We are a community? What is our very first task?

The very first task is the eucharistic celebration, the Mass. It is through it that you exist as a church. You will say: "Father, you are dreaming. Things do not happen that way. People go to Mass; they get bored; they pray well and they pray poorly. There are people who come late or who leave early; they choose the Mass that is convenient to them either because of the schedule or the location, the preacher, the singing or lack of singing. In fact, we behave legitimately like the customers of a public utility."

I tell you that you have to reverse your attitude with respect to the Eucharist. Every Eucharist that is celebrated is an act that searches out each one of us and gathers us together in a body. It is an answer to a call, it constitutes the church and posits that each one of us is converted by the power of God and agrees to be so assembled at this particular moment, by the Spirit, so that we can become the body of Christ. Every assembly is a crucial event in our individual and our common history, punctuating our lives from week to week. Between two persons who have, on the same Sunday, listened from two opposite sides of the church to the same word of God, shared the same bread transformed into the body of Christ, shared the peace of God, there is a greater communion of faith than between two friends who spend an evening confiding in each other.

We must accept a radical vision of faith, making the sacrament of the Eucharist a creative locus of the existence of the church. To attain this vision of faith requires effort and dedication. It entails a common reflection, prayer, penance, a deeper penetration into the mystery of faith. The Eucharist is the creative act of the community establishing fellowship between those that God has gathered in it.

Put the heart at the center

The challenge to our faith is that the heart of faith must be our meeting ground and the strength of our assembly, rather than anything else. In general, we think in an opposite way: we should first know one another, first try to enter into a mutual sympathy, and then, at the end, we will be able to celebrate the Eucharist. I tell you that in our present life we must also be capable of reversing that direction, that is, being open to this action of God to the extent that each brother or sister who appears becomes a surprise and a gift. The Eucharist is therefore the first task of a church; it outlines the first circle of belonging. If you live the eucharistic celebration for a period of time, you well know that a way and a progression come into being among you. Thus the strongest core of the existence of a community and a parish can take shape.

This holiness which innervates the body of Christ is not only expressed in the Sunday Eucharist but also in the joy we have in the possibility of praying everyday when taking part in the Eucharist. In our world where the realities of the Gospel are absent, we must mitigate, with set purpose and the capacity to be together, the absence of daily landmarks, so that the inner force dwelling in us may be nurtured. In the often exhausting life of today one of the tasks of the parish is to set up a certain permanence of prayer, to give to people who have no place to pray at home (most people are unable to pray at home) the possibility to pray everyday, to devote a true moment, genuine and pure, to God. This is a possibility that you must give to one another.

Bear the unbelief or the ignorance of the majority

The other sacraments are also present as fundamental missions of this gathered community and delineate your very specific duties, one and all. Let's take baptism first. You may know that out of every one hundred young parents who bring a child to baptism barely ten—or eight or seven—come to Sunday Mass or belong unreservedly to the Christian faith. If you could bring together in this church all the people who asked for the sacrament of baptism for their child during the past year, you would realize that they are not the same kind of people you are. There are areas of belonging to the church which cross each other's path at times, but they rarely meet.

Catholics who have the grace to take part in the Eucharist, and thus to be in the living communion of faith, must not leave to priests alone the spiritual burden of those who have not received this same grace. In a parish different worlds interact and the big problem is: Is a believing community, which must become fervent, afire with the Holy Spirit, capable or not of carrying the burden of the unbelief or ignorance of those who still come to ask for the sacraments of the church? This is a big problem; this is one of the most serious questions we must be able to answer. And here, we have to deal with practical problems.

I should put in the same category, even though they are not sacraments, funerals. This is indeed one of the most fundamental and universal of human rituals. Should we leave it to paid professionals to face suffering and to offer compassion? Is it a waste of time in a Christian community to take seriously grief and suffering, sorrow and sickness? Don't we have here a humble and austere task that could yet create bonds of greater truth?

These acts of Christ that are the sacraments are truly the birth of a parish; they are your principal task. You will tell me: "This is the job of the priests. What can we do about it?" I will throw the question back at you: "What can *you* do about it?" What can be done—in the case of baptism, for instance—to witness baptismal life to people who know nothing about it? Who will explain to other parents how you live your marriage, how you received the birth of your children, what you discovered in the process? Who, if not other men and women, believers who have had the grace to live such an experience? How could the substance of Christian life be communicated outside of this creative brotherhood? What can be done if you are not fully participating in the preparation of the sacraments—indeed, even in their celebration?

Did you ever think about the situation of a priest who finds himself before a group of people among whom there isn't a single believer? How many times has such a priest asked himself: Where are the believers? You must be the ones who will carry this unbelieving people of Paris whose path will continue at times to cross that of the church. Not in order to lecture them, not in order to inflate your own importance, but in order to offer the brotherly love, patience, goodwill, welcome, and prayer, which makes these acts of faith effectively carried in faith.

A community which begins to exist in such a way becomes a place of spiritual fruitfulness.

The solitude of faith

There is a second point which we must stress. The fundamental attitude of the church is faith. This is what is expected of us as a church. And today there is no Christian existence without solitude in faith. I repeat: solitude. If you have children and they are not completely faithful to what you wanted to transmit to them, if you work in any environment and you have a normal social life, you can very well perceive that, as believers, you are often alone and going against the current. Let me add that one has to expect that Christians almost are compelled to become nonconformists.

We no longer live in the days when one could think that being a Christian amounted to being an honest person who, on top of it, believed in God. The "honest person" was so in the eyes of everybody. Now in our times, when it comes to the most decisive choices of human life, consensus is not in conformity with what the Gospel tells us; and when we want to remain faithful to a demand of Christ, be it moral or spiritual, or one of justice, we are alone most of the time and we perceive that we are in contradiction with what the rest of the world thinks. And even the affirmation of faith is in contradiction with public opinion.

In fact, faith is a struggle in which we find ourselves naked and solitary. It is not a question of having in oneself a certain capacity for affirmation, for intellectual response. We have to be able to make a choice: with the strength that God gives us we want to lean on God's word rather than on what other people think. This is very difficult because we ask ourselves: "Am I mad? After all, isn't faith an opinion, or something obsolete or untenable? Shouldn't the positions of faith be in conformity with what everybody repeats or deems reasonable?" We cannot bear this contradiction. Those who lose their faith are often people who cannot stand this state of contradiction. They lose faith because they cannot keep faith. We must give to one another the means to keep faith. How? Not merely by comforting one another, by reassuring ourselves, but by receiving together this strength of Christ which enables us to believe.

The heartbreak of faith

Here is another fundamental point about faith. He who believes takes part in the Passion of Christ. For the supreme act of Christ's faith—as we read in the Epistle to the Hebrews—is that through which he delivered himself to his Father in the surrender of death: this is faith. Faith does not simply consist in being sure of the catechism, reciting it, knowing it, being certain of it, and if one has a doubt asking someone else for help in overcoming it. Faith is always a participation in the Passion of Christ, because it means that we put ourselves into God's hands and that we accept, in this surrender to God rather than reliance on ourselves, being torn apart by our own contradictions. The heartbreak of our selfishness, our ignorance, our refusals. Faith confronts in us refusals, closed hearts, darkness. We cannot keep faith unless the Spirit keeps us in Christ. It is therefore necessary for a Christian community to be so imbued with the Spirit of God, the love of Christ, faith in the Father, that when we falter, we can find at our side the brotherly support of our companions in the Passion of Jesus who can help us, carry our weakness, listen to our discouragement, give us strength from above.

Speak the Gospel as your mother tongue

Faith is a gift given to the church and the church shares it among her members. In this experience—in the strongest sense of the word— your very existence finds a new structure. You must therefore give to one another the means to structure this experience, and to understand and discover the word of God. To put it simply: you have to read the Gospel together, and not only on Sunday. You have to give to one another the means to read the Bible and to pray: this is the food without which your faith will falter.

You cannot read Scripture any which way. You must read it as a word uttered by Christ among you that gives you the meaning of the history you are going to live. By receiving this living word of Christ himself speaking in his church, you live in a history, the entire history of the People of God which becomes your own. The question is not to make Christianity present to modern cultures: it is so, more than you think. What you, Christians, must do is to acquire this Gospel as your mother tongue and to take as your own the history to which you are the heirs; otherwise you become lost children. This cannot happen without work. The word of God must become your mother tongue, must inspire your heart, dwell in your spirit, nourish your life; this familiarity with God which keeps us in his church must become the very heart of your life.

We must therefore endeavor to welcome and nurture Christian life. Therein lies a most important task without which you cannot respond to your vocation. For you yourselves are the spokespersons of God since you are Christians. The word of God must be so anchored in you that God can utter it through you. We do not have to give you recipes so that you can find adequate words to answer colleagues at work. Ideally, each one of us, according to his or her talent and life, must be so filled with this word that God may be able to use us as he wills.

Witnesses for the young

A parish is also a focus of the contagion of faith. One of the most essential points is the matter of the younger generations. In our society the generation gap is a terrible thing. It is a challenge to society and church. As a Christian community you must respond to this challenge. It is not easy. But a church which is not capable of transmitting—even in a split society—her essential riches to her children, is clearly a church in danger of death.

I know that there are institutional means:

catechism (the role of the church is to have the means to adapt the
    catechism so as to make it effective and faithful)
chaplaincies

Catholic schools (and under our present circumstances, you know that the bishops want to maintain this fundamental freedom which is one of the ways through which the church is able to transmit the faith to young people).

But these means are of no help without the will of Christians to transmit, as a community and with God's help, the living experience of faith. I am now talking about a most painful matter: I am convinced that there are parents among you who have had the sad experience of seeing their children turn away from faith. They may still ask themselves why and how such a move took place.

Things must not be judged in terms of personal responsibility. At no time must you think over and over: "It is my fault." After all, you don't know. Entrust the matter to God's mercy. Only God knows that fruits will come from what you did for your children. But on the whole, when the gap in faith follows the generation gap, there is tragedy.

You will say: "There is nothing that we can do; this is the way things are in a secular society." And I answer: This is a challenge. Take one another's hand, live your faith, help one another, be strongly committed, take initiatives. There is a need for time and energy. You will tell me: "We cannot do it" You cannot? Well, I don't know. It all depends on what matters to you. I am going to be very harsh: What is most important to you? To succeed in your professional life or to keep your home intact so that your children may have both a father and a mother? . . .

The society in which we live does not make it easy. We have to ask more radical questions now than in the past and know what price we are ready to pay for the fruitfulness of Christianity. I find it scandalous that there are no adults capable of devoting more time and generosity to care for the life in Christ of children and young people. Not that this burden has to be carried by all; but Christianity has always been a tremendous source of dedication, vocations, extreme generosity. This is the proof that the Spirit is at work. Remember that masses of people gave their lives for the poor, the sick, remote countries, lost causes.

Who is shirking his or her job? God or you? And if young people do not have the witnesses they need, is it their fault? They are not what you expected and what we expected, true enough. But their life is not that easy. Do you think that it is easy to keep a moral and a spiritual discipline in a world where one is constantly bombarded with noises, images, obsessions of the senses? Do you think that it is easy to lead a moral life without having been given an education, a discipline, a mastery of one's body and one's sleep? To master desire when everything is being done to exacerbate the desire for possessions and money? We must help the young to live concretely the demands of the Gospel and the strength of God's word.

This can only be a collective undertaking. Some parents are totally incapable of doing it by themselves. They have the right to count on others. There are difficult situations in our society: broken homes, sickness, economic problems, enforced separations, moral difficulties. But let all help the others, let all come out of their solitude. This too is a parish.

Renunciation

You must create such a contagion of love and communion that anybody who is "lost" may find a welcome, any sick person a consolation, and anyone in despair a word and a gesture. You will tell me that this is a day-dream. Yes, it is a day-dream: go out in the streets, nobody pays attention to anybody else. We must go against the current and only the power of God's love can help us to do so. Such a love is creative; it is tolerant, welcoming, richly inventive. It bears with everything; it forgives everything; it is patient (1 Cor. 13). It is a source of strength and joy.

A parish, a Christian community, must be a perpetual center of reconciliation because we share continuously the forgiveness of God. In our society people get away from one another, become specialized and push one another away, exclude one another according to ideologies, competences, hierarchies. To find one another calls each time for a tremendous amount of energy because one must overcome separation. The differences are such that it is often impossible to find one another in genuine love. In this divided and hostile world, where people hurt or ignore one another, we must prove that a reconciling love is possible, that Christians are not sectarian, that they forgive one another and that they accept the sufferings they inflict on one another. The pope calls this "a civilization of love."

This capacity to reconcile generations, ideologies, backgrounds, and experiences is the ultimate challenge of the society in which we live. Not in order to do away with differences, but to enable people who are different to find one another again. Remember this sentence of Saint Paul, which is a provocation, because he announces as a present reality what is to come at the end: "There are no more distinctions between Jew and Greek, slave and free, male and female, but all of you are one in Christ Jesus." (Gal. 3:28). In a situation where there are still men and women, slave and free, Greek and Jew, how can one live in such a way that this communion of love, of equality and mutual respect is anticipated, already lived in the Christian community? To love one another in such a way requires all the strength of Christ.

The only real question

The final question that I will leave with you is the following: Have you taken up Christianity or have you allowed Christ to take you over? Are Christians the masters of Christianity, deciding what it should be, or is it Christ who, through his Spirit, takes hold of you and leads you where you do not want to go? The future of the church in Paris and elsewhere does not lie in the wise administrative steps the archbishop could take, or in the competence of decisions or techniques, but in whether we are going to let ourselves be grasped by Christ. This is the decisive problem because it is the sine qua non of freedom. As long as we have not let ourselves be grasped by Christ, we are not free and we do not respond to the call of God.

My hope and my conviction—my act of faith—are that, since you are baptized, since God has loved you, since you are heirs to all the riches of the Kingdom, God will raise from among you poor men and poor women who will respond to this call. God will raise all those who will follow Christ to the end, and they will carry their brothers and sisters and the brothers and sisters will carry them. God will make us capable of sharing in the Passion of Christ and will make us capable of loving one another. Hence I am not worried about the problem of vocations. If there are living Christians, those who are needed by the church will stand up and others too will rise to go elsewhere, where the Spirit will want them to go.

The act of faith I am making is the mission that Christ entrusted to me. But I can make it only by asking you to make it. I am not pushing you. I am not exhorting you. I do not ask you for anything. I am talking to you in God's name. We must surrender to him. Our lives must give glory to him. For our mission is to bring to this world the light that can make human life beautiful, the love that makes life worthy of love, the hope that makes human life desirable. You know quite well that our society does not love life; it does not give life anymore—physically—to its children. At times, too often, it takes it away from them. Love life, and our country will live and men and women will love life. Let yourselves be loved by God who is life and you will be witnesses to life, to generosity, to superabundance.

No Religious Marketing

*T*elevision viewers saw the archbishop of Paris in the street when he stood, for instance, in front of a department store to talk about the temptation of riches and money. Is this not the beginning of a new form of witnessing and preaching?

With your permission, I do not want people to confuse two different moments: the Liturgy of the Word itself and the homilies of the Mass, and the short fifteen minute films made by the team of *Day of the Lord* and shown before Mass.[1]

When I preach—as any parish priest—I am only the servant of God's word for Christians who pray with me, wherever they happen to be. The television viewer does not "monitor" the televised Mass. He or she takes part in it. The word of God acts on the viewer also. In the homily, which is an integral part of the eucharistic liturgy, the priest (that I continue to be) is literally the voice of Christ present in the church. The word of God he has the mission to transmit does not belong to him.

By preaching Lent and the Resurrection of Christ I was not aware of doing something "new." I did my job as a priest, in its most essential aspect.

On the other hand, in connection with this Lenten preaching, the

Interview by Dominique Gerbaud and André Madec in *La Croix* [Catholic daily], 18–19 April 1982.
1. The program *Day of the Lord* appears before the nationally televised Mass each Sunday. (Translator's note)

team of Day of the Lord asked Father Philippe Farin to make short films. He put me in certain situations: in the street, among religious sisters, at Père-Lachaise cemetery. Even if these conversations retain a spiritual character, they are similar to what television can do with scientists, writers, politicians, and ordinary people.

Does this street "preaching" herald a more frequent mingling of the archbishop with the people? Is not your place in the street?

Contrary to what some people may believe, I have to fight against this temptation. If I let myself go, I would spend my time meeting people in the street and elsewhere. Personally, I prefer such contacts and the grass roots to the study of files.

But the responsibility of an archbishop—and my duty is not to shirk it—involves many other tasks which are time consuming. If I do not take care to remain faithful, I know that I might lose my soul. I have to remain a priest who acts like a priest. I could risk losing my soul and also the purpose of my ministry: I would not be what God wants me to be: for me, this is a serious problem.

What impact can certain gestures have: for instance, shaking hands with people, taking a child to one's side?

I do not separate gestures from words. For me, they are truly in solidarity with words and connected in a manner of being. The only way to preach is to be faithful and obedient to a word. Thus I find myself in a situation which is opposed to that of an advertiser. The advertiser or the translator thinks: "There is a message and there is a medium; therefore I must look for the best translation, the best expression of the message, for the one who is going to receive it." They will thus articulate all their logic on the basis of the study of the target.

You did not think about your "target"?

Absolutely not. When I am in church, I talk to the people among whom I celebrate the Eucharist. If God gives me the opportunity to talk to people who are elsewhere, I can address them at the same time. The word to which I witness is a true word, uttered at a given moment, by someone to someone.

And this is a weakness that some journalists hold against me. I am unable to supply ahead of time the text of the words I have to speak.

For the characteristic of the spoken word is precisely that of not being a ready-made text. Otherwise it is not the same type of word. This does not mean that I do not make preparations. Quite the contrary: I reflect, I pray as long as I can, I meditate on the mystery of the word of God. At the same time, I think about the person or persons I am going to address.

In spite of all, television might still help preaching?

To the extent that television can still be the tool of the true word spoken to someone, yes.

Are you pessimistic?

Television can be a major tool used to free oneself from obligation, to put on a show, and thus to go against the spreading of the true word. There are all kinds of traps both for the speaker and the listener.

The one who talks runs the risk of becoming a prisoner to the system of the image, of being lured by the vain desire to show off, to be sensitive to compliments and criticisms. This is difficult because, at the same time, we do tell ourselves: "Watch it! In order to come off well on TV, I have to make such and such a gesture." The technique itself tends to determine the attitude. It is a perversion that comes extremely fast. I fight it as if it were a disease. There really is need for rigorous asceticism of thought, spirit, and heart, which will make us shrug off all this. If one wants to preach the Gospel, one must be a real man.

But isn't there a positive aspect?

Undoubtedly, simply because what I have said can be heard and heeded by millions of people. I have had many positive testimonies to this effect. Yet I spoke to people I do not know: a word tossed like a bottle into the ocean. Many people were able to find and open the bottle, and perhaps profit from it. A word that can go who knows where, reach who knows whom, and produce a fruit we know nothing about—like the Spirit.

On the side of the viewer is another disadvantage: the distance that the screen puts between him or her and reality. The viewer is involved in an imaginary or unreal way, even with live programs. I would even dare to say that he or she is a *voyeur*. And even in the face of the most horrible facts that should call for indignation, pity, or love, the viewer "shields" himself or herself. Everything becomes image and simulation. Including death, slaughter, and destruction. The trap is the distance, the look of detachment.

The church generally responds to the request of the media. She intervenes when asked to do so. But shouldn't she create the event?

If I do something because it will be watched on television, it is not as if I did it for God and it is then filmed. Remember what Jesus said: "Be careful not to parade your good deeds before men to attract their notice. . . . Your Father who sees all that is done in secret will reward you" (Matt. 6:1–4). Many people know how to use television. Thus, while I am sympathetic to the world of the media which is that of our civilization, I do not intend to be an accomplice of it.

For instance, I know quite well that there is a specific law of the media: "In order to be heard," journalists say, "things have to click and must be what we call news."

But we have to keep our independence, otherwise we would transform the preaching of the Gospel into fidelity to the laws of marketing. I have already been approached: you should go into religious marketing. . . .

You don't want to do it?

No. Absolutely not. For I believe that this is something perverted and contrary to the law of the Gospel. It is not impure, but I believe that the means are not proper for faith. The product cannot come through this channel because the Gospel is not a "product"; it is an act of God.

And the first step in genuine preaching is to obey God who creates freedom and truly speaks to another's freedom. God is the one who speaks and even acts. The Gospel is an act in itself. It is the Good News, that is, someone who tells the Good News. God utters it through human lips and it calls for a listening attitude. At the most, it can lead to martyrdom. To carry this word supposes that one is ready to be identified with this word, which is itself martyrdom and gift of life. Christians know that they are open to crucifixion. They know that, in some way, they will be crucified by this word they are carrying. Such is the inner logic of this word.

Will television be able to play any new role in preaching? Will television finally make up for the lack of priests that everybody is bemoaning?

No. A certain type of word in a given network of communication does not belong to the same order of things as the presence of priests within the Christian people.

If the mode of expression by television spreads more than it has done so far, one can imagine in all probability that there will be an increased use of all systems of recording and transmission. This is good because it is a richer, more personal, warmer, more communicative form of expression, if we know how to use it. But it remains completely outside of the order of replacing the priest as such—as a book does not replace a teacher, a novel does not replace a friend, nor a poem a word of friendship or truth. When one feels like crying, one can open a book, but this will not replace a firm handshake. The specific role of the priest in the Christian community, even if there are fewer priests, will remain irreplaceable.

You Do Not Obey Me

The ecclesiastic hierarchy has often been compared with a military type of organization. Do you consider yourself, as archbishop of Paris, some kind of general?

A general or a union leader or a manager or an executive has to rule over others, to organize actions, to manage the specific interests of the organization. Is this the case for a bishop? The comparison is promptly shown for what it is: the object of the church's action, just like the nature of the bond between Christians, remains beyond the grasp of observation. What are the "results" that the church aims at? What could she put on the "balance sheet" of her action? Neither the number of the "members" nor the "turnover" are pertinent criteria. Look at the churches that are wealthy: one can be paralyzed by its riches, while another, on the contrary, is constantly giving to the poorest. Look at the churches that draw large crowds: one presents Christianity only as a complex of social conventions; another, on the contrary, enables people to live the Gospel on a daily basis. Another church, persecuted and naked, insignificant in the eyes of the powers that be, is for a certain people, however, the only guarantee of truth, justice, peace, and freedom without compromise. I will not name any country because it is not my function to mete out reproaches or praises. But I have in mind very specific situations in the past and present. This shows one thing: the "organization" of the church cannot really be compared to other organizations because the church is

Interview by Gérard Dupuy and Luc Rosenzweig in *Libération* [popular Parisian daily with left-wing leanings], 27 September 1983.

23

built on a challenge. Our "boss," Jesus the Messiah, was executed together with "common criminals." He does not teach us hatred or revenge, but love for the life he is giving us.

Nevertheless, your position, whether it be at the head of the diocese of Paris or in the church of France, gives you authority over both people and matters of doctrine. Now the Catholic church does not exactly have the reputation of being a democracy.

She is, as a matter of fact, far *more* than a democracy. All things considered, democracy is nothing more than a form of arbitration for the benefit of the majority and it retains a power of coercion (in principle, that of the representatives of the people). Hierarchical power, in the church, is the service of believers so that one and all can surrender to the authority of God who alone can gather people in a truly free "communion."

I have often thought about the libertarian slogan "Neither God nor Master." It seems to me that it "borders" the experience of Israel and that of the church. We, for our part, know that only God is the Lord of humankind, for only God gives us existence in freedom. All other powers run the risk of becoming abusive and alienating. In the church we are all subject to a radical and permanent critique through our common faith in God. The one who orders is like the one who obeys.

Take the domain of faith, in other words, the domain of "orthodoxy" or "right thought." If I see someone who—it seems to me—is deviating from this line, I can and must tell him or her, while justifying that what I say is truly the faith of the church. But I cannot put myself in the person's place, face to face with his or her own conscience. Therefore such a person will listen to me only to the extent of the credit he or she freely grants, not to myself, but to the "service" that I perform in the name of the "mission" I have received. When he or she listens to me, it is God who is obeyed, not myself. Just so do I obey God if I talk to someone in a just and legitimate way.

If someone does not listen to you, are you going to take sanctions?

What sanctions? It is not a sanction—in the coercive sense of the term—to find and judge that the opinion of one person or another is not consistent with the faith of the entire church. Should such persons stick to their viewpoint, this "judgment" will however bring about a difference: what they say will no longer be considered representative of the Catholic faith. . . .

The One God Wants to
Speak Through Our Mouth

Luke 6:12–26

Now it was about this time that he went out into the hills to pray; and he spent the whole night in prayer to God. When day came he summoned his disciples and picked out twelve of them; he called them "apostles": Simon, whom he called Peter, and his brother Andrew, James, John, Philip, Bartholomew, Matthew, Thomas, James son of Alphaeus, Simon called the zealot, Judas son of James, and Judas Iscariot who became a traitor.

He then came down with them and stopped at a piece of level ground where there was a large gathering of his disciples with a great crowd of people from all parts of Judaea and from Jerusalem and from the coastal region of Tyre and Sidon who had come to hear him and to be cured of their diseases. People tormented by unclean spirits were also cured, and everyone in the crowd was trying to touch him because power came out of him that cured them all.

Then fixing his eyes on his disciples he said:

"How happy are you who are poor: yours is the kingdom of
  God.
Happy you who are hungry now: you shall be satisfied.
Happy you who weep now: you shall laugh.

"Happy are you when people hate you, drive you out, abuse you, denounce your name as criminal, on account of the Son of Man. Rejoice when that day comes, and dance for joy, then your reward will be great in heaven. This was the way their ancestors treated the prophets.

25

"But alas for you who are rich: you are having your consola-
tion now.
Alas for you who have your fill now: you shall go hungry.
Alas for you who laugh now: you shall mourn and weep.
Alas for you when the world speaks well of you! This was the
way their ancestors treated the false prophets."

We are carried by the prayer of Jesus. This church built on our gathered lives finds its shape in that solitary night when Jesus went into the hills to pray so that, at last, when day came, he chose the Twelve, giving them as Saint Luke says, the name of "apostles."

The names I enumerated again when proclaiming the Gospel are not those of the founders of a new genealogy.

I am aware, in this cathedral of Notre-Dame of Paris, of being, with many of you, the heir of the archbishops I succeeded and whom I knew directly or indirectly: Cardinals Verdier, Suhard, Feltin, Veuillot, Marty. But if our lives are thus linked to theirs by the functions they had, the episcopal succession cannot be understood as a family genealogy or a political lineage. One and all, bishops and priests, we are installed by the very act of Christ who chooses and names the apostles. The church is not born of herself, unlike a human begetting or a historical succession. The church does not cease to be born from the act of Christ that constitutes her. And if, in the tradition of the church, the apostolic succession has always been considered a necessary condition for the authenticity of the episcopal ministry, it is precisely because it shows fidelity toward the founding act of Christ; this founding act is not an origin fading away little by little into the past, but the very act of Christ who gives life to the church of today.

We must therefore greet one another as called today by Christ, gathered today by Christ. Only then do we understand that our life in the church is a mission, that the only purpose of our life is a vocation. For, as we found out, we are among the people whom Jesus calls, whom he gathers, who come to bring him their diseases, their listlessness, their sadness, their struggles, their hopes.

The ministry that was entrusted to me and that I share with so many here, bishops and priests (I am keenly aware of this) makes us messengers, spokesmen for the one God who wants to speak through our mouth. The Father in heaven lets us know his Word made flesh

Homily at Notre-Dame of Paris, 13 February 1983, upon Cardinal Lustiger's return from Rome where he had been elevated to the rank of cardinal.

who now echoes throughout the world, and lets us believe in him. The Spirit gathers us and allows us to utter this living word that we had the grace to receive. Yes indeed, brothers, the Gospel we just heard describes the truth of what God wants to do with us today.

And so we can understand the meaning of the blessings that Jesus speaks over us. For the Beatitudes "Happy are you . . ." just like the cries of sadness "Alas for you . . ." are part of the prayer of Jesus for us: they are not inscriptions on a wall, words to be made into slogans, affirmations that could be used in a program. They are blessings or, on the other hand, cries of sadness coming from Jesus. The Son looks at the disciples that the Father gives him, the messianic people we belong to; and in advance, he utters upon his people the words of the Beatitudes. These blessings are for us, if we act with the strength of the Holy Spirit, in conformity with the commandments of the Father that Christ gives us. Yes, the word that dwells in us is a powerful word, capable of making us act in conformity with the holy will of the Father, of making us act as brothers and sisters of Christ, of making us act by manifesting the love with which we are loved. The commandment of Christ dwells in us and also the possibility of fulfilling it and the strength to be faithful to it. And the blessing of Christ is uttered upon us, just as is the sadness in which he will keep us company if, unhappily, we were to become estranged from it.

Happy the poor and alas for you who are rich. This blessing makes us into a messianic people called to find no consolation in all the riches of the world. Consoler is one of the names of the Messiah, one of the names of Christ. God asks us to put our hope not in any of the riches of this world, our strength not in any of the riches of this world, but only in the riches and the strength of God. The Father calls us in Christ to become poor so that the Kingdom of God may be made manifest and be given to us.

Then, if we accept that Christ utters this blessing upon us, how happy we are! Happy are you, you, my brothers and sisters, whose only treasure is God. Then, poor in God, you will know how to share with those who are hungry the riches of this world which do not belong to you; then you will know how to live in the justice and the truth revealed by God as the fundamental law of his love; then you will know that in this world only God is alive and wants all of us to live since he is the creator and redeemer of all humankind. Happy are the disciples of Christ whose only treasure is God.

Happy the disciples of Christ *who are hungry now. Alas for you who have your fill now.* For you are those in whom God brings about a new hunger for the banquet of the Kingdom of heaven. Alas for you if you have stifled this hunger! Happy are you if it dwells in you for then you will be able to witness in this world to the hope given by the Spirit, given by Christ, a hope that is greater than the sum of all the miseries in the world. But you, my disciples, alas for you if you already have your fill now, for you will be hungry when the table of the banquet of heaven will be laid out.

Happy are you, you my disciples, *who weep now, but alas for you who laugh now,* for you will mourn and weep. Now if you are my disciples, your tears are blessed. Blessed are your tears when you grieve over the unhappiness of man, over injustice and sin, the cries of those who reject God, when you grieve over the sadness of the Passion of the Son of man. Happy are you and happy in your tears, if you do not resign yourselves to God not being manifested in this world. Happy are you if you cannot accept that God seems to be deaf to the cries of men and women, silent when they fall into the dumbness of death. Happy are you if you weep because you know that consolation is given, that you will laugh with the very laughter of God who raises the dead. But alas for you if you laugh now, unconcerned with the weight of the trial bearing upon the men and women who do not know the joy that God wants to keep for them.

Lastly, *happy are you when people hate you,* you my disciples, you will be able to know the fate of the master in his Passion, since you are, you brothers and sisters of Christ, called to be, in this time and in history, Christ, Christ manifested in your mortal bodies, Christ manifested in your weaknesses that he took upon himself, Christ manifested in his body that is the church. Then, when you will suffer the Passion that the Son of man wanted first to subject himself to, when you will feel loneliness and rejection in the name of Christ, because of Christ, rejoice and be glad, leap for joy for your reward is great with God. This is the way the prophets are treated. You, beloved disciples of Christ, are called to be witnesses to the only prophet, Christ: you are those through whom God speaks in this time. But alas for you if, in you, Christ no longer speaks. Alas for you if, running away from the Passion of the Son of man, you are nothing but complacency. Alas for you if you are praised for yourselves, for this is the way their ancestors treated the false prophets.

My brothers, my friends, these blessings that Jesus utters upon his church must be a permanent source of strength and courage for us. These words of Jesus help us today, at each step, to go forward with greater fidelity. These words, singing in the depths of our hearts, and the compassion of Christ for our falterings encourage our joy and our faithfulness.

Brothers and sisters, as you see, the mystery of the church cannot be compared to any reality one can point out in this world. It is neither a power, nor a group, nor a history like one contained in a human genealogy. It is Christ making himself present by the very act through which he makes us his church. In his shared banquet, in this Eucharist where the body is given up and the blood is shed, where we ourselves become what we receive, let us be filled with the gladness and joy that Christ meant for us.

OUR JEWISH ROOTS

⸻ ✳ ⸻

Well, If I Must . . .

Translated by Maurice Couve de Murville

Y.B.P.: I would like to ask you, first of all, what difference do you see existing today between the Jewish people and the people of Israel. Is there any difference between them, do you think?

It is difficult for me to answer because those are theoretical questions. Even among Jews there are different ways of stating the relation between Israeli identity and the identity of the Jewish people. I cannot pretend to have a definitive view on that question. But I can express my personal feelings; I would say that they are not identical but that one is part of the other.

The notion of the Jewish people has many different aspects; it can mean a religious belonging or a historical one. For a Jew, the feeling of belonging to a people is both very powerful and very fluid. It has different degrees. Historically, if one is talking about present-day Jewish consciousness, I don't see how one can define belonging to the Jewish people (I am not saying belonging to "Judaism") without some reference to the State of Israel. And I do not see how the State of Israel can be defined without including the wider notion of the Jewish people. I know that in saying that I am disassociating myself from certain points of view; for instance, there used to be a "Canaanite" tendency among Israeli intellectuals[1]; I do not know if it still exists.

Interview by Y. Ben Porat (Y.B.P.) and D. Judkowski (D.J.) in *Yediot Haharonot* [Israeli daily], 6, 15, and 21 January 1982; published in French in *Le Débat*, no. 20, May 1982. Maurice Couve de Murville is the archbishop of Birmingham, England.

1. This tendency existed among the first settlers of Israel and recommended the abandonment of their Jewish character. Later the movement urged the Jews in Israel to merge with non-Jews and to create a local political and cultural system.

33

Y.B.P: Yes, it does.

At the opposite end of the scale, I know that there are Jews, both in Israel and in the Diaspora, who consider that they are not committed to the State of Israel. So there cannot be a clear-cut answer. But for me a link does exist.

Y.B.P.: So you would say that the State of Israel is not a state like other states.

I can quite see that other states, when faced with the particular country called Israel, entertain the same sort of relation with it they have with any other state. I can quite see that politicians in Israel, who are faced with political problems, deal with them in the way that other states do (or in the way that they ought to do if they were honest and respected their proper ends and ideals). But it is none the less a unique state. Its origins, its identity are not the same as those of any other country. It is the outcome of an extraordinary utopia which became a historic reality. That utopia was brought up to date by the dreams of the European nineteenth century, but it stretches back through several thousand years of community consciousness. I cannot think of any comparable case in the whole of history.

However, one must also say that Israel is a state like other states, and it is proper to say this, otherwise Israel would come to occupy a position which would be threatening for other nations. There is also the risk of imposing on Israel a false messianic consciousness; that would be morally perverse and politically disastrous. There have been examples of "messianic states" in history and they have all come to a very bad end. A state must be a state.

However, whenever one hears Jewish people saying, either in Israel or elsewhere, "We want to be a people like any other," one cannot help wondering whether this desire includes a hidden temptation. Is it not for a Jew a way of running away from his or her vocation? So there is a kind of inner contradiction here. I expect you recognize the allusion to the first Book of Samuel where that contradiction already exists.[2]

Y.B.P.: I would like to ask the question at a practical level, a personal level almost. You have in front of you two Israeli journalists who are also Jews. Do you make the distinction? Do you think of us as Jews or do you

2. "The people refused to listen to the words of Samuel. They said, 'No! We want a king, so that we in our turn can be like the other nations'" (1 Sam. 8:19).

*think of us as Israelis, that is, two non-Frenchmen who hold the passports
of a foreign state?*

I find the distinction hard to make. But I can say this. I have often
been to the Near East and to Israel; in fact, I have been there nearly
every year since 1950, as a student first, then as a chaplain to students. Well, it seems to me that Israelis are not Jews like other Jews.

Y.B.P.: Is that a good thing or a bad thing?

I don't know. But I can quote two conversations I had some time
between 1950 and 1960. I met a Belgian Jew; he had been a doctor
and became a teacher in a kibbutz, somewhere in Galilee. He had
lost his entire family during the war so that he was alone in the
world and he made his *alyah*[3] to Israel. As there were too many
doctors, he became a teacher. He was telling me that he liked the
sabras.[4] But suddenly he said, "They no longer have that Jewish intelligence; they are slow, calm, pleasant" *(laughter)*. He was a very
cultured man and that was a most extraordinary thing to say.

At about the same time I had a heated discussion, lasting all night,
with the director of the school of agriculture in Galilee; you know,
that round building. I think Moshe Dayan was a student there for a
time.

Y.B.P: Ygal Allon went there.

Did he? Anyway the director I am talking about was an extraordinary person, an old man of Russian origin. I had shared some of
my misgivings with him. I said: "You are creating here a national
consciousness. That's a good thing, I can quite see the negative side
of things for Jews in Europe, and it is in reaction to it that you exist
here. You are developing a utopia; only here it has become a reality.
You and your contemporaries are rooted in the consciousness of a
particular historical situation. But what about the generation which
will come after you? Where will its strength come from? Will nationalism alone suffice to provide the will to survive? What will the inner
coherence of the people be? How will people be motivated for sacrifice? This drive to become "people like other peoples," does it not
come finally from the fact that you were not like other people? Comes
the day when you are just like other nations, when you are just Is-
raelites, where will the will come to live differently from other na-

3. *Alyah,* literally a "going up"; the return of the Jews to the land of Israel.
4. *Sabra* is the Barbary fig, which is hard on the outside but sweet inside. It is the nickname
for Jews born in Israel.

tions? And what will your contact be then with the Jews throughout the world?

Υ.B.P.: That's exactly the question I am asking you. But how do you see the Jews? Do you see them as having special attributes?

What do you mean by that?

D.J.: Are they considered particularly intelligent?

I shouldn't rely on that judgment as it is made by non-Jews *(laughter)*. I would tend to give a theological definition of what a Jew is; that is, a religious definition.

Υ.B.P.: Go ahead.

It is given in the Bible; "a gathering of individuals whom God has made into a people." God made them into a people of his gift, and it was not for their sake but for the sake of the whole world. Now, one has to ask: "What was the effect of this calling on the historical consciousness of the Jewish people?" For a culture was born as well, and that culture is not irrelevant to Jewish consciousness. It is part of *the* commandment which is: to transmit the *commandments* to one's children and to guarantee the future by means of one's children. Here you have both the promise and the commandments. It is not by accident therefore that Judaism has survived. It continues through history, brings forth its own culture, and creates an attitude and a way of existing which are unique. That too belongs to its essence. The Jewish people is conscious of its past in history and it knows that it has a future for which it is responsible, not just for itself but by reason of the gift which it received at the beginning. That is where you find the basis for the Jewish people's attitude to history; it is an attitude which enabled it during several thousand years to cope with existence in diaspora, and that was long before the coming of Christianity. That surely is something quite unique. There's nothing like it in history. I know there are gypsies, but they are migrants, and it is not as migrants that the Jews have maintained their unique character throughout the centuries.

Υ.B.P.: What about the idea of being a "chosen people"? Is that an idea that Christians can accept? Do Christians still think of the Jews as the chosen people? Do you?

I think that it's a key idea for the understanding of faith. If you don't have that concept, you cannot understand either Judaism or Christianity. But if you leave the area of faith and secularize the concept, you end up with things like the German army having *Gott mit uns* on their belts. It becomes intolerable.

D.J.: Do you agree with General de Gaulle's comment on the Jews: "An elite people, self-assured and dominating"? Was he right?

At the time, I thought it a humorous expression, because the picture of the Jew projected by the period I had witnessed was one of the Jew persecuted and done to death. And here he was calling the Jews "an elite people." I don't mind if that's the new image people have of the Jews *(laughter)*; anyway it blotted out a caricature which had lasted for many centuries. But it's also true that General de Gaulle spoke with a certain touch of grandeur, not necessarily pejorative coming from him. That is what was remembered of his witticism, and no doubt he meant it to be so understood.

D.J.: Do you think he was anti-Semitic, perhaps unconsciously?

No, I don't think so. I think that by upbringing De Gaulle belonged to that section of conservatives who are both republican and socially conscious. It is only after his time that anti-Semitism tried to come to the fore in France. It could not do so in De Gaulle's time.

Y.B.P.: Your Excellency, there is a question which everyone in Israel is asking since you became archbishop of Paris and appeared on Israeli TV, where what you said was much appreciated. The question is: What do you think is the difference between Judaism and Christianity? I know that it's a rather complex question.

It's very complex.

Y.B.P.: But I've come all the way to Paris especially to ask it!

In order to answer I have to overcome a great difficulty, which is that I am not speaking to you two only, but to all your readers as well, and I don't know where they stand. All sorts of misunderstandings are possible. I respect Jewish people; I am very conscious of the indignation they might feel toward my personal position and of the feelings of opposition they might have; so in trying to answer I might be hurting their legitimate feelings. I do know what some people think of a Jew who becomes a Christian. I don't want to be provocative and I don't want to offend anybody, so it has always been with very great reluctance that I have given any personal explanations.

There is a preliminary point I would like to make. I have claimed to be a Jew, but that was not at all in order to enter into a theological debate. I never claimed to be at the same time a good Jew according to the requirements of the rabbis and a good Christian according to the requirements of the church. But I am sure you understand that I cannot repudiate my Jewish condition without losing my own dignity and the respect I owe to my parents and to all those to whom I belong; that is true both in times of persecution and in times of peace. I claim to be a Jew not to hurt anyone, but because I respect the truth and what is due to the truth.

I knew when I claimed to be a Jew that a certain number of misunderstandings would occur and that I would not be understood. When I say that I acted out of respect for the dignity of being a Jew and for my own self-respect, I meant that I could not cease to be Jewish. Obviously I am not an observant Jew in the sense understood by those who define Jewish orthodoxy. But what I can say is that in becoming a Christian I did not intend to cease being the Jew I was then. I was not running away from the Jewish condition. I have that from my parents and I can never lose it. I have it from God and he will never let me lose it.

Y.B.P.: But surely you were prepared to move on to something else, even if you did have a deep respect for the Jews.

That's right.

Y.B.P.: Doesn't that mean that you thought that something else was more correct, better, more divine—I don't know how to put it.

Yes, my way of putting it was: a better way of being Jewish, according to what I knew then of Judaism.

Y.B.P.: But you did move on from one condition to another, and you chose the latter.

That's true; but I did not move on from being Jewish to "not being Jewish." That would have been impossible.

Y.B.P.: Didn't you move on to another religion because you thought it true?

Yes, but as if carried in the womb of the first one.

Y.B.P.: Can I ask you some personal questions; I hope you won't mind? Did you become a Christian at fourteen?

Yes.

D.J.: Do you remember how it happened? Was it the result of a revelation or of evolution? Do you remember how you felt at the time?

Up till now I have always felt slightly embarrassed about answering questions like that. I hate exhibitionism. But of course if one says nothing people imagine all sorts of things. There was another reason for not saying too much, which was that parents could have been blamed. People could have said: "They were a bad lot. If they had given their children a Jewish education, things would not have turned out as they did." I know there must be some people who think that way. Anyhow, since you have asked the question, I will try to answer.

When I was a child, I was conscious of being Jewish in exactly the same ways as any son of Jewish immigrants in France. There was nothing special about me. I wasn't called Durand or Dupont; my first name is Aaron, after my paternal grandfather. I was called Aaron at school. My mother had come to France as a child. My father came at eighteen and never spoke perfect French. We were hard up; I wasn't dressed as well as the other children, but I was fairly often first in my class and that was another thing that made me different from the others. At the entrance to the Lycée Montaigne I had my face bashed in because I was Jewish. Sometimes when I came up to a group of boys who were talking, they would say, "Push off, you filthy Jew." I know about all that. I also knew that being Jewish was something special. My parents were not believers; I still remember some of the things they used to say: "Rabbis, priests, they all talk the same rubbish. . . ." But I had the sense of the presence of God; I remember that very well. Very little is needed to awaken the sense of God's presence in the mind of a child. What I remember is the way my mother used to say the blessing over the first fruits. That was all. It was enough for me. And then, aged ten, I secretly read through the whole of the Bible. . . .

D.J.: What, at ten years old?

Yes, I was supposed to be practicing the piano or doing my home-work. My parents were down in the shop and they couldn't see what I was up to.

D.J.: Was this before the war?

It must have been 1936 or 1937. My parents had a bookcase which was locked and I was not supposed to read any of the books in it. It contained all sorts of books which my parents had bought. They had a great respect for books and bought more or less anything. The key was kept on top of the bookcase so it wasn't very difficult for me to stand on a chair and find it. I opened the bookcase and read all sorts of things. I read Zola; I read Abel Hermant. I read all those boring novels which came out between the wars; you know, a series brought out by Flammarion and bound in green. But I also found the Bible, a Protestant Bible, and I read it right through.

D.J.: The Old Testament?

The Old and the New Testaments. I read the Bible passionately and I didn't say a word to anybody. I cannot remember whether I was eleven or twelve at the time, but from then onward I began to think about these things and to mull over them. I always went to public school and not to a Catholic school. My teachers were completely neutral in matters of religion. When I was eleven, I had a Latin teacher who was Jewish but I only found out after the war. I also remember the history lessons when I was eleven. When we were taught about the Hebrews in class, I thought it wasn't much compared to what I already knew. Literature too was important; it influenced me and started me thinking. I can remember too a holiday at Berck when I was thirteen.[5] I was only a child but I was faced then with the suffering of other children, the problem of something obviously evil, the problem of death. I seemed to receive in my understanding an absolute confirmation of the existence of God, God who is the only just one in contrast to the injustice done to human beings.

But before that I had come across Nazism in real life. For two years running, when I was eleven and twelve, my parents sent me off to Germany for a month during the summer all on my own, to stay with a family and learn German. I don't know whether they realized what they were doing or whether they were just daring. I had my real name on my father's passport. The families were anti-Nazi, but the second year I stayed with a family of teachers and their children, who were a little older than me, were in the Hitler Youth, which was compulsory. So at the age of eleven I saw Nazism as it really is. Can you imagine what it meant to a boy of eleven to be talking things over with a lad of thirteen who was in the Hitler Youth; he showed me his knife and said, "At the summer solstice we are going to kill all the Jews." I heard that with my own ears. I read the anti-Semitic placards that the Blackshirts put up in the streets. I knew Hitler for what he was; I wasn't at all surprised by the way Nazism turned out subsequently.

By 1937 everything was perfectly clear for that particular French Jewish boy of eleven who had had the opportunity of talking with German boys of twelve or thirteen. I could see what other French Jews, adults, could not yet see perhaps. Perhaps German Jews could not see it either. So you see I was deeply marked by all this; nothing of what happened later surprised me. What I mean is that I could not be surprised by what I had understood outright and intuitively as a child.

It was in Germany too that I first met adults who were Christians and I was impressed by the fact that they were anti-Nazi; that was the one thing which struck me about them. It was in Germany too

5. Berck is a resort on the North Sea. It was famous for its invigorating air, and many sick people, especially children, went there in hope of cures. (Translator's note)

that I guessed why God has committed himself to the Jews because of the Messiah. It is the opposite of *Gott mit uns* on soldiers' belts.

So it was in those years that I began to draw near to Christianity, by thinking, by reading. Those were the only influences on me, books and the culture I was imbibing at the Lycée from different teachers. Later on I found out about the beliefs of those teachers; some were Jewish, some were committed Catholics, some were unbelievers, others were agnostics. But I had a long interior path to follow and, fundamentally, it was Christ who gave me the key to my searchings, Christ as Messiah and image of the Jewish people. At the same time, I knew that persecution had been the lot of the Jews in history and that it had also been the source of their dignity.

At the time I wanted to become a doctor, because I thought that was the best way of helping humankind. My parents had taught me that, if people thought of us as different, we ought to be better than others, more just, serving all, defending the poor and the unfortunate. I couldn't see any better way of serving humankind than being a doctor. That's what I thought at the time, or else I might have wanted to become a great writer like Zola so as to defend the oppressed.

D.J.: But you said you were influenced by the Bible.

I was.

D.J.: Were you shocked by anything you read in the Bible? What happened exactly?

I cannot remember. I found everything in the Bible surprising but nothing shocking.

D.J.: Did you share your thoughts with your parents?

No, not at all.

Y.B.P.: So it was a real conversion?

It was more like a crystallization than a conversion. Through the circumstances I have mentioned, I found that, when I first really confronted Christians, I knew their beliefs better than they did themselves. When I reread the Gospels at that stage, I already knew them. I say "at that stage" because it was then that my parents absolutely refused to accept that I was convinced; they thought it was disgusting. I said to them, "I am not leaving you. I'm not going over to the enemy. I am becoming what I am. I am not ceasing to be a Jew; on the contrary, I am discovering another way of being a Jew." I know that Jewish people think that's a scandalous way to talk, but that's what I experienced. When I chose my Christian names I chose three

Jewish names: Aaron-Jean-Marie. It's obvious if you look at the Hebrew forms. I kept the name I had received at birth.

D.J.: Earlier on you spoke of the way the values of Judaism persisted in Christianity. Now you are saying, "I discovered the values of Judaism in becoming a Christian." What exactly do you mean? What values are you talking about?

I mean God's calling of a people, so that they could know him, love him, and serve him. I mean the promise of universal salvation, prepared for all men and women. I mean the joy of being with God and of being loved by him. I mean the understanding of the history of Israel as the history of salvation, as opposed to the history of damnation that the war was displaying at the time. I also mean the value of that historical belonging which is not just due to chance but is the unfolding of the love of God, our love for God and God's love for us.

Y.B.P.: I believe that you became a Catholic at Orleans when you were fourteen.

At Orleans, that's right.

Y.B.P.: Did you decide to become a minister then?

Yes, I did.

Y.B.P.: Right at the start then you knew that you would become a priest?

Yes, for me it was clear right from the start. But I didn't mention it to anybody.

Y.B.P.: Was it the same idea of service that you'd had previously when you decided to become a doctor?

Yes, it was.

Y.B.P.: But couldn't you have served humankind from within Judaism?

For me at the time, the contents of Judaism were no different from what I was discovering in Christianity. I saw Judaism then as a historical condition marked by persecution; I did not think for one moment of leaving it. But it found its fulfillment in welcoming the person of Jesus, the Messiah of Israel; it was in recognizing him, and only in recognizing him, that Judaism found its meaning.

Y.B.P. Did you see the persecution of Israel as a punishment?

No, I did not.

Y.B.P.: Didn't you accept the view that God had punished the Jewish people because it did not recognize Jesus?

No, I never thought that way at all.

Y.B.P.: I think I told you that I was hidden by a priest during the war. I shan't tell you his name as he is probably still alive. I used to serve his Mass during the three months I was there; it was in the South of France. I was fifteen at the time; I was in hiding at his house and he saved the life of many children. He never tried to convert us, not at all, but what he tried to get across was: "You see, my child, you are being persecuted because your people did not recognize the Messiah." Isn't that Christian doctrine?

That sort of thing has been said. It was one of the ways of understanding the fate of Israel in Christian countries. But I never accepted that view.

Y.B.P.: Don't you think the Vatican will be after you for having said that in an interview?

Saying what?

Y.B.P.: Saying that phrase, "the Jews are persecuted because they refuse to acknowledge Jesus," is not a sort of creed.

No, I don't think it will, because that statement is not part of Catholic faith.

Y.B.P.: So if a priest said that sort of thing to me, it was his personal interpretation?

It was his personal interpretation. It is an interpretation which is quite widely diffused and accepted but it is not part of faith. So in telling you that I do not accept such a view, I cannot be suspected of professing a deviationist opinion.

Y.B.P.: But isn't what you are saying going against common opinion?

What I am saying will no doubt surprise those people who go no deeper than generally accepted ideas and prejudices. That is because Christian thinking on the destiny of Israel, on the Jewish condition, and on the place of Judaism in the history of salvation is only just beginning to emerge in modern times.

Y.B.P.: But surely you ought to be saying to us: "Look here, if you want to be good Jews, if you really want to be saved, you should become Christians." And yet you aren't saying it, and I am not trying to get you to say it. But I do think it would be logical if you did.

Not necessarily and for this reason: it is not up to us to decide what we should be. It is up to God. It is up to God to decide who I must be and what I must do; God decides first and I decide afterward.

But there is another, deeper side to your question which I want to look at with great fear and trepidation, and then I will come back to the question as you formulated it. What is the meaning of being Jewish today? How should one be a Jew so as to be faithful to Judaism? The answer isn't as obvious as all that. Similarly, it isn't obvious exactly what being a Christian means and there are different ways of being a Christian.

I think that the situation of Jews in the Diaspora today is very different from what it was before the destruction of the temple. Judaism has had a unique spiritual experience. During those two thousand years the unique phenomenon called rabbinism has occurred. As a result, something of great value was safeguarded, which is Jewish identity; but in order to achieve this the rabbis had to choose between various options. As a result, there were many aspirations which were disregarded by the official majority; many questions and many trends within Judaism were not identified or recognized.

Moreover, new problems have arisen since the beginning of modern times, since the eighteenth century and the beginnings of emancipation. The problem of Jewish identity does not only concern Jewish identity from the legal point of view; it is a problem of Jewish fidelity. That seems to me a very important question. It has a bearing on the question which you have raised because historically the controversy between Judaism and Christianity has had two sides to it. There is the aspect which concerns the way in which Judaism relates to its own claims and to its own traditions. There is also the way in which Christians, or shall we say groups within a Christian culture, identify and recognize the specific Jewish heritage, with its richness and diversity as they exist today.

In modern Christian theology, the relation between Judaism and Christianity has hardly been tackled. All the elements of the problem are there; they call out for a fundamental examination, but for historical reasons these questions have been put to one side and passed over. This is especially true of the questions concerning the origins of Christianity, its relation to Judaism, and the way in which Judaism reacted toward it. When the New Testament was written the lines were already partly drawn up, but only partly so. Afterward the differences became more serious. The first problem is to understand the relation between Israel and the nations. That's a vital point; the revelation made to Israel is also for the nations. In the tradition we find a series of covenants, the covenant with Noah, and so on.[6] One has

---

6. The covenant with the sons of Noah (Gen. 9:8–10) is considered in the rabbinic tradition as a covenant which is continually on offer to the nations.

to ask: "Was the covenant with Noah the only kind of covenant which was offered to the nations? Were there not other possibilities in the Prophets? The covenant with Noah already implies a great deal; in fact, since it involves moral rectitude, it already implies everything. But were not the Gentiles called to receive something from Judaism itself: Does not the Bible itself announce something more than the covenant of Noah when it proclaims the promise made to Abraham and the revelation on Mount Sinai?"

Y.B.P.: Yes, other answers may be found in the tradition.

So you agree that other answers may be found. Well, that was precisely the cause of the crisis which occurred from 70 to 140 during the first century of Christianity. The question was whether pagans, people coming from the *goyim*,[7] could enter into the Covenant. And one also has to ask to what extent were some of the promises fulfilled at that time and which ones they were. When the messianic titles were applied to Jesus, what happened to the image of the Messiah as far as Jews were concerned? And what image of the Messiah did Christians accept, then and now? These are the questions that Christians and Jews inevitably put to each other.

Most of the Christians when they entered into the Covenant were pagans in origin, but they forgot that they were born into paganism. As you know the word *church* translates the Hebrew word *qahal*.[8]

Y.B.P.: That's why the Book of Ecclesiastes is Qoheleth in Hebrew.

Exactly. So the church is a gathering together which is summoned by God.

Y.B.P.: Right.

When we talk about the *Catholic* church, we are using a word derived from the Greek *kath' holon* ("according to the whole"), which means "according to the totality of Jews and Gentiles." That's different from talking about "the universal church," meaning only "the totality of the nations." Yet you often find it translated that way. For example, in translating the Creed Protestants substitute the word *universal* for *Catholic*; universality would then be a horizontal notion, like the United Nations.

Y.B.P.: Quite.

But the Greek phrase *kath' holon* really means the *qahal*, composed of Jews who have been the object of God's choice. So that "totality" of humanity according to God's plan is made up of Israel and the

7. *Goyim*, the plural of *goy*, the "nations," used of non-Jewish peoples.
8. *Qahal*, "assembly," "convocation," "congregation."

nations, who are to be finally united in the one and only Covenant. If you put things that way, it is clear that the last days have not yet been fulfilled.

You might say, "But where can you see the promises of the Messiah actually fulfilled?" That is the real question between us. In a way they haven't been fulfilled. History continues; its present condition is that the fulfillment remains hidden. That is the Christian belief. The figure of the Messiah is a hidden one. Christians tend to forget sometimes that they are still waiting for the coming in glory of their Messiah.

Israel on the other hand must remain faithful as long as the times are not accomplished; it is still loved by God because of his election and because of the Patriarchs. God's gifts and his call cannot be abolished. It is obviously a very difficult question because, from the Jewish point of view, Christianity has anticipated things and is in too much of a hurry. And that's true too; Judaism retains a valid point of view on Christianity; what it says is relevant.

What one cannot say, as the Marxists do, is that Christianity has sought refuge in spiritual things and in the next life. On the contrary, Christianity is very realistic in its outlook. But this is an area where one has to challenge a good many prejudices and assumptions; if I were to go into it fully, I would need more columns than your paper is prepared to give me.

Y.B.P.: So what you are saying is that Christianity is a sort of "open" Judaism, a Judaism which has been opened to the world and to the pagans. Christianity consists in making the Gentiles participate in Judaism. It is this achievement which has given us Christianity.

Yes, in a way, but in a way which was unexpected both for Israel and for the pagans.

Y.B.P.: And were the pagans told, "You can now join in"?

Yes, that is what the first Christian community of Jerusalem, which was composed exclusively of those who were Jewish by birth, eventually came round to accepting, after much controversy. The person of Jesus, once he was recognized as Messiah, brought into focus a whole range of Jewish expectations which were seen to have a special spiritual content and which were experienced, at that moment, as fulfilled in the Christian experience.

D.J.: So, if you can remember what you thought as a child, you considered Jesus the Christ as a Jewish Messiah?

Yes.

D.J.: And do you still think of him that way?

Most certainly I do, and I am not alone in this. The Christian Scriptures say that Jesus is the Jewish Messiah. It is only translation which obscures the fact that Jesus Christ means Jesus the Messiah.

Y.B.P.: So, if I understand you, you are saying something like this: on the one hand, it is right to be a Christian but, on the other hand, it is right to remain a Jew because we need the Jews precisely as Jews.

Yes, according to what God decides.

Y.B.P.: So that this view of the future may be fulfilled?

Yes. You are leading me on to theological and spiritual questions.

Y.B.P.: But isn't that what we are talking about?

All right, but then you have to accept certain presuppositions, otherwise the dialog takes on a certain wild and extravagant quality. That is why I am being cautious. We are in that period of history in which God is fulfilling the promise made to Israel "until the fullness of time is achieved." The church too is grappling with a historical question. In the early church, the church of the first two centuries, there was a "church of Jerusalem," that is, a Christian church composed of Jews. It was the same throughout the Roman Empire. One of the constant problems of the early church was the coexistence of Jewish Christians and Gentile Christians within the new church, the new *qahal,* the *qahal* of the Messiah. The great difficulty, where this coexistence was concerned, was provided by the ritual laws. Were the Gentile converts to Christianity bound to keep all the prescriptions of Judaism? Should they be circumcised? Did they have to keep the dietary laws? What obligations were they taking on? Those were the questions that Christians were asking about Gentile converts, just as Jews were asking them about their proselytes. But they were not rejecting Judaism as such.

Y.B.P.: This respect that you have for Judaism and for Jews, doesn't it come from the fact that you are a Jew yourself and that your name is Aaron? After all, lots of other Christians don't speak with such respect for Judaism, nor do many priests and church people.

That may be so, but it's so much the worse for them. It is a pity that Christians, who nearly all are from a Gentile origin, should have kept a Gentile mentality. Jesus never claimed to be "king of the Jews"; that title was given to him by a pagan, the Roman Pilate. At the time, the Jews in Israel did not refer to themselves as "Jews"; they used the expression "the people of Israel." It was outsiders who called them Jews. The Gospel of Matthew, which was composed in a Jewish milieu, is very precise in its terminology in this respect.

If Christians were faithful to the gift which God has made to them, they would understand that God has made them "children of God," "sons of God," as are the children of Israel but in a different way; they would see that this gift takes place in the person of the Messiah who welcomes them; they would understand that they have benefited in a superabundant way from the gift made in the first place to Israel, although Israel itself does not always realize the full greatness of that gift. My deepest desire is that there should be on both sides gratitude and mutual recognition. I wish that Christians would not forget that they have been grafted on to the one and only stock of Israel; and that stock lives on. I am commenting on the words of Paul, of course.[9]

Y.B.P.: It's a metaphor.

That's right and it's an unusual one because he says that the wild olive shoot had been grafted onto a cultivated olive. But in fact a gardener does the opposite; it is the stock that is wild and it is the graft which is taken from the cultivated plant. Whereas what Paul does in describing the relation between Gentile Christians and Jews is to say, "You, the pagans, are the wild shoot and you are grafted on to the cultivated olive root, the Jews"; and he adds, "and you have become the branches of the tree according to your nature."

There's another aspect which gives great hope, I think. Thanks to the spiritual and cultural freedom which Israeli nationhood has brought about and thanks to a different outlook on the part of Christians, it is now possible perhaps for Judaism to recognize Christianity as an offspring of God. After all, could Judaism while remaining faithful to its call from God, recognize one day that the nations which have become Christian are also like unexpected children for the Jewish people? It would be like the gift of an unexpected offspring who has not yet been recognized as such. Since Christians have not acknowledged that the Jews are as their older brothers, and the stock on which they have been grafted, perhaps the Jews themselves could recognize the pagan nations which have become Christian as their

---

9. "No doubt some of the branches have been cut off, and, like shoots of wild olive, you have been grafted among the rest to share with them the rich sap provided by the olive tree itself, but still, even if you think yourself superior to the other branches, remember that you do not support the root; it is the root that supports you" (Rom. 11:17–18).

younger brother. But there has to be forgiveness first because of all the persecutions, all the fratricidal conflict. Precisely because they are so alike there has been a kind of war of legitimation. It is the old story of wanting to kill one's brother so as to have the whole inheritance. The reason for persecution has been jealousy, in the spiritual sense; but jealousy could become emulation and so become a source of blessings.

Y.B.P.: Have you studied Judaism?

I have done some reading out of interest but I have not been through a course of Talmudic studies in the proper sense. That needs excessive specialization; but I have read quite a lot.

Y.B.P.: Have you learnt Hebrew?

Hardly. I can read biblical Hebrew but I have not learnt modern Hebrew. I started, then I had to give up.

D.J.: Have you been aware of any prejudice against you because of your Jewish antecedents?

You mean from Christians?

D.J.: Yes, from Christians, and from your colleagues.

It's hard to say because I do not worry much about what people are thinking about me. I think it's unhealthy to be always wondering what effect one is having. I would be furious if there were an opinion poll to find out what people think about me because of my Jewish origins. That would seem to me to be an indiscreet question and an unhealthy one. But of course there may be pockets of anti-Semitism here and there; it could hardly be otherwise. It is also possible that in a period of emergency I might become a target and a scapegoat. But one thing I do notice; I stand for a good deal more than what I am as an individual. It is not only me as an individual who matters but everything I stand for historically. I can see that the decision which gave me such a notable responsibility has been for many Christians a reminder of that historical and spiritual reality which I have called "the roots." It is like a living reminder of their past history which they have often been tempted to forget.

I am alluding here to a problem which is peculiar to Christians. After all, it is because of Judaism that Christianity recognizes Jesus as Messiah, the son of God, meaning by that what the Bible means by calling him Messiah-king and also eternal Wisdom. It is only because of certain criteria, inherited from Judaism, that Christianity is preserved from the temptation of appropriating Jesus as a mythological character and adapting him to all circumstances and to every culture. Such is the criterion which has allowed Christian faith to preserve its true and authentic character. There has always been a tendency, which is particularly strong today, to accept Christ as a divine personage and to deck him out with whatever qualities a particular culture is endowed with. But it is the Bible which tells us the real nature of God's choice and that is what makes it impossible to identify Christ and Apollo or Dionysos. Judaism is the witness of that unique choice. For Christians it is the Jews who are the living witnesses of the unique and historical character of Christian faith.

It is impossible to understand anything about Christian belief if one does not accept God's choice of a Messiah, and one cannot understand God's choice of a Messiah if one does not accept his choice of Israel. It is when people want to do away with this foundation of Christianity that they start persecuting Jews and wanting to blot them out. The history of Christianity shows us an example of this negative attitude toward Judaism which has been condemned by the church; I am alluding to the heresy of Marcion, who wanted to produce a version of the Gospels without any allusions to the Old Testament. Although this view was condemned by the Church as heretical, it turns up again in modern times. You know that certain Protestant German historians argued from the fact that Jesus was a Galilean that therefore he must have been an Aryan.

There can be a similar temptation for Western Christians when they present Christianity to African and Asian peoples; they are tempted to pass over Jesus' Jewish nature. They say, "The Gospel is a way of life." So there is a risk that when Africans become Christians they may say, "Our African culture takes the place of the Old Testament as far as we, African Christians are concerned." and Asians might say, "The sacred writings of Asia are the Old Testament for us." Are they right or wrong? Where does the Christian religion find its balance? During the Synod of Bishops in Rome in 1974, Cardinal Marty emphatically recalled the obligation of accepting the whole of Scripture; one cannot jettison the Old Testament under the pretext of being faithful to the New Testament in its confrontation with pagan culture, its "inculturation" as we call it.

Y.B.P.: Because the Ten Commandments are in the Old Testament after all.

Yes. The Ten Commandments and their twofold summary which is traditional in Judaism: "Listen, O Israel, you shall love the Lord your God" (Deut. 6:4–5) and "You will love your neighbor as yourself" (Lev. 19:18); these are central to the prayer and to the teaching of Jesus and to the faithfulness of Christianity (Luke 10:25–8). It is not an accident that the whole of Christianity's understanding of humanity refers back explicitly and insistently to the beginning of the Torah, the first chapters of Genesis; this has been brought out especially by John Paul II.

One must admit that there is a real danger of altering the Christian faith from the inside and making it into a form of paganism. Many periods and cultures have been tempted to submerge Christianity into a form of paganism. It is true that Christianity has to live out a certain tension from the very fact that it is called to be a "light for the nations." But in the present state of things it can only be true to itself if it continues to receive the gift which was made to Israel. However, there was a twofold break in the past; it occurred when the Jewish authorities said, "One cannot be faithful to the synagogue if one is a disciple of Jesus"; and the Christians said, "One cannot be a Christian if one belongs institutionally to Judaism." There was a deep break, a parting of the waters.

Y.B.P.: So one could suppose as one listens to you (perhaps you cannot say this but I can say it for you) that you feel in part more Jewish than not.

I don't know. I certainly do feel very much a Jew.

Y.B.P.: If one moves away from the spiritual and religious aspect, can you say that you feel solidarity with Jews throughout the world? What are your feelings when you read newspaper reports about Jews being persecuted in Soviet Russia because they are Jews?

How can one not feel solidarity with father, mother, or cousins if they are ill or persecuted? You cannot possibly expect that I would answer your question in any other way. They are my brothers.

D.J.: Would it be very indiscreet if we were to ask you to tell us about the main stages of your life? You have told us what happened when you were fourteen, but what happened afterwards, in 1940 and 1942?

I do hate talking about myself in public.

D.J.: I know, but it's a very understanding public.

No, really; I don't feel. . . .

D.J.: And it's a public which is very well disposed toward you.

I am sure of that; but everything one says gets around. It always does.

D.J.: Not necessarily.

Y.D.P.: Since we publish in Hebrew.

Well, if I must, I must. I will try to share some of my memories. It was wartime. I had to flee from the town I was living in and to hide, otherwise I would have been betrayed. There were precise threats to that effect and I had been warned about them. One had to register with the police; at first my parents hadn't registered, and then in the end they did.

D.J.: Was this at Orleans?

Yes, but my parents had stayed in Paris. In 1940 they had given me permission to be baptized, but inwardly they did not agree at all. I had asked for it repeatedly and they gave in. Perhaps they thought it might afford some protection against the persecution which was already threatening in the summer of 1940. But for me it had a quite different meaning. Then it became obligatory for Jews to wear the star of David. We tried everything, false papers, and so on. Anyway I won't go into details. My father went off to the unoccupied zone of France to go into hiding and prepare the way. My mother stayed behind to mind the shop and maintain some sort of livelihood; food was short. Then she was arrested. First, the shop was put under the "oversight" of an "Aryan" administrator, like all Jewish shops. Then it was confiscated. The flat was pillaged and then occupied by "Aryans." My mother was arrested because she had been reported for not wearing the yellow star. She was interned at Drancy.[10] We tried every possible way of getting her out. Then she was taken away and finally deported. Later I learnt that she had gone to Auschwitz when I read the memorial of French Jews edited by S. Klarsfeld. At the time we had no news of any sort. But she knew that all the Jews were going to be killed; people knew it at Drancy. She told us so in a letter which had been smuggled out of Drancy by the guards, in return for cash. I had left Orleans and was in a boarding school where I finished my secondary education and got my baccalaureate. I crossed secretly into the nonoccupied zone and joined up with my father. For a year I worked in a factory and I also started studying for a degree in chemistry. I took part in underground movements; I used to distribute copies of *Témoignage chrétien*. It was no more than what numerous young people of seventeen and eighteen were doing in France at the time. Then came the Liberation. I wanted to be a priest; it was my own idea. My father was utterly opposed. So for

10. Drancy was a transit camp, harshly administered by French police, where Jews awaited transportation to Auschwitz. (Translator's note)

two years I read for a degree in literature. I took part in the work of the student union.

D.J.: Was that in Paris?

Yes. Then in 1946 I entered the university seminary, the Séminaire des Carmes at the Institut catholique in Paris, and in 1954 I was ordained a priest. I was student chaplain until 1969. My responsibility was the chaplaincy at the Sorbonne and other universities in Paris. I met a lot of people in the intellectual world of Paris at the time. Then for ten years I was parish priest of a place on the edge of Paris, near Boulogne. And then, to my great surprise, I was appointed bishop of Orleans by the pope; but I was even more surprised when I was appointed archbishop of Paris. So there you are.

D.J.: How do they make these decisions? Do you know the process by which you were chosen as archbishop of Paris? Did you know the pope personally?

No, I only met him after I became a bishop. The decision was his. The nuncio submits a certain number of names and says "These are the people one is thinking of" and he finds out about the candidates.

Y.B.P.: So he must have said that this one was originally Jewish?

He must have.

D.J.: Do you think that's why you were chosen?

I don't know. How could I?

D.J.: Haven't you ever talked about it with the pope?

No, never. But when I had been appointed, I wrote to him telling him that my parents came from Bendzyn and that most of my family had been killed at Auschwitz or elsewhere in Poland. He had known all about it when he decided to appoint me.

Y.B.P.: That really is very important for us.

Quite.

Y.B.P.: What is an archbishop supposed to do? We don't know.

If only I knew! I seem to be caught up with hundreds of problems. I have to help the Christians who live in Paris to live in the Christian faith and to live up to their Christian faith. There are other sides to it as well. Since France is very centralized and Paris is preponderant, the archbishop of Paris is, in a way, an official person. He is in contact with all sorts of people; that's the best known side of my work, so I mention it first so as not to forget it. The ambassadors of foreign countries announced that they wanted to pay courtesy calls; I haven't accepted yet as I just haven't got the time. If I were not careful, all my time would go on official functions. Many I cannot get out of. For instance, every foreign bishop passing through Paris wants to pay a courtesy call, and so on. It's due to the importance of Paris in today's world. Then there is all the work which has to be done by the French bishops, and sometimes by all the bishops of the world, because decisions have to be taken. Our discussions are very democratic, in spite of what people might think. I know a lot of people think the Church operates like the Central Committee of the Communist party *(laughter)*.

Υ.B.P.: Do you have a large administration?

No, it's small and not really adequate. But may I come back to what I consider to be my main task? I have to be faithful to the mission of priests and a man of God in relation to all the people I meet. I meet mostly people who are believers but some unbelievers also. I have to help communities, parishes, movements, and groups to live their faith, to live the Christian life. The faithful are facing very difficult problems because of the rapid changes which have occurred in the way people behave, in living conditions and in the place of the church in modern society. There have been enormous changes over the last ten years or so. It would be very easy to become confined to an official role. Everything tends in that direction, especially the way we do things in France. I don't want to be but it's an uphill struggle.

Υ.B.P.: Do you have time for meditation?

I make time.

Υ.B.P.: Do you manage to get into your timetable: no interviews between such and such a time?

Yes, that's it. It's the only way to do it. Each week I have a whole day off and each day I take at least an hour, over and above the recitation of the Divine Office. That's all the freedom I get.

Υ.B.P.: Would you allow me to ask: Does an archbishop read nonreligious books? Do you go to the cinema? Do you watch television and read France Soir?

When I was a parish priest, I considered that it was my duty to devote about one-third of my time to personal study, reading, and reflection. Now that I have been catapulted into the responsibilities of an archbishop, I spend all my time dealing with emergencies. I am in grave danger of becoming an intellectual cabbage *(laughter)*. It's no joke; I know it's a real danger. I get home very late and I don't have time to watch television anymore; not that I ever did much. I don't listen to the radio any more. I don't go to the cinema and I don't read. It all adds up to an abnormal situation.

Y.B.P.: Do you read the papers?

I look through them. I read the weeklies very quickly. But things cannot go on like that.

Y.B.P.: Being an archbishop doesn't sound much fun!

Well, it's a question of duty. It's not a job I would have chosen and I don't do it for fun, but because God asks it of me. That's the only thing which makes that sort of life possible in peace of mind and heart.

Y.B.P.: So really it's better to be a parish priest.

Much better!

Y.B.P.: Because one is in direct contact?

That's it. You can preach, say Mass, have discussions with people who have problems with their faith; one can help people in their lives and proclaim the love of God for humankind.

Y.B.P.: Don't you have an official position too?

Not directly. What are you getting at?

Y.B.P.: Aren't you in touch with the government?

Yes, I think I have to do that. The mission I have received requires that I speak out at the right times on issues of conscience and morality. These are human as well as Christian concerns. I don't start off by making a statement to the press. Often a public statement of that sort means that things are past mending *(laughter)*. If one wants to make an impression on a political figure, it's much better to speak to him personally. So I think it's my duty to get to know the leading personalities in the social, political, and economic world so that we can understand each other and size each other up. I hope that the people I have to deal with can see me primarily as a man of God, so that they can appreciate that when I speak I do so as a believer who is trying to witness to justice, peace, and truth. I need to convince them that I am not defending the interests of a pressure group by means of the political power game. So I think it is my duty to have contacts with the president of the Republic, with members of the government, with the opposition, and with members of public bodies.

Y.B.P.: Are Vatican politics discussed at the archbishop's house?

More or less. I mean by that that we are concerned about the welfare of the church. But we are not directly involved in what the

Vatican will say or do about South America, for instance. But we can give our opinion on the matter.

D.J.: How close are your links with the Vatican? Do you send in frequent reports?

Not really, but I am rather new to the game. Some links are part of the institution; so, every five years every bishop pays a visit to the pope.

D.J.: Every five years?

Yes, every five years. The bishops of each country have to go to Rome and they give a report of the situation in their country. But John Paul II has started another sort of link. He goes to the various countries himself and this means that the leaders of the population come together. On particular problems there are special study groups; the national conference of churches delegates somebody. Rome has an age-old tradition where the management of the church's affairs are concerned. One of the problems after Vatican II was to renew these traditions so that the various national churches could take part in them. One of the major concerns of the present pope is to prevent the Vatican administration from becoming top-heavy. He wants to follow the indications of Vatican II so that bishops from all over the world can take part in the government of the universal church and can bring their own contribution to it.

Let me give you an example. Canon law is very important. It has been reformed several times through the centuries. The last text dates from 1917; at the moment it is being recast. For the last ten years a commission has been working on this, made up of international experts, bishops and cardinals. Before promulgating it, the pope asked all the bishops of the world to come and criticize the text and to submit it to a final revision.

Y.B.P.: I expect you know that in Israel we have some political parties which are religious parties.

I do.

Y.B.P.: At least three of them, if not more.

Yes.

D.J.: What do you think of this combination of politics and religion?

That question is a trap. I don't want to make a pronouncement on the internal politics of the State of Israel.

Y.B.P.: Would you say that a Christian religious party would always be a right-wing party?

No, it could just as well be a left-wing party. It is quite possible to have a party with Christian ideals which is progressive. But what you are really asking is whether it would be right to transform a democratic state into a theocracy.

Y.B.P.: Our question is about Israel.

It's different with Israel; there the question is more serious because of the religious meaning of kingship in Israel, a meaning which has been inherited from the Bible.

Y.B.P.: We have political parties which we consider to be extremely right wing and they want to impose their rules on the state. Have you followed the affair of the excavations in Jerusalem?

I have.

Y.B.P.: Our "church," if you will excuse the description of the rabbinate, has been in open conflict with the government over it.

How can I answer without sitting in judgment?

Y.B.P.: So what is your considered view on the question?

That you mustn't try to use me to settle your quarrels *(laughter).*

Y.B.P.: Could you imagine a Christian leader forbidding excavations at a spot where there might have been burials two thousand years ago?

Certainly not.

Y.B.P.: He wouldn't see these archaeological digs as a lack of respect for the dead?

Certainly not.

Y.B.P.: Our religious parties said the opposite. When we attacked them in the newspapers, they said: "But all other religious communities, including the Christians, are the same. None of them allow excavations where there might be bones."

Actually it's the opposite with us. Pius XII and his successors are the ones who wanted the excavations at the Vatican which is on a burial place. There would only be sacrilege and profanation of the dead if there were an intention of insulting them or if there were lack of respect toward one's beliefs or toward what one cherishes. That was not the case I imagine. I know that the excavations in Israel caused fierce reactions on the part of Muslims as well as Orthodox Jews. But the excavations yielded fascinating results from the point of view of Jewish and Christian history.

D.J.: When did you last go to Jerusalem?

In 1977.

D.J.: When you go, what sort of people do you meet?

As many people as possible, all sorts of people.

Y.B.P.: Not only church people?

No. I went in different circumstances. For ten or fifteen years I went nearly every year with groups of students.

Y.B.P.: Were these educational visits?

They were pilgrimages. We went to "discover" the Holy Places. We also planned meetings with Muslims, Palestinian Christians, and Israelis. We used to have regular meetings at the University of Jerusalem. We always used to visit one kibbutz. We did all the things one does on a two- or three-week visit when one wants to show youngsters a different world from their own. These yearly visits gave me many possibilities for establishing contacts, although, as leader of the group, I did not have much time for making visits on my own. But when I could, I tried to meet people in ordinary life and casually.

D.J.: Did you meet Israeli statesmen?

Hardly, but I met Ben Gurion on his kibbutz.

D.J.: Was that at Sde-Boker?

Yes, but I could hardly claim to have known him.

Y.B.P.: Did you like Israel?

Oh, yes *(laughter)*. What do you mean exactly by "like"?

Y.B.P.: Well, the Israeli solution for Jerusalem?

I would say that the least one can hope for is that the Holy Places be accessible to all and be taken out of belonging to one nation, in one way or another. This would mean an international guarantee for their accessibility to people from the different creeds involved, Muslims, Jews, and Christians.

Y.B.P.: Are you in touch with the Jewish community in France? Have you met Chief Rabbi Sirat?

Yes, I have met him and also Alain Goldmann, the chief rabbi of Paris; also Chief Rabbi Chouchena. But don't forget I am only beginning my time as archbishop of Paris . . .

Y.B.P.: Is there mutual suspicion between you and the head of the Jewish community?

I know that some of the things I said were hotly contested by Chief Rabbi Sirat, in certain articles which you obviously know about. But when we met afterward he was extremely friendly. He had understood what I had said to journalists in a different way from what I had intended; I was not speaking in legal terms. I was using everyday language and expressing my personal feelings and sense of belonging. So I think things have been clarified; I hope so anyway. As for the Jewish community, I have not really had the chance of meeting it yet. You see, I am not Sephardic; I do have Sephardic friends, but I know the Jews of Europe better than those of North Africa.

Y.B.P.: Is the French Jewish community more Sephardic than Ashkenazi today?[11]

Yes, surely you know that.

Y.B.P.: No, I am not all that clear about it.

Really? Well, in recent years there has been a certain shift in the trends of French Judaism.

Y.B.P.: I am not so clear about things because every time the French Jewish community is mentioned the name of the Rothschilds comes up, Alain and Guy. And people talk a lot about the Jewish revival, about political conflicts.

You are alluding to Hajdenberg?

Y.B.P.: That's it.

I see. Anyway I don't know him. Let us say that I have not yet had contacts with the community as such.

D.J.: Could we have just a few more minutes with you? Who would you say are the greatest figures of the Old Testament and what is their message?

I'll take another ten hours to answer that one *(laughter)*.

D.J.: Just quote three names.

Only three? That's not enough. I could say Abraham and Isaac, or Moses and Aaron, or David, or even the greatest sinner among the kings of Israel, or the prophets, or many others. How can I choose? Your question is too journalistic; it is as if you asked me in French literature what is my favorite book.

D.J.: You would say Victor Hugo, alas!

Certainly not *(laughter)*. Really all the parts of Jewish history convey something of God's revelation and love, his truth and his message. So it would be very hard for me to choose.

D.J.: I have another question. You lived through the time of the Holocaust and you suffered from it. How do you see the Holocaust fitting into the pattern of history? What is it that made such a thing happen? How can a believer like yourself make sense of it?

In this present world, humanity is struggling with the worst. It is struggling with the negation of itself. In this world the absolute for which humanity is made and which is its state as divine has a nega-

---

11. Since the Middle Ages the Jews of Spain were called Sephardic and the name was extended to the Jews of the Mediterranean areas generally. Ashkenazi applies, since the same period, to the Jews of Germany and Central and Northern Europe.

tion that is its hellish condition that can neither be understood nor endured. In this case of the *Shoah*[12] (I prefer to say the *Shoah* rather than the Holocaust, because Holocaust means something else; it is a free offering given to give glory to God), there was the will to exterminate. What was even more unbearable was that not only were human beings massacred and exterminated, as is still happening all over the world today for all sorts of reasons, but they were exterminated for no other reason than that they were Jews. The Nazis had other enemies and opponents and they did not suffer the same fate for the same internal reasons. The only reason was that they were Jews. It is therefore a crime that goes beyond anything that one can imagine; it is a denial of the other. At the beginning you asked me, "What is a Jew?" I said, "A man who brings the news of God's choice to his neighbor." And here he is being rejected and killed for no other reason. It is the uttermost limit of homicidal hatred. It is only when we see hatred like that that we can see, in its unbearable starkness, the destiny of the Jews and the destiny of humankind. That harsh light gives a glimpse of the dark depths of humanity itself. The only possible response is silence. One cannot talk of such a thing. Nor should one want to, because it is unbearable. The only thing that I can think about it, in my deepest self, is that from what is completely evil God can nevertheless bring something completely good. I don't know how he will do it, but I believe that all those who are victims of this horror were most certainly well loved by God.

Y.B.P.: One needs faith to talk like that.

I know, I speak as best I can. But there is a further consideration. I think that somehow they belong to the sufferings of the Messiah. How, only God can say, not me. And one day their persecutors will see that it is through them that we are saved. I don't know. I suppose it is better not to say such things. But it is what I think; of course it's not a justification of what happened. Once again Israel is a bearer of revelation; it reveals something about history and it reveals something about the nature of humanity.

Y.B.P.: But it could happen again.

It could happen again and it is happening again. One trembles at the thought that a disaster like that could happen again. But it is not just an accident; what happened exposes the human condition. We must therefore remain always on the watch. We know now what can exist deep down in human society. So those men who are on the side

12. *Shoah:* Hebrew for "annihilation."

of goodness and dignity, and who believe, those men must remain always on the watch.

The worst aspect of the whole business is not only that crimes were committed but that men tried to justify themselves for having committed them. So there were two sorts of evil; there were the crimes committed and of course one already knew about human cruelty. And there was the evil of trying to justify these crimes, looking for the reasons which motivated such acts and finding a cause for them instead of denouncing them; I think that is a greater evil, and it is widespread in our own day. Only the other day someone was trying to explain the assassination of President Sadat by looking for the reasons which motivated the murderers. No one looks for the motivation behind the courage of innocent victims. It is always violence which people are trying to justify. This points to a sort of blackout of the human mind; a kind of veil over people's judgment. The *Shoah* did not occur in the Dark Ages, in the time of the Huns and in a remote corner of the world; it took place in Europe, after the great eighteenth century, the century of Enlightenment.

Y.B.P.: I read in a newspaper something which you had said and which struck me as particularly fine. Could you say it again for us and explain it. You said, "My nomination as bishop meant for me that all of a sudden it was as though the crucifix were wearing the yellow star."

I can say it again but I can hardly add anything.

Y.B.P.: By that remark you were paying homage to the Jews who were persecuted and who had to wear the yellow star.

Yes, in spite of themselves and without knowing it, they became the image of innocence in this world. Without knowing it; no one chooses to be a hero. I know that all those who died over there were not heroes; but since they were persecuted unjustly they bore the figure of innocence and right. Some people want to deny what happened, the concentration camps, and so on. By doing that they not only reveal their bad conscience but also their secret desire to deny innocence and to avert attention from it. That is the way things happen in this world. First of all, the flouting of innocence is accepted and then one denies that there is such a thing. But taking on oneself the image of the innocent victim, that is at the center of the faith of Israel. That is the figure of the suffering servant in Isaiah.

D.J.: Do you as one of the prelates of the Catholic church feel a moral obligation toward the Jewish people?

Of course. But I have always felt like that, and so would anyone, I consider. The fact that I have a different office does not make any difference to that feeling or to that duty. I would add that every time there has been persecution of the Jews, there has also been rejection of Christianity. Those Christians who persecuted the Jews, whether they were politicians or churchmen, sinned grievously against God and against the Jews. Their actions amounted to a denial of their attachment to Christianity. It was not a national or ethnic quarrel; it concerns the essentials of the faith, as is shown by the fact that their attitude was often disguised under religious reasons.

Y.B.P.: Do you intend to visit Israel?

I would like to but I don't know yet.

Y.B.P.: Do you know if the pope is going to Israel?

I don't. He has said that he would like to go but I don't know exactly when that will be.

Y.B.P.: You don't know?

Didn't he say he was coming?

Y.B.P.: Yes he did.

Well, if he said it he will do it.

D.J.: What sort of man is the pope? He seems very nice and he is very popular in Israel. Can you tell us how you see him?

Well, first of all, he is an extremely cultured man. To understand a man like that, you have to know something about his past. Firstly, he is a Pole; everyone knows that but it implies a particular culture and a historical context which are different from those of Western countries. I am sure that everyone in Israel knows about contemporary Polish history, how Poland had to recreate its national identity, Polish nationalism between the wars, and so on. I am sure you understand that better than the French because you also had to live through the problems of recreating a national identity. So, from that point of view, the pope is in a good position for understanding you.

Secondly, the pope has had twenty years of wartime experience. He was in the Resistance; he was deeply affected by the most dramatic episodes of contemporary European history, much more than the English or the Americans could imagine, or Italians or Spaniards, more than Frenchmen even. His country has been much more deeply affected by the war, by the German occupation, by deportation, and then by the movements of population after the annexation of part of their territory. Lastly, the communist ideology has affected his country.

Thirdly, the pope is a man whose philosophical upbringing has come from German philosophy; phenomenology has been one of the sources of his philosophical thought. That's already three extremely unusual things for a pope to be. So he has a very personal view of contemporary history. He is not an Oriental; he is a man from Eastern Europe. But he is a much traveled man; he has visited the Polish Diaspora which is scattered all over the world, more or less. He has a world vision, rather than a Roman one. He is in Rome now but Rome is no longer the center of the world. The world has its center wherever humanity is. The pope gives symbolic expression to this truth by moving about everywhere.

Fourthly and lastly, he is a mystic; I don't mean in the sense of people who have visions.

Y.B.P.: You mean a deeply spiritual man?

That's it; a man who is completely in the hands of God, so that he is extraordinarily free. He couldn't care less about what people think about him. He never plays to the gallery. He is a free man; someone like that can face any situation; he can also welcome anyone. He is a mystic; he is not afraid.

Y.B.P.: So how can someone like that become pope?

It shows that miracles still happen *(laughter)*. I don't believe in providential personalities, but I do believe that God's providence provides the right man. In that sense people become providential. That being said, it's still true that times and periods change. John Paul II is a different sort of pope. Previously people from Western Europe didn't know that beyond the Oder is still Europe. They just ignored that part of Europe which is made up of the Slav nations. I wasn't surprised that it was the people from the Third World, from Africa and South America, who related readily to a pope from a country which has such a different image. He really is a sign of modern times.

Y.B.P.: Were you already a bishop when you met him?

Yes. I met him several times. Never have I met anyone with whom I have felt more at ease. He doesn't necessarily agree with you, but he is a man who can be completely attentive and who has an extraordinarily well-stocked mind. He understands what you are trying to say because he is so well disposed toward you. But you couldn't pull a fast one on him. He listens in silence but his supreme skill is saying what he thinks.

Y.B.P.: One more question, rather a fanciful one. Christmas is near and it nearly always occurs at the time of Hanukkah.[13]

13. Hanukkah was instituted in 165 B.C. by Judas Maccabeus to mark the purification of the temple after its profanation by Antiochus Epiphanes. It is the feast of Dedication or of Lights. Jews light candles on eight consecutive days, starting on 25 Kislev.

Yes.

Y.B.P.: What do the candles signify at Christmas? Is there any connection between the two festivals?

There could be.

Y.B.P.: Could one find a symbolic link between Christmas and Hanukkah which could express the connection between Judaism and Christianity which you have been talking about?

I don't really know. I think the similarities are due to a coincidence, but there could be more to it. It's different with Passover and Easter; they are the same festival.[14]

Y.B.P.: Jesus himself celebrated the Passover, didn't he?

Yes, and Christians celebrate the Passover of Jesus.

Y.B.P.: The feast of Hanukkah came much later.

There are different views about how Christmas came to be observed at the winter solstice. It looks as though originally the heavenly conception of Jesus was celebrated on the same date as his death and Resurrection, that is, at the time of *Pesach,* 14 Nisan, the spring equinox. That would put his birth at the winter solstice. The date was also chosen to replace pagan festivals because all pagan European peoples celebrated the winter solstice. So the feast of the Nativity of Christ was used by the Church to sweep away the idolatry of the Romans and the others, and to christianize these winter festivals. There is no historical evidence about the date of the birth of Jesus. I wonder whether my colleagues, the rabbis from Pharisaism, didn't do the same thing about finding a date for Hanukkah *(laughter).* Someone should study the historical origins of these two festivals. Hanukkah stands for the reversal of history, the overturning of false gods. Christmas may have had that meaning to begin with, thanks to the belief of the Jews and Pharisees that the meaning of history could be reversed. But I really don't know; there is something obscure about the whole thing.

Y.B.P.: Do you have any family in Israel?

Yes, I discovered it after becoming archbishop of Paris. I did not know that I had cousins over there.

Y.B.P.: Did they get in touch with you when they learnt that you had become archbishop?

14. After the ten plagues of Egypt, the Hebrews were allowed to depart and to *pass through* the Red Sea. Passover *(Pesach)* is the feast of passage which commemorates the Exodus; Jews have their meal that day in traveling clothes. To it has been associated a feast of first fruits which involves the sacrifice of a lamb or a kid whose blood is put on the doorposts and lintels.

That's exactly it. I received lots of telegrams and letters from cousins whose existence I did not know about. Ours was a very large family. They all said they were first or second cousins. I have one first cousin who survived the extermination and who knows more about the family than I do. He is researching it.

Y.B.P.: Did they send you photographs?

Yes, although not all of them were actually relatives. The name *Lustiger* is quite common. There were only two or three who were really my cousins. Nut Armand really is my first cousin and I was really surprised to learn of his existence.

Y.B.P.: One more question. Do you think that the church could have done more to save Jews during the war?

There is quite a lot of research being done on that. After the event, the judgment which can be made is always different from the one made at the time. Don't forget the attitude of the leaders of the Allies on the question during the war! Both Saul Friedlander and Léon Papeleux have been doing research on the subject; that research must go on. There was a whole Christian network which was created in order to save Jews. I think that the church saved more Jews than any other social or charitable institution. Of course that was her duty. Some people think that it took a long time to come round to a condemnation of anti-Semitism. But Pius XI had already condemned it before the war.

Y.B.P.: Do you know what the attitude of the present pope is toward Israel and the Jews?

I am quite sure that historically he is the pope who has had the best opportunity of understanding the situation of the Jews. He has true sympathy because he saw the Jewish situation through the experience of Eastern Europe; that is completely different from experiencing it in Western Europe. An Italian can only have a very imperfect notion of what the Jewish condition is like. The pope knows about it directly and in a special way because Poland was the focus of Jewry in Central Europe; the pope understands the prejudices against Jews and anti-Semitism in its most irrational and anti-Christian form because it flourished especially in Poland and Lithuania. In order to understand the origins of Jewish nationals and Jewish national feeling before the creation of the State of Israel, one has to remember that it was born in Poland and Central Europe. On the other hand, the pope has a very high regard for Judaism and he respects it spiritually.

Y.B.P.: One final question. How do you explain the way in which the State of Israel had such an appeal for Christian public opinion when it was set up?

When it began, the State of Israel was a utopia. Its creation was to be the realisation of equity and justice. I well remember what people were saying in Israel in 1950: "Here the police are honest. Here no one cheats. . . ."

D.J.: Things have changed since (laughter).

There was a kind of primal innocence. In Israel then there were no thieves; there were prisons but no criminals. Israel was intended as an exemplary creation because it inherited the patrimony of the Jews. But later on the same gap developed as the one we see between so-called Christian nations and their politics.

Y.B.P.: But don't you find that when you read something about Israel in the papers, something about its behavior as a state toward the Palestinians, for example, don't you find that it is always judged very severely?

I do; it's as if the condemnation were doubled.

Y.B.P.: So that means that people expect more from Israel than from other countries?

Yes, that's because people have an idealistic and unreal view of Israel. They still have the view that its founders had, a view which derives from the biblical requirement for absolute justice and truth.

Y.B.P.: But isn't it unfortunate for us if people expect too much from Israel?

Yes, I agree, because Israel, like other countries, cannot help making mistakes sometimes.

Y.B.P.: And committing sins too (laughter).

Yes, sins too. But one must not forget that the prophets of Israel called humankind to repentance.

Jewish and Christian Traditions Confronted with Universality

I am deeply moved by being among you tonight, but my time is limited. I will therefore leave unspoken the personal feelings I would have wished to express and go immediately to what seems to me to be the core of the matter.

Hidden resistances

This work of encounter between Jews and Christians that you have undertaken is historically decisive. A few years ago perhaps, half a century ago certainly, one could think that this work would finally ensure the triumph of reason over prejudices, over irrationality. In fact, it has been in such a way that Jews and Christians alike understood the problem of the struggle against anti-Semitism, as a struggle beyond religious boundaries. And after all, these very philosophical concepts of enlightened rationalism were those that enabled the birth of Zionism and had already, after the French Revolution, inspired the Emperor Napoleon in his measures with regard to the assimilation of the Jews. Today two centuries of experience have made us aware of the bloody failure of this Western delusion.

I will borrow a comparison from psychology in order to situate the problem of the relationships between Jews and Christians in the face of the historical failure of Western rationalism. One often speaks in Jewish literature (not in the sacred or scholarly literature, but from

International meeting of Christians and Jews at Heppenheim, West Germany, on 30 June 1981. The text was published in *Una Sancta* [Catholic monthly review] of February 1983.

the pen of modern novelists) of "Jewish angst," which others call "Jewish neurosis." There is no need to explain it. Kafka gave it its most fascinating expression for the Christian West, which has not yet clearly identified its Jewish source. In my opinion, anti-Semitism is the bloody neurosis of Christian societies. It is symmetrical to what has been called the Jewish neurosis.

The neurotic aspect of Hitlerian anti-Semitism has already been studied several times in the past thirty years. I am aiming here at a wider understanding of Western history with its temptations, its trials, its sins, in order to bring to light its spiritual pathology and thus to pave the way for its salvation. I have considered here the Jewish world and the Christian world as two partners, two historical subjects, prisoners of a double neurotic relationship.

One can also explain in another way this psychological comparison, if one considers the Jewish world and the Christian world as being only one historical subject. It is then necessary to talk about the West in the totality of its history in which are mingled, without confusion, all the currents of the Mediterranean civilizations marked by the presence of the Jews and kneaded together by Christianity. If the West is thus seen in its entirety as one sole historical subject, we would have to admit that it suffers from a morbid division which can be described as schizophrenic. For the West seems to be living a historical dissociation of its components, a mutual denial leading to its own destruction.

We can see this very well: we cannot be faithful to the inheritance we have received if we are not cured of this fatal disease. Christians must cease denying the existence of the Jews, thus denying themselves. Through pardon and mutual recognition, Jews must also discover that Christians are participating in the blessing that was entrusted to them and they must recognize the inner consistency of this blessing. Only a mutual recognition of Jewish fidelity and Christian fidelity may allow each one to be what it really is, getting closer, in the darkness of history, to the messianic relationship between Israel and the nations.

Do not therefore be surprised, while you develop relationships between Jews and Christians, if you unveil historical resistances which are the measure of humanity's sinfulness, if you bring to light a fatal historical pathology, if you touch the roots of a murderous madness through which, down the centuries, the peoples who inherited the biblical revelation tore at each other. I am not only talking about the persecution of the Jews by Christian nations; I also speak about the wars that divided Christian peoples and Christian nations. And here, in this place, we cannot ignore the historical role of the fratricidal relationships between France and Germany. And does not the State of Israel, now that it is a state like all the others, participate in its turn in the very same historical conflicts of the nations?

The challenges of the future

Provided we go back to our mutual identity, we must face together several contemporary challenges.

The first one for the West is the crisis of secularism. It has been said that it is the fruit produced by the Christian and Jewish West because of the struggle against idolatry. But if one sees secularization and atheism as the ultimate progress in the struggle against the idols, it amounts to giving in to a self-idolatry of human reason. There is, indeed, a fundamental category brought to light in the Jewish tradition and which is part of the patrimony without which Christianity is not Christianity: the sacred, defined not in sociological terms, but in terms of revelation. The delusion of secularization is opposed by holiness, the sacred element invested in us by God's call. The mystery of God and fidelity to the mystery of God as it is revealed is truly the key issue of Western societies, which tend to become structurally atheistic. Such is the first challenge, the challenge of secularization.

The common conscience we have of the eschatological character of God's Kingdom responds to the second challenge which is expressed in a double temptation of our civilization:

(1) The totalitarian temptation. This is the negation of eschatology. This totalitarian temptation can be called Pol Pot, Stalin, Hitler, and many other names. . . . Faith alone enables us to see that this world is not the Kingdom of God.

(2) Its opposite, the skeptical temptation. Only faith enables us not to give up the ethical obligation of the law, the fidelity to the word God gave us, our task in this world.

I will conclude by pointing out a third challenge. The dignity of every human person is one of the fundamental demands of our society, of our time. But nothing can be said about this matter as long as we are not capable of hearing, of situating within ourselves the source of our true dignity, which is our formation in the image of God. The rock on which the dignity of man can be founded is there and there alone.

For there are no borders that human persons could draw at will, limiting their rights, deciding where respect for themselves stops or starts, as if it depended on them to determine the limits of good and evil. The true dignity of persons is not in a human convention about the law, but in their nature, created by their relation with God. And this is what we must witness to, be martyrs for. Such is the third challenge which is perhaps the most urgent.

All the nations

We have evoked our common past. We have looked at the challenges of the future. The present sends us back together to the most fundamental question of faith.

At the end of the second Christian millennium, we have, as Western peoples, placed ourselves in the presence of other peoples whose history we discovered only a few centuries ago. Now the peoples of Africa, Asia, and America put us to the test of truth. Are the Jewish and Christian traditions only a form of the sacred in the West or do they have a universal vocation? Does an African, who must study a Western language in order to participate in the forum of the nations, also have to learn to read Hebrew, Greek, or Latin to have a share in the blessing? Can he truly say: "If I forget you, Jerusalem? . . ." Must he learn to say it?

Finally, in the face of the word that God spoke to us in the concrete situation of history, what is our true vocation? Is it a particular, ethnic, and perishable history? Or is it universal? If it is a particular history we are nothing but imperialists. But if it is universal, then we must offer proof that it is the gift of the Holy Spirit. . . .

Im eshkaḥēk Yerushalayim![1]

1. "If I forget you, O Jerusalem": a reference to Ps. 137:5.

Christianity Is Indissolubly Linked to Judaism

What is the essential mission of a bishop of Paris?

As any bishop, the bishop of Paris witnesses to the faith. Because of his ordination, he has a sacerdotal role. He is the shepherd of a people, the witness of a people.

He is also, in a certain way, the successor of the biblical priests?

Yes, which entails a theological problem. Nowadays, and especially in the West, there is a debate among the Christians. Some of them see a Judaization of Christianity in the idea—which they deplore—of a sacerdotal caste. In general, this comes from the fact that they have not properly understood the meaning of the priesthood in the Bible. The concept of separation has a decisive role in the Bible: first the separation of the people as such, then a separation between sacred and laity within the people. Even within a "priestly people," the priests are set apart. In Christianity, this concept was retained in a peculiar way since the sacerdotal function is concentrated in the person of the Messiah, Christ. But as is the case in Judaism, the priesthood is shared by the totality of the people, and there is no such thing as a real sacerdotal caste. Ordination brings to the fore for certain men and certain acts this sacerdotal function that belongs also, and first of all, to an entire people. The basic idea is therefore the same, but the priesthood does not belong to a specific family. It is received through ordination.

It remains true that this debate brings to light the retreat—if not

Interview by Rabbi Jacquot Grunewald in *Tribune Juive* [Jewish monthly published in Paris], 4 September 1981.

refusal—of a certain number of Christians before the idea of a "setting apart," "election," perceived as being exclusively, and pejoratively, Jewish. While it is the very foundation of the "Christian vocation." While, without this reality of the election, it is impossible to hear correctly what the Gospel says about Christ. This amounts to seeing the election as a privilege. This paganizes the election. Thus on the belt of the German soldiers was the phrase *Gott mit uns*. One forgets that the election was made for the service of others and not for the benefit of the chosen who would think of themselves as members of an elite.

Let us return to Paris. Setting aside its tremendous numbers, does the Catholic community of Paris present specific problems in comparison with other Christian assemblies? And what are its immediate problems and its general problems?

The specific problems of Paris stem from the originality of its position within France. The diocese of Paris is hypertrophied with regard to the whole of the French body. There are difficulties coming from the megapolis, the large city. There is no need to enter into details.

But can it be said that there is a particular problem which is specific to those who are responsible for French Catholicism?

Certainly. I would define the historical problem of Catholicism in French culture as follows: France is a country of Catholic tradition. Her kings were "most Christian" kings. It has been said that she was "the eldest daughter" of the church, which means that, among the barbarians, she was the first Western people baptized, thanks to the baptism of King Clovis.

But France, since the beginning of her history, since the early Middle Ages anyway, has carried in herself the relics of an inner division. Due to the presence of a strong "secular" tradition, it can be said that French culture has a double face.

Everybody has learned to confront Voltaire and Pascal. In the seventeenth century there were libertines and a party of *dévots*.[1] Already in the fourteenth century the jurists of Philip the Fair brought back Roman law in its most pagan aspects. This double tradition never ceased to exist and it expressed itself in the first secular revolution of the West.

---

1. Literally "devout party," a group of influential people who sided with the church and Catholic orthodoxy against "freethinkers." (Translator's note)

Besides, France does not have much of a biblical tradition, contrary to the Anglo-Saxon and Germanic countries that were influenced by the Reformation. Through its translation, the Bible was the matrix of the German and English languages. Nothing of this kind occurred here.

The church of France drags along a nostalgia, the image of a unified country, while it happens to be a country whose citizens have multiple origins and tendencies. How can one retain a strong awareness of one's spiritual identity, of the Christian faith calling to universality when it is perceived at this moment of our culture as an unjustified difference, an incomprehensible peculiarity?

How can one learn not to be like everybody else out of fidelity to God? Such is one of the crucial questions that the Catholics of France must learn to ask themselves today in order to be able to answer the questions posed by their contemporaries.

(Then we talk about French Judaism. His Excellency Jean-Marie Lustiger credits it, for the same reasons, with a "unique" place.) But is there in fact a French Judaism? The Jews of old, when they were precisely confronted with this twofold secular and Jewish tradition, did they not capitulate in one or two generations, as soon as the gates of emancipation opened wide before them? Did they not prefer the tradition of Voltaire to that of Moses?

As to the Jews of today, in their vast majority they were not really nourished by this "bi-faced" culture. Others, who keep their place in the heart of Judaism, were better armed to overcome the secular current with the teachings of Moses.)

It remains true that France is today the most "secularized" of all countries, though this concept is not a French but an American one. The matrix of American culture is pluralism. Or to be more precise, America is a majority made up of minorities in flight. Every American is thus endowed at the same time with a majority and a minority consciousness. In France, the regal tradition is unitarian and the Jacobin tradition is uniforming. Yet, the country has inner divisions. This explains the features of French anti-Semitism in the nineteenth century: it was bourgeois and liberal. It was a nationalistic anti-Semitism that, unlike what happened in other countries, Russia, for instance, did not issue exclusively from a religious tradition as, to continue with the same example, Russian messianism.

It was said that if the pope appointed you in Paris, it was so that after the incident in Rue Copernic[2] the parishioners of the French capital might be aware that their bishop was of Jewish descent. In such a way, he was said to want to halt an anti-Semitism that some people saw as a resurgent force.

People also said, and for identical reasons, that I had been appointed bishop of Orleans because it is a town of "rumor." I have no idea whether these viewpoints have any factual basis. I never discussed the matter with the pope. I suppose that he must have, among other considerations, taken these types of significance into account. As I know him, I would say that my Jewish origin did not determine the choice of the pope; but once he had made his choice, it certainly contributed to his insistence in appointing me to these positions, in case my Jewish origin were to be presented to him as an objection.

And how did the Catholics of Paris make you aware by their reaction that they knew their bishop was a Christian of Jewish descent?

The situation is so unusual, unthinkable, that the reactions of the Catholics of Paris are difficult to perceive and to understand from the outside. My appointment and my presence in Paris brought to light abruptly the part of Judaism that Christianity bears in itself. It is as if crucifixes had started, all of a sudden, to wear the yellow star. Many Christians told me or wrote to me, quietly and discreetly, the religious love they had for the Jewish people in the name of Christian faith itself. My presence thus enabled them to express feelings they dared not voice publicly, either because of anti-Semitic stereotypes or because of the bad conscience of France since the Nazi occupation.

The Jews should know, and also the majority of the French people for whom Christianity is first of all a form of social belonging, that the most fervent Christians have for the people of Israel a sincere and humble love nourished by their faith and prayer. It is not for nothing that Christians pray the psalms and continue to meditate on the Bible.

As to the attitude of the Catholics with respect to anti-Semitism, it has evolved considerably. But anti-Semitism is a secular phenomenon. The behavior of present Catholics with regard to the Jews is the consequence of various cultural factors, though there are reflexes which were transmitted to them since childhood.

---

2. A restaurant of Jewish ownership and patronage was bombed in the street of that name in the fall of 1980, and there were several victims. The incident stirred up anti-Semitism and, at the same time, reaction against it. (Translator's note)

Can one consider that there is a Christian anti-Semitism in today's France?

No, not if we talk about a deliberate anti-Semitism. If you show to Christians the anti-Semitic texts that were published under the Nazi occupation, they will not accept them.

And the anti-Semitic writings of the Christian theologians of the past centuries?

No more. But there are stereotypes that are unfavorable to the Jews, buried deep in consciousness and memory. It can happen that, under the influence of political factors, they are reactivated.

Do you consider your situation as a priest of Jewish descent an exceptional or exemplary one?

Neither exceptional nor exemplary. There are and there have been other priests and other Christians of Jewish descent. In Israel there are quite a few Christians of Jewish origin. I was struck by the fact that they feel comfortable in the Israeli mosaic. Perhaps the majority of Israelis tend to see them as sweet dreamers, but they do not refuse them the right to exist as such.

Such an attitude is characteristic of this category of Israelis for whom the nationalistic element became more important than religious considerations. But let us come to an essential question. When you were appointed archbishop of Paris, certain words regarding your attachment to Judaism which had been credited to you caused some emotional reactions in the Jewish community. You were supposed to have declared that, when you embraced the Catholic faith, you "achieved your Jewishness," which could mean that the normal destiny of a Jew who wants to achieve himself or herself is to become a Christian.

You know, many people said many things I was supposed to have uttered when I was appointed archbishop of Paris. I don't think that I used the word *achievement*. It seems to me that I said that, as a Christian, I took upon myself my Jewish condition and that I did not intend to deny it. What I meant by evoking this achievement was not a theological reflection, which belongs to another order than an interview, but something pertaining to my autobiography. As a child, I perceived my Judaism only as a social identity, since all the education I had received was essentially secular. I was the son of immigrants who knew that he was a Jew and belonged to a community persecuted for no other reason than the evil of human beings. In the Lycée Montaigne I thought that I was the only one to know the meaning of the word *pogrom*. My father told me that his grandfather was beaten and the hair of his beard plucked when he ventured in the streets of Poland on Christian feast days.

As to the election of this community and its moral superiority, it was for me a call to struggle for justice and the respect of all, to help all the unfortunates. To become a doctor seemed to me the best way of doing so at that time. Or else a "great writer" like Zola whose books I read around that time. How many Jewish children throughout the world must have had the same ambitions!

It is in Christianity that I discovered this biblical and Jewish content that had not been imparted to me as a Jewish child. Thus it happened that in the course of my life I thought that I became a Jew because, by embracing Christianity, I finally discovered the values of Judaism, not denying them in the least. I saw Abraham and David on the stained glass of the cathedral of Chartres.

Contrary to certain Jews who came close to Catholicism without necessarily becoming converts, such as the philosopher Simone Weil, you do not seek in any way to extirpate Judaism from the Christian faith. You consider, quite to the contrary, that through the Christian faith, Judaism is valuated.

Christianity is indissolubly linked to Judaism. If it separates itself from the latter, it ceases to be what it is. The relationships between Judaism and Christianity are complex and offer a great opportunity for the worst misunderstandings. It is not a substitution, as in the case of a political empire replacing the preceding one, nor a cultural transfer as when a culture is accepted by another (Greece in Rome, antiquity in Europe, and so on), nor a succession as when a son takes the place of his father in an enterprise. The parable of Luke's Gospel opens a new understanding: "A man had two sons. . . ." Certain exegetes explain that the elder son is Israel, while the younger, the *goyim*. An old Jewish story. . . .

But in becoming an adult, didn't you think about studying Judaism since you had not done so as a child? Did you not feel a need to know Judaism better?

In 1945 and 1946 I was twenty years old. To whom could I have gone spontaneously to learn about traditional Judaism? French Judaism was barely reborn out of its ashes. What really concerned the Jewish collectivity, as I understood it, was the creation of the Jewish state that washed away an immemorial humiliation. As a Christian, I was then asking myself the question of its spiritual future. But you know what things were at that time. . . .

Does Catholicism not have a policy of conversion for the Jews anymore?

If you mean by this a missionary activity specifically geared to the Jews, no. Nobody among today's Catholics is aiming to take the Jews away from Judaism at all costs. But if a Jew wants to convert and takes the initiative in this direction, we do not reject him or her.

Are you in full agreement with the 1973 declaration of the French bishops about relationships with Judaism?

Yes. I would perhaps have used other words, but I accept this declaration. You see, there is a dispute between Jews and Christians that we must manage to overcome. On the one hand, Christianity has rejected the Jews from the outset; and on the other, the Jews rejected Christianity. However, I want to be clear on this point. There can be no equal sharing of wrongs and responsibilities. I stress this: these rejections were in no way symmetrical, as some may have heard it said, not in any way and especially not on the level of physical consequences: persecution to the extent of annihilation!

What I mean is that, at the point we have reached today, some Christians may have been led to believe that the Jews have become a meaningless entity. Which is what the bishops' declaration wanted to redress. But a similar reasoning exists among Jews: they too might be brought to consider Christians meaningless. In the face of such a temptation, must we not stand up today?

It is true that there has not been a declaration by the French rabbis about Christianity, so that the leaders of Christianity in France are often asking themselves questions about the exact position of the French rabbis. One can fear that, only too often, people are content with platitudes about friendly relationships between Jews and Christians. How could and should Jews and Christians work together?

The duty of Judaism is to bring about justice. For this purpose, God gave his commandments to the Jewish people. Christianity inherited them, but in their ethical meaning. Today we are struggling against paganism that leads to the rejection of humankind. We are witnesses to life. We must boldly confront the death wish of our time, remind again and again the world that it was created by God and that God has sole sovereignty. And that humankind is created in his image and likeness. This is the only absolute foundation of humankind's dignity for which one must be ready to sacrifice everything, including life. In the world of today we find ourselves partners in a common witness. Through our common origin we have learned to struggle against misfortune since God has entrusted us with the blessings that Christians received through the Beatitudes. We must never surrender, never. And we have nothing to lose by struggling together.

Anti-Semitism: Irrationality

*Y*ou *were born in a Polish Jewish family, you converted to Catholicism as a youth. And even when you became a bishop, you declared: "I remain a Jew." Isn't this a contradiction?*

In my view, to become a Christian does not mean to deny the Jewish condition. Not in any way. I did not run away from it in the days of the yellow star and the concentration camps; I don't see why people would pull it away from me today.

Are there any objections on the part of Rome when you say such things?

No, and there are very good reasons for this in Scripture. I will send you back to the New Testament in its entirety.

What passage of Scripture are you talking about?

The New Testament is incomprehensible if it is not founded on the Jewish vocation, the vocation of Israel, the vocation of Christ to the pagans. This is a fundamental given of the Christian faith which embarrassed part of the West all though its history.

No doubt. Which is why it surprises us all the more that your reflections were not contested within the church.

There is a constant drift in the West: the desire to cut off its own historical roots. A balanced Christian faith would commit suicide in rejecting these roots. Marcion's heresy, wanting to uproot from the Gospels all traces of the Old Testament, is a testimony to this. Just like some of your scientists who claimed to be able to demonstrate that Jesus was a pure "Aryan." . . .

Interview by Klaus-Peter Schmid in *Der Spiegel* [German magazine], 11 January 1983.

As to me, how could I separate my destiny from my parents, my family, all my dear ones? I don't see how I could have denied my own history, were it only from the viewpoint of my own honor and the honor of humankind. Don't forget that this history, forever marked with the "final solution" of Hitler, remains a burning issue for all of humankind, and especially for the West.

Were your family observant Jews?

My family belongs to that generation that had invested its hope in the liberalization of the early twentieth century in Central and Eastern Europe. The trend was much stronger yet in Germany than in Poland or Russia. My young father, my young mother rejected the religious world as if it had been made of absurd constraints, antique curios, in order to enter into the modern era without denying anything of their identity and their social or familial boundaries.

You spoke about the honor of humankind. Now, as early as the time of your childhood, this honor was terribly violated by Nazi Germany in the murder of the Jews. When did you become aware of this secular perversion?

One of my first contacts with Christianity took place during summer vacations with two German families in 1936, in Ziegelhausen near Heidelberg, and in 1937 in Freiburg-am-Bresgau. I was ten and eleven years old. These families were anti-Nazi and Christian. I then saw with my own eyes what Nazi anti-Semitism was. I used to read *Der Stürmer*[1] which was posted in the streets.

Were you already reading German?

Yes, I was in Germany in order to improve the German that I had started to study in school. I met for a whole summer with teenagers who belonged to the Hitler Youth and the B.D.M.[2] They were simply in love with Nazism. The parents distrusted their children. I remember a boy who was two or three years older than I. When he showed me his Hitler Youth dagger, he told me that he would kill all the Jews.

But you are talking here about personal memories. As a Jew, don't you think that the attitude of the official Catholic church toward the persecution of the Jews in Nazi Germany was too accommodating?

What I found out was that the people who were anti-Nazi were most of the time Christians. Simultaneously I encountered violent

---

1. *Der Stürmer,* anti-Semitic periodical of Julius Streicher, an early Nazi leader who was convicted at the Nuremberg war crimes trial and was hanged.
2. B.D.M., Bund Deutscher Mädel, was an association for girls similar to Hitler Youth for boys.

anti-Semitism and the concrete testimony of people who claimed to be Christians. What was a scandal to me later on was not the slowness of the church but the blindness of almost all the intellectuals and the political leaders of the West before the rise of irrationality, of the Nazi madness. For it is easy to accuse the church alone, but what happened to the German university scholars during that time? Who among them did protest? Where were the liberals, the democrats? What happened to the left-wing parties during the last years of the Weimar Republic?

But isn't it the vocation of the church to protest earlier and more forcefully than intellectuals, for instance?

This was part of the spiritual and intellectual collapse of an entire people. The same thing happened in France. During the war, we also encountered terrible equivocations and excesses of irrationality. The accusation against the church from some quarters, even if it is justified on certain points, seems to me a good way to rid oneself of the true question, which is that of the resignation of the entire West, or the impotence of the West as a whole in the face of such monstrous happenings. Even the Allies, when they saw the aerial photos of the concentration camps taken by the American airforce, hesitated to speak out. What can one say about the Russians? Read again the autobiographical novels of Manes Sperber and Mendel Mann, for instance.

Christian Life:
Reenactment of the Passover

What Jesus celebrates during the Last Supper, is it actually the Jewish Passover?

Jesus celebrated with his disciples the Jewish Passover—the feast of *Pesach*. The exegetes are still debating whether the Last Supper was a paschal meal, an anticipated paschal meal, or else a Sabbath meal identified after the fact with the paschal meal. In the Gospels, especially the Gospel of Luke (22:14–20), every detail of the Last Supper finds its full significance if it is based on the ritual celebration of Passover. Jesus celebrates the Passover with his disciples as with a new family; he is the head of the family. At the end of the *Seder*,[1] adds Mark, they sang the psalms, the *Hallel*. The Eucharistic celebration of Christians draws all its meaning from this origin. Nowadays the Eucharist is often presented as a meal. This is quite right. But people think about festive meals as they take place in our society. Festive meals, even sacred ones, were numerous in the pagan era. Even today the pagan roots of our culture are quite close. The Eucharist is neither a sacred pagan meal nor a "festive meal" as we conceive it today. It is the shared and hasty meal of the Passover rooted in a sacrificial symbolism still very real in the time of Jesus: the lamb of the feast was sacrificed in the temple. Without this reference, the very Eucharist loses its meaning.

Interview by Jean Daniel in *Le Nouvel Observateur* [leftist Parisian weekly], 1 April 1983.

1. *Seder*, the dinner meal on the first night or first two nights of Passover, during which the *Hallel* or "Halleluja!" psalms are sung, specifically Pss. 115, 116, 117, 118, and 136. (Translator's note)

Because there is already, in the Jewish Passover, an evocation of the flesh and the blood.

The blood in question is a textual echo of Moses' formula: "This is the blood of the Covenant" (Exod. 24:8). Jesus recited it (Mark 14:24). For the Eucharist is a memorial (*zikkaron* in Hebrew), "Do this in remembrance of me" (Luke 22:19). This is much more than a mere memory: it brings back the past and ushers in the future, for the significance of the Passover is messianic.

How can one say that the Eucharist is a memorial?

It is a double memorial. First in the meaning of the Jewish Passover: the Christian Easter adopts the memory of Israel. . . .

Meaning the celebration of the Covenant and the Exodus from Egypt?

Yes. During Holy Week, and especially during the celebration of Holy Saturday: the whole history of salvation, of creation up to the fulfillment of time, is liturgically commemorated in the readings. In its turn, the Eucharist is a memorial of Jesus' memorial. Thus do the pagans gain entrance to the memory of Israel by sharing in the memorial of Jesus since, by doing this, they participate in Jesus' thanksgiving, the Son who obeyed the promise. A Christian who would not adopt this memory of Jesus, which includes the memory of Israel, would not welcome the grace given to him or her. In this, it must be said, Christian liturgies are faithful to the Jewish ritual of Passover celebrated by Jesus.

Jesus brought Judaism to unbelievers?

He brings the pagans into the grace given to Israel. He enables people to share in the Covenant with God. According to us Christians, this was the event foretold by the Prophets.

And what is the second aspect?

Precisely that this memorial lived by Jesus became a memorial of Jesus himself, of the offering of Jesus who grasps us in a state of rupture and sin, of distress, living apart from God, and who invites us to come back to him instead of locking ourselves up in refusal and despair. As Son, he offers his own life and freedom to the only Father in heaven. He brought all men and women into the filial condition . . . It is much more than this. We say that Jesus is the Son of God, the "only Son" of God. Before giving to these words the meaning which brings us to the mystery of God himself and his eternal Word, we should not forget that Isaac was the first to bear this title of "only son" of his father Abraham (Gen. 22:2) and that Israel was called "the beloved child of God" (Hos. 11:1, cf. Exod. 4:22). Jesus presents himself as the obedient Son who "does the will of the Father in heaven." This is a phrase of revelation, a "voice from heaven," said about Jesus when he was baptized, during the Transfiguration: "This is my Son, the Beloved; my favor rests on him" (Matt. 3:17; 17:5).

Except that the Bible talks about "the people."

The Bible says "servant," "chosen," and "son." Israel is personified as son and, at the same time, the Messiah-king is presented as son. Son is therefore a term whose significance is collective and personal at the same time. But let's be clear: true filial condition is perfect obedience to the will of God the Father. It is within this obedience, this human condition which has become filial and not servile and fearful, that the condition of son is achieved. To say that Israel is the son or to say that Jesus is the son in his human condition does not mean that humankind perceives itself—as was the case in the pagan cosmogonies—as the physical issue of God, but as a partaker of the life of God through grace, through a gratuitous choice and through the free love of God. Thus can humankind reach its fullness. We enter, with regard to the unknowable God, into a relationship enabling us to know the mystery of God and to find by grace the achievement of freedom, as Jesus told his disciples in the Sermon on the Mount.

In this part of your analysis you do not speak about the divinity of Jesus.

I am talking about both the filial condition of Israel and the human filial condition of Jesus. There is no separation between Jesus and Israel. The evangelists witness to the history of Jesus while referring it constantly to the history of Israel. It is in this meaning that Jesus is the fulfillment of Israel (Matt. 5:17). The word is terrible because it has often been understood as meaning the annihilation of Judaism and justifying the persecution of the Jews.

You mean to say that the blossoming of Israel in Jesus does not imply. . . .

Does not imply the historical disappearance of Israel and does not turn into futility its historical existence or its spiritual vocation.

Nor its survival. . . .

Nor its life or mission.

Would you go so far as to say, in your evocation of the memorial dimension of the Passover, that in this act of Jesus the will not to make any proselytes was violated, that is, that there was an access to universality?

The access to universality is at the same time anterior and posterior to the last Passover celebrated by Jesus. Jesus himself affirms it in a phrase taken from Isaiah—"for all men"—at first enigmatic for his disciples: "This is the cup of my blood, the blood of the Covenant, shed for you and for all men for the forgiveness of sins." From the outset of the Covenant with Israel, as early as the promise to Abraham (Gen. 12:3), and in the entire continuity of the Covenant and the hope given by the Prophets (Isaiah, Jeremiah, Ezekiel), as well as by Daniel, access to the nations is the constant meaning and key of the vocation of Israel."

But with a mission, kept by Israel, to be a witness among the nations?

Yes, of course. With the concept that all the nations will come to worship and Israel will have the surprise of children "it did not beget."

Universality is inscribed as a hope as early as the vocation of Abraham: "In you all the nations of the earth will be blessed." The uniqueness of the vocation of the Jewish people, in its very constitution, has its meaning only within this universal opening. This is not a promise of universal hegemony: this is not a people at the center of the world who will see the totality of the universe coming to it. It is a mission toward all, because God is revealed as God of all peoples and not only of Israel; he makes himself the God of Israel only because he chose Israel, which is nothing by itself, in order to make it the instrument of his love for all the nations. Look at the story of creation. Genesis shows how the God of Israel is the God of all men. He is the same and only one.

Secondly, universality is inscribed in the life of Jesus himself. During his life, foreshadowing elements are carefully noted by the evangelists. Jesus himself said: "I was sent only to the lost sheep of the House of Israel" (Matt. 15:24). He accepts from his Father in heaven this limitation of Israel as the domain of his action. The opening of the Kingdom of heaven to the pagan nations will be achieved only after his own death; however, in the time of Jesus there are prophecies and adumbrations of the conversion of the pagan nations that the evangelists strongly emphasized.

I present one which is very well known: the parable of the prodigal son (Luke 15). The meaning of the parable is the following: the elder son, who remained with the Father, is Israel. The Father is God. And the elder son is always with the Father and must rejoice in the love of the Father. The younger son, for his part, has claimed his share of the inheritance, and the inheritance is the sum of the divine goods, the knowledge of God. He went away to a remote country, to the country of the dead. He squandered the inheritance and had nothing left. He is the pagan. As a result, he becomes a slave and would like to eat the food given to swine. In the Middle East swine are sacred animals symbolizing death, which is why the Jews are forbidden to eat them. Death is not a god. He who is in God's hands can have no complicity with death. Thus the younger son becomes a slave to death, brought down to the level of the animals. He said: I want to go back to my father because there I will have life. The father welcomes him, and you know the rest of the parable.

The meaning of the parable is that the younger son is also a son. This is to say to Israel: watch it, the pagans are lost sons, and God finds joy in getting his sons back. They have as many rights as you do to the goods of the Father, they have even more! They have more because they are repentant sons, lost sons who have been found again, dead sons brought back to life. And you, who have remained just and faithful, you have no reason to complain: "you are always with me," and thus you must rejoice with me in finding your brother who was lost. And you must not be jealous of his portion of the inheritance. This parable is clearly a Jewish one and could not be explained outside of this context.

Then, there are in the very life of Jesus precise moments pointing to the entrance of the pagans into the Covenant with God. For instance, we are told about the cure of the centurion's servant in Capernaum (Luke 7:1–10) where the differences in attitude between pagans and Jews is clearly seen. The Jews come close to Jesus, surround him on all sides, touch him; they are physically in contact (Luke 6:17–19). As to the pagan, he comes from a distance and says: "Lord, I am not worthy that you should come under my roof. Do not trouble yourself to come." Jesus admires this and says: "I tell you, not even in Israel have I found a faith like this." Thus the pagan has access to salvation through faith, and the story announces the salvation which will be given to the pagans.

Everything happens as if there had been a promise, in the life of Israel, and an adumbration in the life of Jesus, of this opening of salvation to the nations. But this event occurred only after the death and Resurrection of Jesus. It happened on Pentecost through the gift of the Spirit who widens all at once the circle of the disciples of Jesus and creates a new people (Acts 2), somewhat as in Ezekiel in the episode of the dry bones when the rebirth of the people was predicted (Ezek. 7).

Here is the event that gave birth to the assembly, the *ecclesia* of Jews and non-Jews, which caused a break from the synagogue. The Passion is not the moment of the break: the Passion of Christ, quite to the contrary, reveals that all, without distinction, are imprisoned together through their complicity in sin; Saint Paul stresses this forcefully at the beginning of his Epistles to the Romans.

The evangelists stress that all men and women are compromised in the death of Christ, Rome as well as the people of Israel. There is a special and very lucid analysis of Roman power that claims to be just. And Pilate, the representative of law and order, commits the supreme iniquity: "I find no case against him" (John 18:38; 19:4–6). "I am innocent of this man's blood" (Matt. 27:24). While he is responsible and pretends to ensure justice, equity, he knowingly condemns an innocent. This is the essence of lie justifying itself through skepticism. "What is truth?" Pilate responds to Jesus. In this trial certain representatives of Israel were also compromised: elders, priests, scribes. And the people, according to Saint Luke, are reduced to a silent role. They look on as if they did not understand. The Greek word used by Luke (23:13; 27:35) is *laos*, the sacred people, the "holy people."

They are holy and they do not understand?

They are silent. They were present, looking on. Everybody was compromised, including the disciples who were afraid and ran away. Such is the universal dimension of the cross of Christ. The Passion of Christ serves as an instrument of revelation of the totality of evil which exists in the world and in each one of us.

At what point in time do all those people who will recognize him understand the meaning of his death and understand the promise of Resurrection?

Jesus remains unfathomable, incomprehensible for all until the day when they receive the promised "gift," which enables them to enter into the knowledge of the Wisdom of God.

Thus the disciples on the road to Emmaus in Luke (chap. 24). The two men are on their way, having left Jerusalem right after the Shabbat-HaGadol, the Great Sabbath, therefore on Sunday, and they walk in sadness. Someone catches up with them on the road and asks: "Why are you so sad?" Then they tell him: "You must be the only one in Jerusalem not to know what happened! Jesus, a prophet who was powerful in word and deed—we were hoping that he would be the one to deliver Israel—died three days ago. It is true that some women came to tell us that they did not find him in his tomb. But . . ." At that point, the stranger gave them a commentary on the Scriptures: "You foolish men! So slow to believe the message of the prophets . . . Don't you know that the Messiah had to suffer to enter into his glory?" And, starting at the beginning, he explained all of Scripture to them. The men do not yet understand. Then comes the last episode at Emmaus which is very mysterious. They say: "Stay with us, it is getting late . . . We are reaching an inn, come with us." Then when they are going to sit down at the table, they recognize him "at the breaking of the bread," and "he vanished from their sight."

Then the disciples think: "Was not our heart on fire while he explained the Scriptures to us?" and they return hastily to Jerusalem "to tell the Apostles what had happened to them."

Thus the disciples do not understand until the moment when they receive what the Passion of Christ and his Resurrection were meant to give to humankind. The promised gift is the Holy Spirit changing the hearts of humankind. It is the Spirit who sets "afire" the stony hearts of men and women, in accordance with the oracle of the prophet Ezekiel. Only this Spirit enables the disciples to have access to the mystery of the Passion, to understand why the Messiah had to suffer.

The Last Supper is the food of the messianic people who already see this transfiguration and the birth which is taking place.

Which means that without the Passion and the Resurrection there is no fulfillment?

Only the gift of the Spirit of the risen one foreshadowed the fulfillment of time.

Then what does Judas symbolize in this absolute of the Passion? He is the tool of the divinity. . . .

This is the extreme paradox. I think that Judas is, with regard to the disciples, what death is in the experience of Christ himself: an apparent victory of the evil one, of evil over good. The idea that the Messiah suffers and dies is in itself a scandal. It is a negation of God. It is the greatest scandal. The idea that, among the disciples, there is, as it were, the expression of definite refusal and of imprisonment in despair is another scandal, inseparable from the death of Jesus. But Jesus overcame death, he also died for Judas.

His symbol remains an enigma for you?

An enigma and a scandal like death. Judas and Peter cannot be separated. Peter denies and repents. Judas betrays and despairs. These are the two faces of human beings. We are not told anything about the behavior of the other disciples during the Passion of Jesus, except that they run away, that they are not present. The two apostles who have a personal face, who play a role in the Passion are Peter and Judas. The others appear only as a group . . . except one, who is nameless: "the disciple Jesus loved."

In the human and historical dimension it all happens as if Judas still played the role of evil, sustaining a sin, bound to pay for it and to be punished for it.

Yes. Saint Luke says: "Father, forgive them for they know not what they are doing" (Luke 23:34). The prayer of forgiveness uttered by Jesus for all those who were the tools of his Passion, executioners, people, everybody, is a word of mercy; it is not a facile and irresponsible amnesty. Mercy is the other face of justice.

When people condemn the just one, his innocence brings to light the hidden evil which is in all people; it unveils to what extent evil can exist. In this crime it is clear that evil has complicity with death. This is the ultimate coherence of the human condition revealed by the crucified just one. He manifests our wounded freedom, our will to do evil which leads to homicide, the death of the other, or to suicide, one's own death. The figure of the innocent unveils evil by accepting its consequences to the very end. At the limit, the innocent dies not by decree, but because he accepts to be subjected to the complete consequences of evil so as to unmask this evil, to bare it, and have it caught into God's pardon.

The one who still doubts and "looks on" the crucified has to have a revelation of the abyss of freedom and the depth of hope. And also the depth of pardon.

In this Jewish and Christian vision of suffering, nothing can surprise us coming from human persons. Whoever shares it cannot despair of them, since he or she went to the absolute bottom of despair and rose out of it with the crucified. Then, the disciple of Jesus can no longer say that someone is good or bad since the disciple knows now that anyone—including himself or herself—can go to the extreme of evil; and yet, knows that this same person is destined to the extreme of good, and that pardon is given to him or her.

Except that for people who are outside the church, it seems that in Judaism death remains a scandal, while Christianity integrates it.

It remains a scandal for the Christian as well as for Jews. And Judaism is the first answer to the problem of death, a promise of life. In the great prosopopoeia: "Death where is your victory? Death, where is your sting?" (1 Cor. 15:55), Saint Paul quotes Isaiah and Hosea (Isa. 25:8 and Hos. 13:14). But death remains a scandal, a double scandal, an inconceivable madness in the case of a crucified Messiah. The scandal of human mortality is expressed by astonishment in the face of the inevitability of death. Death and its unpredictability always appear to me as an injustice, even if I manage to reason by thinking that I am a biological being or if, at a given moment, being tired of life, I feel sated. But the scandal of death— this is a phrase of Saint Paul—appears in all its magnitude in the scandal of the cross (1 Cor. 1:18–25). The scandal of the unjust death of the Messiah. No man loves death. The disciple of the resurrected Christ who has learned to love life because it is given by God sees this as a double scandal, and it cannot be overcome except when it is associated with the suffering of Christ. To make of Christianity an exaltation of death is to be contemptuous of the awareness that Christ and the first generation of Christians had of the sacrificial (and redeeming, in the meaning of liberating) role of Christ's offering in his death. I think that Jewish consciousness is tremendously important here to understand the suffering Messiah; the Jews know the price of such an experience. Jesus himself read or heard in the synagogue of Nazareth the scroll of the prophet Isaiah: "But we, we thought of him as someone punished, struck by God and brought low. Yet he was pierced through for our faults, crushed for our sins" (Isa. 53:3–4). These verses are among the most moving of the whole Bible. One cannot understand the sacrifice of Christ without keeping in mind that God himself has a sort of deep fear in the face of death (Matt. 26:36–46).

And is not the Resurrection a way of imagining a duplication of this world?

The Resurrection is faith in the power of God who gives divine life to human persons in the fullness of their historical condition, including their bodily one. It is literally impossible to represent, even if it has been the source of some phantasmagorias.

Yet there is a Gospel reference to the Resurrection of Christ where he appeared much as he had been before. . . .

In order to show his identity while manifesting himself as the first fruits and the guarantee of a new creation. This does not enable us in any way to imagine our own future as resurrected people. Faith in the Resurrection comes from faith in God, not from an imaginary belief in what we will become.

Which means that the rare witnesses to the Resurrection of Christ could not hope for a similar resurrection?

Yes, but the only thing that is clear is that in participating in the divine life, death has been vanquished in him. "I was dead and now I live" (Rev. 1:18).

But for them, it was possible to represent it?

The only analogy of the Resurrection in this present life, the only anticipation I have now, is what God already gives me in allowing me to live with him and in him. In my mortal body he already puts a divine energy which I know is capable of overcoming my death, but in a way that I cannot imagine. I can receive a foretaste of resurrection because in walking in the footsteps of Christ, the Messiah, I can be united to him in the Holy Spirit, and I remember that he lived this life, that he went through our life and our death on his way to the Father. He remains present in human history, but not as a ghost, a survivor. There is no mausoleum containing his body. The first fruits of the resurrection that he brought into history and into the hearts of human beings to whom he gives the messianic anointing of the vivifying Spirit, lead to the growth in history of his body: the church.

Do you realize that in saying this you go against all the arguments that were used by secular proselytism, and even Pascal's wager?

I don't believe that Pascal placed a bet on resurrection, in that page written during the course of one night.

It is implied in the wager. . . .

Perhaps. But in any case, I do not believe that this "probabilist" wager could be decisive. It might even be fallacious, since the prize was not correctly identified. For eternal life, as the Gospel sees it, starts now. I could not believe in the power of resurrection in which I do believe, though I cannot represent it at all, if it did not come to me as a word that God gives, as a hope that God gives me with his Spirit of adoption. What I am talking about here is not a marginal experience. This is not a "rare experience" reserved for initiates. It is the ordinary condition of the women and men who are called to be one in Christ by participating in his resurrected condition (Rom. 6:3–11). This life is woven in the ordinariness of daily life, in human weaknesses, in the gaps of existence.

The celebration of Easter, in this meaning, becomes in fact an identification with the essence of Christianity.

Yes, because Christian life is a reiteration of Easter.

Now then, how can you see any justification for the survival of Israel given the importance of what happened to Jesus, according to you?

The survival of Israel—but I would rather simply say, the life of Israel—is inscribed in the promise of God. God cannot deny himself. When God gives, he does not take back what he gave and promised: "God never takes back his gifts or revokes his choice" (Rom. 11:29).

What about the coexistence of Israel and the nations?

The relationship between Israel and the nations seems to me to be described in the parable of the laborers who were hired by the master of the vineyard at different hours of the same day (Matt. 20:1–16). The first are the Jews, the last are the pagans. Yet they receive "the same wages" as the first while they were hired last. One day God will wipe away all our tears (Rev. 21:4); humankind will be like a family pulled back from death and reconciled. Such is, for Jews as well as for Christians, the ultimate eschatological fulfillment of all things. Now it is clear that this fulfillment is not yet given to us as a possession, but as a hope. In our waiting, the relationship between Israel and the pagans remains one of the constitutive tensions of our history whose fulfillment is awaited like "a resurrection from the dead" as Saint Paul says (Rom. 11:15).

Moreover, not all pagans did enter into the Covenant. Many refuse it, and Israel must perdure until the end of time, as witness to the promise of God, with its proper vocation of elder son.

In the Christian concept of history the world remains divided between Jews and pagans. The Jew is one who has received the Covenant; who is the historical witness to God's initiative. The pagan is one who has not received this mission; who will testify to the superabundance of the primal mercy.

Jews must recognize the gift they have received, a gratuitous gift, and pagans in turn have access to this gift only by admitting that it was first given to Israel. The people of the "Christians," that is, literally those who belong to Christ, the Messiah, is made up of the gathering of Jews and pagans, as witnessed by Saint Paul and the Acts of the Apostles.

In other words, there is always an interdependence. If you do away with one of the terms, you will do away at the same time with the very domain in which the divine initiative and action are exerted. Then there is a conflict. In the Gospel, there are several references to the "jealousy" between the sons: one or the other claims the whole inheritance. One and the other must recognize by accepting the gift made to his brother that he himself has no other claim than the gratuitousness of the love God has for him. Each one is the witness of love for the other. Both therefore must perdure, Israel and the pagans. Not as archeological entities, but as constitutive givens of the history of the church.

There is more yet. In the Church of Saint Sabina in Rome, the public can admire two complementary figures of the church: *ecclesia ex circumcisione* and *ecclesia ex gentilibus* (the church from the circumcision and the church from the Gentiles). This is quite a different image from the one in the cathedral of Strasbourg. Inside the church herself Jewish identity remains as an element of the grace she received, as a permanent reminder of its absolute gratuitousness, as the sign of God's love.

At Chartres anyway, on one of the portals, all the apostles are on the shoulders of the prophets. . . .

Yes, but in Rome the idea is that the church is Catholic (*kath' holon*) only because it is first made of the Jews and the nations.

You mean to say that, for the church, as long as the pagans exist, Judaism will perdure?

The ancient tradition of the church understood the history of salvation that way. I just referred to it with the Epistle to the Romans. And this is actually what is being brought to light at the time we are living, a time of redemption and liberation. Otherwise we would declare an end to history. And who can do so if not God alone? It is true that another understanding of history and the place of Israel in the economy of salvation appeared in Christian thought after the patristic era.

Would not the fact that Christianity needs Judaism induce you to call for conversions?

Everyone is called to turn back to God, to "convert." In which way? This is everyone's secret, known by God alone, and which is part of the secret of history's fulfillment.

What would you say to people who might perhaps be groping toward God?

I think that the real debate is about life and resurrection. I feel like telling everyone I meet: "Let yourself be grasped by life." If we have a hard time believing in resurrection, it is because we do not want to let ourselves be grasped by God who gives life.

I would say that the real question, which is asked at times, is this: Is our life something else than what we can master? Today we think that we are more in control of our life. But then we discover that to live is not that easy. The tragedy of our civilization is that it begets death in the measure that it wants to improve or even save life. We discover that it is difficult to love life. To love life is to be transformed by God, the living one who raises the dead. I think that Freud was right when he stressed the importance of the death instinct.

To have faith in resurrection is first of all to root out from one's heart complicity with death. And this is a miracle.

If I had to make a choice among the people I would like to address today, I would chose as a priority, even if this comes as a surprise, two types of women and men. The first ones are those who are tempted to commit suicide, whatever the reason or the means be: moral, psychic, or physical (you can destroy yourself in many ways and not only physically). To those people I would say: Your life is more than what you think. Accept this life not because it is such, but accept it to receive life; it comes from farther away than you do; it is more beautiful than you think; believe in the life you received and accept its trials.

And the second group would be those who want to kill. There are many ways to kill. In the Bible hatred is part of murder. Contempt, refusal of the other, revenge are part of murder; to deprive one's brothers or sisters of what they need, of the right to speak, and so on, is to kill them. To those people I would say: These others who are before you, whom you hate, are given to you as signs of life and of God. Stop. Accept them, don't kill them, love them (Matt. 5:21–26, 43–48).

DISCOVERING
GOD

✳

Do Not Despair of Man

F *ather Lustiger, we wish to meet the believer in you. How have you experienced the discovery of God?*

In fact, the discovery of God and Christ is a very mysterious reality. One cannot relate it in a logically constructed discourse. If I rely on my personal experience and what I think I have understood from the experience of other people (I have been in contact all my life with unbelievers and atheists), I see two aspects which, for an outsider, could seem contradictory.

First of all, a total adhesion that God gives and through which one discovers faith.

Then, the presence or reappearance of all that is contained in the doubts, refusals, escapes of anyone in the face of God's existence. As far as I am concerned, atheism (including atheism as a philosophical doctrine) is not only a cultural given which is a feature of modern times; it is also something which must be classed among the temptations of man. To put it in a different way: the thought process of faith is not a deductive logic whose first step would be to determine whether or not God exists, and whose second step would be to situate oneself as a consequence. The discovery of God entails inner difficulties which have to be overcome. Atheism then takes the meaning of a spiritual trial in the itinerary of the believer. It appears as a temptation to be afraid of God, to concoct a personal notion of God, to doubt. All the people of our century have sooner or later gone through this.

Interview by Remi Montour in *France catholique-Ecclesia* [Catholic weekly], 27 February 1981.

What I also would like to say is that, in the final analysis, one does not discover God. He discovers you. He disconcerts you. When the seeker realizes that he or she is sought, that is faith. Which does not mean that all that came before was futile. When the unbeliever accepts God's grasp, then that person realizes the meaning of the road he or she had been walking. It is somehow like a person who does not discover what waiting for love means until he or she is loved.

Therefore you too have known the temptation of which you speak. Could you indicate the form it took?

I remember a time, which I look upon today as naive, and after I had already chosen the life I would lead but aware of nascent hesitations, which I was tempted to answer myself with the following reasoning. After all, the Christian vision of the world, were it only because of its humanistic content, its content of love and peace, is the most beautiful that can be. It is worthy of giving one's life for it. But that reasoning was a miserable failure.

It meant reducing Christianity to an ideal?

Yes. The temptation to give oneself purely humanistic reasons in order to remain faithful. I say that this is a miserable answer. It is true that the Christian vision is the most beautiful that can be. But only a believer can say so . . . I also think about another stage of my life. I remember a strong temptation which is rather common today, especially among young people. It concerns the church. People think: "And what if the church were, all things considered, only some kind of human secretion?" She could have encased the Gospel, like a kind of sediment seen on the shells at the bottom of the sea or on the hulls of ships. And the hard shell would have to be broken in order to rediscover the Gospel. This is easily understood: it is a purely human reading of the life of the church, such as that of a nineteenth-century rationalist like Stendhal. In the most extreme case, people have the viewpoint found today in some newspapers: the swindle-of-the-church, the hypocritical pretenses of Christianity.

How can one overcome such a temptation?

One must decide to receive the ecclesial reality, including that of the sinful persons who make it up, as a mystery of grace. Indeed, the answer is not the one I gave myself in a naive and finally illusory way: Christianity is the best way to live, and even if it is not true, one would be better off acting "as if."

If it is not true, it is not true at all?

Yes. To exorcise this temptation is not to affirm that Christians are better than other people. It is to accept that, in the mystery of sin, there is a mystery of mercy; that the holiness of God is revealed in a church made up of sinners: this church is therefore not an institution external to the mystery of Christ, but it is the very body of Christ bearing the wounds of the sins of men and women. This does not deny the temptation I referred to; it means going all the way in it and going beyond what it offers. I remember a formula of the theologian Hans Urs von Balthasar, applied to the church: *Casta meretrix* which can be translated as "chaste procuress."

This is an image that appeared all along the history of the church. Already the Fathers. . . .

Yes, it was from there that he took it. But I would like, since you asked me about it, to talk about another objection which has, as a matter of fact, marked my whole generation. It concerns the interpretation of the Gospel. For instance, a Marxist kind of objection: Would not all of our life be summed up in political efficacy and should not the Gospel be reinterpreted in this perspective? Or yet, the question asked by German liberal exegesis, with Bultmann at its head (his masterwork was published in 1926): Can one trust the Gospel and how can it be interpreted? I knew these debates when I was in my twenties. I overcame them thanks to two decisions.

The first one was truly a decision of faith. I realized that this way of posing the problem of understanding of the Gospel was rooted in the hypothesis that the master of the Gospel, the master of the word of God was not God, but human persons themselves making interpreters, judges. While it is the opposite that matters. You cannot have access to the word unless you let it interpret you; indeed, if you accept that it is the word that speaks to you.

On the matter of exegesis, I am very thankful—as are many of my generation—to Father Starki, a genuine guide. He put our nose to the grindstone of the Synoptics; he made us work in a rigorous way. Rather than get stuck on Bultmannian ideology, he made us adopt an empirical attitude to the texts while retaining our respect for them, somewhat like the physicist who takes up some datum and examines things again just to see if they will work out. This was very enriching for me.

My second decision was made when I saw myself with my back to the wall during a trip to the Holy Land. In the reality of the country of Christ, I perceived a kind of physical brutality of landscape and facts which did not, of course, give me proof, but compelled me to take a position with regard to a "word." The struggle with the angel had lasted long enough. I had to get away from indecision. There was a need for a victor and a vanquished.

Father Lustiger, as much as others and perhaps more, you have known the trials of our time. A time when evil is catastrophic—this is the least one can say—and without human solution; evil in all its magnitude, the evil that some people believed they had overcome through revolutions. . . .

You are right to evoke this tragic condition of life that poses the problem of evil. It leads us to the mystery of Christ as a suffering Messiah, as the mystery of humankind marred by human beings and transfigured into God, mystery of death in the mystery of life transmitted to the humanity of the Son by the Father, and by his Son to our humanity. We are always tempted to dodge the issue because it is unbearable to us. We are always tempted to transform Christianity into some kind of euphoric drug.

The trial of our time . . . This time has been that of the greatest human ambitions (and they were not achieved) . . . But also of the worst disappointments. People thought that the power of human reason would be enough. And they discovered that everything can be turned upside down. Pacifist ideologies beget wars, theories about collective happiness bring the Gulag, liberalism enslaves the weak to the strong, the progress of science gives birth to the atomic bomb, and so on. The question can be posed as follows: At what price can one not despair of humanity? At what price though can one not lapse into delusion? How can we face our ambitions and also the evil that dwells in us? How can we go on working?

Which is why I believe that Christianity is experiencing a new dawn. It is capable of reaching us such as we are, to accept our dignity and not to despair of us. Christianity knows that in this world there is evil and death. It allows us to name them. It knows that there is also a power of love, of pardon, of resurrection enabling us to confront evil, to confront death.

To name evil is already to fight it?

Yes, if one goes to its source which is the heart of humanity. Real evil comes from there: desire for power, possession, hatred, homicide, denial of God. It has the face of Satan. And it is constantly being reborn.

This is what I wanted to say about revolutions. They aim at the suppression of evil, and they recreate it . . . is it a spiral?

Evil is that with which we always have to deal and for that reason

God gives us the strength for victories that are seemingly difficult or impossible. One who would despair of humanity would be sinning against God. Of course one is not called to believe that tomorrow morning wolves will become lambs; but that one can and must fight with the strength of a lamb, of the sacrificed lamb. And that if one is the victim in this struggle, it will be as if Christ were the victim. In other words: that God will manifest his power of resurrection, will give us life.

From now on and until the world has taken on the final form of the agony of Christ, the divine strength which enables us to go through time is the very strength of the risen Christ. It is the present mystery of the eternal Son made flesh which opens in our history the path to resurrection.

All things considered, everything starts with Easter and the Good News: he who was dead is alive?

Yes. But there is a way to understand this which is somewhat mythical—like the time of the Liberation when people spoke about better tomorrows. People then say: "He is risen: it is all over then."

And all the while, humankind goes on in tears?

Exactly. But in reality "He is risen" means that you Christians have the strength to enter into the Passion of Christ. For his power of Resurrection will enable you from now on to be united to his death. Thus you will yourselves be the Easter of the world. Remember what Saint Paul said to the Colossians: "What you are is not yet apparent, and now the life you have is hidden with Christ in God" (Col. 3:3).

If we look at past tragedies and present dangers, should we think that Christians have had and still have an awareness of this "Easter of the world"? That they truly live it?

In any event, they are called to it. The evils that plague the world today are greater than ever. There are many more people than in the past. At the same time, we have considerably better means to solve our problems. The scandal is therefore even greater. When humankind lived in a sort of intellectual childhood and was fragmented and scattered, its ambitions were necessarily limited. Today we have to face the possibility of the greatest calamities of all times.

Then what of the church in this situation? I think she would be totally deluded if she mistook herself for one of the princes of this world. She has a very specific role to play: that of Christ himself, and has no other function. This means that from the Christian people resources of love, pardon, and identification with the crucified Christ have risen and will still rise; and their peace will come through the times of violence in which we live.

The answer of the church to the challenges of time. . . .

She has no answer except that of being a sign of Christ.

And to be a witness to genuine humanity?

Yes, in the way of Christ. The church proposes the model of humanity that is Christ in his Passion and Resurrection. She holds him up as a model to be imitated by Christians who have received the Spirit. Which means that Christians are called to become the mediators of forgiveness, mercy, and redemption.

One would wish that, in certain situations, the refusals of the church be more absolute. . . .

They are. Look at the speeches of the pope. I was recently rereading those he gave in France. They are extraordinarily forceful. But who listens to them? The same is true for the word of Christ. The church must accept the fact that people do not listen to her any more than they do to Christ. A person of faith knows very well that he or she will succeed fully in his or her work only to the extent that the solitude and the agony of Christ are shared. This is true for the whole church. But in doing so the church saves men and women. And this, through a grace strong enough to give birth to saints.

Is it not the permanence of sanctity which gives its true measure to the history of the church?

Yes. And this particular measure is perceptible only to believers, in faith. Either humankind is only a pigsty full of filth and its ideals only lies or Christ at work in his Passion gives back to humankind its dignity. Saint John, when he looked at Christ on the cross, saw in the Passion the revelation of God's glory, the resurrection of man. In the same way, the believer, in the passion of this world tried by sin, already sees the active force of God. Which is why Christian faith can never present itself as an ideology competing against other ideologies. It is the work of a concrete historical individual, that is, Christ. The church not only offers a concept of humanity, she shows the human being.

The Secret of the Beatitudes

*A*rchbishop Lustiger, how do you understand the text of the Beatitudes?

These are words that are very difficult to penetrate. On one level they cannot be understood. They sound like a call to resignation, to passivity . . . or like some kind of profession of faith that would be somewhat vindictive, like: "At the moment, I have no luck, but watch it, a day will come and it will be my turn!" One day, therefore, the poor and the oppressed will ride over the rich and the oppressors. Which is clearly absurd: each time the poor take the place of the rich, it is a new oppression. The text is fascinating: we are fully aware, when we have the grace to have a simple enough heart and a pure enough ear, that it touches an extremely deep truth.

Precisely what truth?

In the Gospel the Beatitudes cannot be dissociated from the curses, even if they do not come immediately after. Thus in the Gospel of Matthew the blessings are at the beginning of the Sermon on the Mount and the "alas for you" phrases come at the very end of chapter 23. In the same way, when God gave his commandments to Moses, he added blessings for those who would obey them but also misery for those who would fail to heed them. What does this mean? That the commandments are life and that to fail them is to go in the direction of death.

For whom are the Beatitudes?

Interview by Claude Goure in *Panorama aujourd'hui* [French monthly with a stress on spirituality], March 1982.

The Beatitudes are blessings given to the disciples of Jesus who will observe the commandments of God, such as Jesus gives them. The Beatitudes are not commandments. Commandments are found in other parts of the Gospel.

The Beatitudes can only be understood as a kind of verbal encouragement for those who are going to follow the way of Jesus. The Sermon on the Mount is indeed given to the followers of Christ. Those who will, because God calls them and gives them strength and courage, faith and love, share and follow Christ in his Passion, out of love for God and love for human persons. If we truly think about it, who is the first recipient of the Beatitudes? Jesus himself.

He is "the one who hungers and thirsts for the justice of God and who is sated with the will of the Father." He is the one who weeps; this is quite clear in his Passion. And he receives the consolation of God in the Holy Spirit. This is a first way of understanding the Beatitudes. They do not apply to the suffering person because the suffering person is a scandal that Christ himself does not approve. They apply to the disciple of Jesus who wills to make himself or herself an act of love and who will share in the Passion of Christ to deliver humankind from its suffering, its alienation and sin. This is to say to the disciple: "Don't be afraid. Happy are the pure of heart; those whose heart is totally open to God; they will see God." They are blessings for the disciples who will fulfill the words of the Covenant by being identified with Christ. Therefore they describe believers in the church. In the history of this world they share the Passion of Christ and bring the hope of his Resurrection to whomever they witness.

This word does not answer for misery in the world but encourages those who share in the Redemption given by Christ. Therefore we must not start with this word. In the same way, the Law was not given at the beginning of the Old Testament, but only when the people suffered through the desert and reached the foot of the mountain. Only then is revelation given to them. And the new Covenant is given to those who have already followed Jesus and who will still have to follow him to understand what this commandment means. This is what is meant by these blessings, and also these curses for those who would not receive all their holiness from God.

Do the Beatitudes offer a ready-made human program?

No. If one presents the Beatitudes as a practical economical or social program or simply a human ideal, one is a liar or a fool. In the Gospels, the apostles are scared by the demand of truth, of generosity, of gift that Jesus offers to them. They say: "But after all, who can be saved?" Jesus answers: "For men, it is impossible. But everything is possible for God."

In the last analysis, what is one's vocation? What is one called to? Christians receive from God, in Christ, the revelation that they are children of God. And to live as children of God, they receive the very strength of God, the Holy Spirit enabling them, as a grace, to do what is impossible. This is the price of the Beatitudes. Human persons must be freed from their own servitude, freed from themselves. They must become what they must be, what God wants them to be: Children of God who want to live in the love of the Father because they receive the gift of the Holy Spirit freeing them from their complicity with death.

Not only with physical death?

No, the death which is in us. Death represents for us absolute evil, supreme injustice. It is conceived as something coming from outside. It is the enemy about to attack us, to inflict injustice on us. But Saint John says: "To hate your brother is to be a murderer" (1 John 3:15). Which means that death finds a complicity within us. It is already in us. And when we do not live in love, not only is hatred dwelling in us—and hatred is potentially the will to see the other dead—but also a complicity with death. It is in this meaning that there is a suicidal temptation: despair is complicity with death. We must be cured of this.

The power of love, such as Jesus gives it as a grace through the power of his Resurrection, gives to Christians the strength to believe and to do God's will in spite of their weaknesses. This is our deliverance. This deliverance occurs quite precisely in the Passion of Christ where we see the normal logic of the world or the powers turned upside down. The law of the mightiest is upset. When Jesus, the suffering Messiah, obeys God to the extent of giving up his own life, he is vanquished in the eyes of the world. He lost. The law of the mightiest silenced him. But Jesus did not want to take the place of Pilate. He did not want to take the place of Herod. He does not fight with their weapons. And because he entrusted himself to God, God raises him up from the dead, gives him life where others give death.

Jesus forgives and gives life, including to Herod and Pilate. The "least" as Jesus called himself, is the savior of those who believed themselves to be the strongest. And the Passion of Christ, like the passion of Christians, necessarily provokes incomprehension, because it reveals in the heart of the other the hatred for which the victim will forgive the executioner. We believe naively that love is loved. What characterizes love is that it wills to receive the hatred dwelling in the heart of the other so as to cure the other's hatred. Thus the paradoxical aspect of the Beatitudes. And this is an incredible vocation, a superhuman one, which is precisely a work of our deliverance.

How?

By unveiling the truth. And truth and justice were really unveiled in the Passion of Christ. In the Passion of Christ (and therefore in the passion of Christians) there is not only a victory of the weak over the strong. But Christ, Son of God, innocent, just, confronts all his adversaries: political power, soldiers, the people, the pagans, Israel, and so on. In brief, all of humankind is present in the suffering just one: he is the one who reveals what is in the heart of everyone. It was Pilate who asked: "What is truth?" The issue of truth is at the core. But Jesus himself, by his silence, leads the Roman to raise the question of truth. While Rome represented the highest human enterprise of justice undertaken so far in the world, totally based on the concept of legality, Jesus reveals that under this pretense of justice, injustice is manifested since Rome legally condemns an innocent man. Lie must therefore be unmasked so that we may be freed from it.

As to us, we imagine that we must do violence to human beings in order to free them. Now what God does is to accept and himself bear our suffering condition in order to deliver us. We conceive deliverance from death as an execution of the evil one. The image that Christ gives is a birth; giving birth, not death. And the Passion of Christ is a birth to new life, the birth of a new humanity. This is what the Beatitudes mean. They bring a new birth into this world that seems closed, where relationships of strength determine the logic of things. All through time humanity is being born in its true dimension. Thus one could write another history. We are incapable of doing so because it escapes us. It is the secret of God, the secret of the saints, of those who weep, who await consolation, who live the Beatitudes and who wait for the comforter of Israel, the Messiah.

This is the world's real strength; it influences political choices. Cynics and the powerful do not realize that, around the corner of history, God is always mocking us. Through the poor who are slaughtered and who, in fact, bring about a new balance in the world. And the process is never completed.

Father Lustiger, some Christians could at times be tempted to see an end to this spiritual struggle, an order that would finally be just. At times Christians think: if we truly live the Beatitudes, we might be able to establish a society, a world that would be absolutely perfect.

It is a real temptation. If you think this way, you think: all or nothing. Now it is neither all nor nothing. I am thinking about a comparison to be found in Bernanos, in the *Diary of a Country Priest*. The pastor of Torcy, the old pastor, talks to the young country priest and tells him: "Listen, the church is like a housewife." In his country church there is mud and a nun helps him. She despairs, because every Sunday people come and dirty the church with the earth clinging to their shoes. Every Monday the nun washes the floor thoroughly and she is exhausted. Then the pastor of Torcy tells him: "That's what the world is all about: we have shoes full of mud and we drag along our misery and our sin. God must continually wash his people." The calculation of the cynics who would sink into despair is countered by the capacity of faith to struggle incessantly, to start all over again. And to believe that human persons are capable of the best. But without being surprised if, at any moment, the worst can be reborn in them, because this is a realistic vision of humanity. In the message of peace of John Paul II on 1 January is a passage where the pope explains (to sum it up) that to know that perpetual peace is a chimera does not mean that we should not do all we can to avoid wars and to bring more peace into the world. Even if people get crazy, one should not despair of sanity. In other words, Christians arc those who have enough realism and strength to struggle, even against despair. Those who base their life on a utopia end up as cynics. It is unavoidable, because all generations have been disappointed by their ideals. What is asked from Christians is precisely to have also the strength to struggle against this despair. While knowing that nothing will ever be settled and that we will have to start all over again. That nothing is won, precisely because we live in the time of struggle and battle. And the place where all things are counted is precisely in the secret of God's treasure. If we are capable of accepting this, without becoming discouraged, it is because we believe that the true price of things is not determined by human beings.

You said that the Beatitudes are for disciples. What should we say then to unbelievers?

For many years, I have met people who were not necessarily within the church, nor even former Christians. The question of the unbeliever to the Christian is: "What is the meaning of life? Is there truly a meaning to life? Why do we, who want to struggle for justice, have to struggle for justice? What force is strong enough to enable us to fight against injustice?" The real question that people ask themselves, the people of our time, is this one: "Is there really something more than ourselves, something that enables us to do what we have to do? Why should we not despair of humanity?"

For Christians, the way to live the Beatitudes would be to answer the question asked by others. It is the real stake of our time. This is the hour for which the bells are tolling. Christian faith brings about in humankind the renewed awareness of its own dignity, and indirectly is a gift given to all humankind by the very act of the Christian who is closest to Christ. At the same time, this dignity that humankind claims appears to it as a utopia, incredible and denied by experience. It is normal for Christian ferment to provoke a question about Christians themselves and about Christ. There was a good reason for Christ to ask: "And you, who do you say I am?"

The ultimate question is not what Christians do, but *who* is the one who enables them to do what they do? Who is their master?

In the state of civilization and culture that the world has reached, we find ourselves at an extremely dangerous point. The risk of humankind's self-destruction is not at all a delusion. Were it only for physical reasons: the stockpiling of destructive means, the fragility of our civilization, the danger that a lack of wisdom can bring to all. Thus the issue of humanity's wisdom in the face of its own folly, or of justice and truth in the face of lie is more acute than ever.

The experience of God's word which is thousands of years old has reached the moment when it must be delivered. It is a word that humankind needs now for its own survival. For in order to ensure our dignity, we need God, and our humanity is revealed only through this dignity, the dignity we receive from God the Father: the dignity revealed by the humiliated and glorified Christ, and by those who became brothers and sisters of Christ.

How Can We Believe
in God Today?

How can we believe in God today? Exactly as our father in faith, Abraham, did in his time! The problem has not changed: it always arises under the same conditions. To say such a thing is clearly to take a provocative stance, to behave as if one ignored the new givens that constitute the wealth of our time and the glory of our generation. An explanation is in order.

I will try to be as brief as possible. To study the problem in real depth would require much more time, commitment, and work. But the work would be yours, not mine. I am quite willing to answer for this question in your presence, but not to answer it. Indeed, if you want a genuine answer to such a question, you are the ones who should be asking it. As to the price this will cost you, nobody knows, not even yourselves. In any case, it would be more difficult to tackle than anything you have handled so far in your life. Let us be clear: in order to answer this question, a lifetime is required. Therefore the topic is such that the most I can do, in all honesty, is to share with you some of my thoughts about it.

Saint Augustine gave us the following phrase: *Si comprehendisti non est Deus,* that is, "If you understand it, it is not God." Here Augustine plays on the meaning of the word *comprehendere:* if you have seized it, if you have mastered it, then, by this very fact, it is not God. In the same spirit, I would like to read to you a beautiful literary text. It is literary, and I offer it to you as such in the official

Lecture at the École Polytechnique, Paris, 2 December 1982.

framework of this lecture, said to be one of "general information", but you must know that for me it is a prayer. The text was written by Saint Gregory Nazianzen, a great Christian author, bishop, theologian, and mystic who lived in Cappadocea during the fifth century:

O you, who are beyond anything, are not these words all
  that can be sung about you?
What hymn could tell about you, what language? No word
  can express you.
What could our mind cling to? You are beyond any intelligence.
Only you are unutterable, for all that is uttered comes from you.
Only you are unknowable, for all that is thought comes from you.
All beings, those who speak and those who are silent,
  proclaim you.
Universal desire, universal groaning calls you.
All that is prays to you, and to you any being who thinks
  in your universe, raises a silent hymn.
All that remains, remains through you; through you is sustained
  universal motion.
For all beings, you are the end; you are all beings and
  you are none of them.
You are not one sole being, you are not the totality of beings.
Yours are all the names, and how will I call you, you, the
  only one who cannot be named?
What celestial spirit could penetrate the clouds covering
  the sky itself?
Have mercy, O you, who are beyond everything,
Isn't this all that can be sung about you?

I offer three points for your reflections, which will enable us in this framework and summary to follow more than a single thought process.

First point: the "relevance" of Christianity today. I use the word to mean something like "pertinence" or "suitability." Fifteen years ago, the "theology of the death of God" in the United States claimed to show that God is "not relevant." I, on the contrary, affirm that Christianity is "relevant" today, even though some may believe it to be obsolete.

Second point: How can we understand the crisis of secularism and rationalism? Is this an opposition to revealed faith? Or a crisis within revealed faith?

Third point: What conditions should be observed in posing correctly the question you addressed to me: "How can we believe in God today?"

First point: Christianity is "relevant." Without going into a great deal of history, I can still say that when I was a young student of twenty, and then a chaplain of students at the age of thirty, I used to visit frequently the holy places of Mount Saint Geneviève.[1] At that time, it still seemed evident to many people that belief in God could only be against the efforts of human reason.

In my teens I knew a graduate from the École Polytechnique with whom I used to have long conversations. That engineer was a great teacher and one could always ask him questions: he always answered them. Now I was asking myself about God. I found it normal, since that man was for me the acme of knowledge, to ask him about the matter, all the more so that he was Catholic and went to Mass with his wife: "Do you believe in God?"

I noticed that he blanched and told me: "Never ask me this question!" For him, the only way to handle this life was to build an impenetrable wall between the rational universe, that of his intellectual development, and the religious universe. Separating completely the two domains, knowing full well that if he ever permitted himself to reflect about the issue, he would necessarily end up rejecting God.

During those years, when I was a young student and then a chaplain, this type of mentality was rather common. Seeking Christian witnesses, we were only too happy to refer to Prince Louis de Broglie and Louis Leprince-Ringuet, for these two great and world-renowned physicists professed publicly their Christian faith.

The gigantic effort of human reason, such as it developed since the seventeenth and eighteenth centuries in Western thought, and which enabled us to take fantastic scientific and technological leaps, took place while pushing aside a whole series of questions that people believed to have been solved. Now, in the space of less than a generation, the West sees the unbelievably strong reappearance not only (as one might think) of wild resurgences of irrationality or obscure forces from the past but also of all these questions that we thought

1. Saint Geneviève is the patron saint of Paris. The church erected in her honor is still on a hill overlooking the Sorbonne, but it has been secularized and is now the Panthéon, a mausoleum for illustrious Frenchmen. Next to it is the Saint Geneviève library, a cherished studying and meeting place for students, nicknamed "Sainte Ginette." (Translator's note)

had been solved—and that come back all the more strongly for not having been mastered.

Let me use a comparison to explain myself. At the beginning, the problem of pollution and the environment seemed to many people to be the bucolic claims of slightly perverted folk who did not clearly understand the necessities of economic and industrial progress; nowadays these problems of the environment and the relationship between man and the world have become crucial and have a bearing on industrial and economical development. There are many problems and areas that we do not perceive when we go full steam ahead with an action or a thought in a specific direction. Indeed, in order to push development in one direction, we are often compelled to eliminate all the rest. This comment is valid for intellectual life: if one should determine a goal and push aside anything else, a point will be reached at which one will become aware of being not only a mind, but of having also a body, a sensitivity, a social life. The real conditions of existence and the situation of human beings in the universe do not let themselves be locked in the goal that human beings have determined for themselves nor in the outline they drew for their own life. Human persons are greater than the goal they can propose for themselves, and if they themselves limit their objectives in order to succeed, they always have to pay an unavoidable price. Thus does American public opinion react strongly to the consequences of the conquest of the moon: the social price paid for this conquest remains an issue for a whole generation in the United States these past twenty years.

While Western civilization was achieving the goals it had determined, pretending or naively thinking that in such a manner it brought happiness to all and a reasonable way of life in justice, right, and equity, it appeared in fact that this triumphant human reason begat its very opposite. Technical progress does undoubtedly bring a better mastery of the world, but also the capacity to destroy it. Economical progress offers a better possibility to fulfill the needs of people, but at the same time it exacerbates the desires of some and increases everybody's sensitivity to the problem of injustice. Mastery over the human body increases the ability to cure or control biological mechanisms, but at the same time robs persons of any norm of behavior toward their body or the bodies of others: the maddest dreams of the Auschwitz physicians have now become subjects of studies and banal experimentation in some medical laboratories.

Thus there is a resurgence of fundamental questions. For at the same time, the religious tradition of the Bible and the revealed word appears today as a force of questioning and protests, and also as an available wealth of meaning, while people thought it totally invalid and obsolete. Yet it does not appear as a simple alternative or substitute, but as resource of meaning. What are some examples?

Biologists and medical researchers are aware of the tremendous ethical problems brought about by their capacity of intervention, but they refuse to settle these problems themselves because they think that universal society should not burden them with the responsibility of what should or should not be done. For it is not a scientific but an ethical problem to know what is right and what is wrong, where the human person begins and ends, what is just and what is unjust. Scientists cannot answer these questions as scientists. And indeed, this is the beginning of a fundamental question: What is the human person? What is the meaning of the person's relationship to his or her body? This is a matter of fundamental choice that compels us to draw on resources other than scientific reason. The fundamental word I referred to, the Bible's "At the beginning God created man in his image and likeness . . ." appears not as an obsolete myth of creation, but as a resource of meaning, helping to ask the fundamental questions that are confronting us once again, if we want to master our power over the cosmos and our own body.

Let us consider also social and collective life. Our era, for at least a century and a half, certainly has been one of social utopias, of the will to master the social evolution of large bodies of people. In this respect one can say that the Marxist-Leninist empires of the Eastern countries certainly represent the most far-flung enterprise of mastery over social life ever conceived. It is at least as great and ambitious as the will to master matter as Western society developed it. This is an ambition which, at least at the outset, wants to pursue rationally derived objectives for the good of humanity. The word *scientific* is claimed not only as something reserved for a handful of scientists in a laboratory or some intellectuals in an ivory tower but as a tool for the transformation of reality and social life, in order to solve the problems of society. Now we see that this tremendous, ambitious, and noble enterprise leads paradoxically to its reverse on certain very fundamental points. When human reason wants to take over social life, its enterprise begets totalitarianism. I would suggest that you read the remarkable works of Hannah Arendt on this issue.

How can we face this reversal of human reason in its results? I had the opportunity to say it in the presence of some friends who had worked with Emmanuel Mounier[2] and are very sensitive to what is happening today in the East. Since 1920 to 1930 Western intellectuals have not accepted this questioning. It was necessary, and the great surprise of these past years is that the spiritual force of Christianity dwelling in a people—I am talking about Poland—was able to do this questioning and raise the lid of merciless and totalitarian reason. What some intellectuals and persecuted Jews and Christians are individually doing in the USSR and other countries, this people was able to do—who nonetheless has as much drunkenness, cohabitation out of wedlock, and abortion as any other people. But this people was able, because it is imbued with a spiritual force, to pose the key problem of the meaning of civilization. Confronted with the question "What is the meaning of humanity and what is the meaning of social life?" Christianity, including its popular dimension, intervenes, not in order to contribute its own ideological solution as "ready-made" but at least to dare to propose going beyond taboos and borders.

I gave only two examples: about the mastery of the body and social critique. But I am struck by a global phenomenon—in the United States as well as in the East (perhaps somewhat less in France, though we should look more closely into the matter), at least in the advanced sectors of academia, but also in a more diffuse and capillary manner. The prophecy of Malraux that "the twenty-first century will be religious or will not be at all" might not exactly see its fulfillment; however, it seems at least evident that the revealed word is offered today as a resource of plausible meaning, not as an alternative to social life but as a wealth in which one should be involved in order to face the question arising today, while it had been thought that it pertained to an invalid and obsolete universe.

Second point: I will for lack of time only phrase it without any demonstration, like the first point.

Indeed, one could think that what I just explained represents a swing of the pendulum. For a while people thought that Christianity and the biblical tradition were nothing but mere superstition and that, opposed to them, human reason arose from the depths of his-

2. Left-leaning scholar and philosopher (1905–1950). (Translator's note)

tory. In other words, modernity—with respect to secular society, the power of human reason, questions about the human condition—then modernity would be a culture alien to the Judeo-Christian tradition, a new America to be colonized. In brief, we would have to reconcile two opposed universes. It might be that some of you feel this way either because you were born in a biblical tradition (be it Jewish or Christian) and have rejected it as one normally rejects the world of one's childhood, or because it seems purely and simply alien to you (I am still talking within the framework of Western civilization, within our own cultural and geographical realm; for I cannot ask all the questions, or study the relationships with other cultures, other traditions; but I know that some of you are seriously asking these questions too).

My thesis is quite the opposite: modernity, seen in a critical sense, is not an adversary of the biblical word, another that would stand facing us and that we would have to conquer again or convert. In fact, this crisis of secularism and rationalism, in brief this crisis of modernity is an inner crisis of Christianity; it is a crisis of faith in the collective and cultural meaning. Indeed, atheism, however paradoxical it may seem, is the fruit of belief, not as its dialectical opposite, but as a trial of faith. Scientific development is a trial of the development of faith in creation.

The Western world, through Judeo-Christian tradition, received the fundamental concept that the universe is given to it. The universe is not God; it is divine because it shares in the splendor of creation, but it is not God. Nothing is God but God (this is the formula of the *Shahada,* the creed of Islam). There is no God but God. Or else: only God is God. Therefore we cannot, in any way whatsoever, grab a creature and call it God. Therefore, also, the universe itself is homogeneous to human thought. The universe is like a counterpart, an object given to human beings. But when revelation says this, it situates human beings in the reciprocity of a look facing God: those who take hold of the universe in order to conquer it never cease to be connected with the God who gives them the power to do so.

It is indeed the Western world, sprung from this biblical word, that gave birth to the scientific, modern, and secularized world. And this is why the crisis of this world is a crisis of faith. The rationalist is a tried believer, the Western atheist is a tried believer (there is a great difference between a Western atheist and the atheists of pre-Christian antiquity or the atheism of some people in Asia, Buddhists or others: it is not the same atheism, for it is not the same cultural universe). The crisis of our century, to the extent that it draws its sustenance from the triumph of the West, is a collective crisis of Christianity itself. Understanding and possession of the world, which are the key to scientific and technical enterprise, were brought forth by the gift of the world that God bestowed on us. And to solve the problem of the mastery of science supposes that we solve the question of this relationship with the world. I truly think that the Western crisis that spread like a disease to the whole world—by the way, the disease is not a total evil—is a crisis that only we Christians can solve. Not "we, the Westerners" but only the believers can help solve this crisis insofar as they alone perceive its origin and key. Which does not mean that we have the personal capacity to do so, but that we can pose the problem correctly, and this must be done if we want to master it. If this is not done, the temptation to self-destruction is very strong: self-destruction either through a phenomenon of old-fashioned rejection or through violence due to the very excesses of technology, that is, weapons, and so on.

When I explain that an atheist is a believer who has been tempted and tried, I do not claim to win him over. I am merely putting a name on his particular brand of atheism. The rational crisis of the West is the crisis of reason that was freed by revelation. Therefore the key issue of modern civilization is the problem of God: it is in fact the only problem! Let us not forget that to pose the problem of God amounts to posing the problem of humanity, which is another way of saying the same thing. What are human beings? What should justify and found their personal and collective action? To what value judgments must they adhere? And by the same token, how can they master this fantastic energy that has been given to them? How can they control the obscure forces that dwell in them? How can they solve the problems that we are facing today? The problem of faith is the key issue of our time.

I shall conclude with the third point, which is the true topic of this lecture and which might be the most interesting. Given what I have said, how can one advance in the knowledge of God? What does belief in God mean? And here I go back to my initial formula: what is true for us today was true long ago for our father Abraham. I hope that this phrase has acquired some meaning for you. I do not say that all the developments and all the manifestations of reason as we experience them today are not an innovation, but that they pose fundamentally, albeit in a new way, the same problem. And because a problem is posed in a new way, it does not mean that it does not involve identically the same elements. The fundamental elements are already present in the gap brought into the universe and the history of man by the revelation of God.

The problem of faith in God is not first of all that of knowing whether there is an unknown object one can conveniently call God and whose probable or certain existence can be demonstrated with more or less security. God is not an "unidentified object," or an unidentifiable one, with regard to which one could establish a calculation of probability. The problem of faith is to accept that human persons, to discover God, are compelled to situate themselves differently with respect to themselves, with respect to the world, and therefore with respect to him whom they do not know. Abraham was a deist: he believed in idols, he believed in gods of whom he had a certain concept. In the same way, when we read the Gospels, we are aware that people in those days were deists in one way or another. Now revelation is precisely this: God himself is manifest as totally different from any idea that we can have about him. For God reveals himself by allowing human persons to receive themselves from God and also to receive God as other. To believe in God is therefore for persons to open their heart and their intelligence to a purification compelling them to accept that they are not master of the one who comes to them, and to accept that they are not their own master.

To discover God is to enter into a way of faith measuring humanity in comparison to another, who is always present, already present, who is present at the very source of its being. Humanity is not absent anymore from the world, like a subject judging all things; it is in the world, receiving itself from God and bound to discover God throughout a long way supposing that human intelligence itself has been freed. Reason can discover God if reason itself is free. Humanity can know God if it wills to recognize him and be recognized by him. Humanity can discover God if God discovers humanity, strips it down to his truth so that it be made "capable" of God since God created humanity in his image and likeness. In other words, the solitude of men and women must be pierced by the creative and loving presence of God, which is at the root of the communion among them and of the gift that God gives to them: the universe. The act of faith, the search for God will thus necessarily be like an itinerary in which reason will be all the more triumphant in that it will accept, not resign to or submit to the one who can free it. Or yet: light can be given to men and women to the extent that they recognize their own darkness. This is the whole paradoxical meaning of the prayer of Saint Gregory Nazianzen that I read at the beginning of this lecture. Logically, we reach here a threshold where reason, to ensure its sovereignty, must recognize another sovereign. The problem is the same for Abraham as it is for us: by recognizing God, Abraham converted to God.

Questions

In the first part of your lecture, you spoke about the relationships between us and the world, and you presented God as the key to the problems brought about by these relationships. Don't you think that this is a subsidiary problem, given the supernatural dimension existing in religion?

Yes and no. I will start with no. Revelation deals with God. But concerning God, it also concerns us. To say that God is creator is to say at the same time that we are creatures. Faith is the relationship between human beings and God, God and human beings, in history. The two subjects, God and human beings, are correlative: this is what revelation is all about. Humanity is not sovereign unless it receives itself from God.

You lead me to stress what I wanted to say in my first point, and now I can say yes to your question. Long ago, during the age of rationalism, one could say that the word *God* was the causal explanation allowing us to hide our ignorance. In other words, one called "God" all that could not be explained. One could say that this was the Western frontier that the Eastern states would conquer little by little, in a triumphant march of reason against God. And God was like an Indian, progressively pushed away to new and still unknown territories. Now today we see more clearly (though that concept was already in the Bible) that the domain of reason does not have in itself a limit in creation: I spoke about this in my second point. By right, human reason is homogeneous with the world; thus by right, human reason can claim to conquer it.

However, when we decide that there are only our reason and the world, and that our reason overcomes the world, we wind up with horrible things and ask ourselves the following question: Why does my triumphant reason obtain results that are the reverse of those I had planned? We cannot therefore eliminate the question of God, even though (by hypothesis) we had eliminated it in order to be able to conquer the world. Once again, God is not the frontier of meaning to our ignorance: God is the other before whom we are and without whom we are not.

According to your lecture, modern atheism came from Christian society. Do you think then that non-Christian religions are not involved in this crisis?

On the contrary, I am quite certain that non-Christian religions are caught in this crisis.

Truth to tell, few among us will say this: atheistic rationalism is in fact a trial of the believer. However, let us not forget that Voltaire had been educated by the good fathers and Spinoza by the rabbis. This is not a rejection, but an inner crisis. Besides, the strongest denials of God are to be found in mystical writings. The most obscure trials of faith are also those of the mystics.

Now about the relationship with other cultures. I will remain within the biblical tradition. Of course other cultures can be considered from the historical viewpoint: Chinese civilization and Indian civilization seem to be much older and more refined than the West. In spite of extraordinary analogies on certain points, showing truly that there are constant, invariable factors in the evolution of the human species, it remains true that these civilizations are what the Bible calls "pagan nations," that is, nations which historically did not feel the shock of God's historical revelation. Now the confrontation between revelation and paganism is something which is absolutely universal. It took place in the conscience of Abraham, first in Israel, then in all the Mediterranean world and the neighboring cultures where a confrontation took place between revelation and spontaneous religion. That confrontation is the very fabric of the entire holy history: between God who reveals himself through his envoys and witnesses and paganism which is a constant factor in everyone (there is a pagan in every one of us). This conflict, this conversion of the pagan to believer is a fundamental historical dimension that Father Fessard, a very great Jesuit who died recently, succeeded in bringing to light, while modern theological thought had somehow forgotten this point.

In the non-Western world modernity brought about the collision with revelation. But instead of being revelation as it is, it turns out to be the crises stemming from revelation: we export the by-products of our crisis. The relationship between the West and other cultures took the form of conquests, by war if necessary, of colonization (even in the positive meaning of the word, that is, transfers of technology and mores). Modern technology, rationality, science, the Western concept of law (nations, the right of man, and so on) are now exported in a fantastic way thanks to technology, the diffusion of thought, including telecommunications, satellites, movies, television, and so on. The cultural collision of the nations I call "pagan" by convention, that is, the collision of the "Gentiles" as the Bible calls them, with revelation occurs through these by-products. What is happening now in the countries of non-Western culture is a terrible tragedy, that of their own identity, their survival, and perhaps of a contact with revelation happening under the worst circumstances. For to discover the universe of revelation (made to Abraham, and what ensued with Christ) through mercantile societies, the multinational corporations, the problems of corruption, the development, through the wild urbanism of the enormous cities of the Third World, to discover it through the by-products of technological society and its mercantile enterprises, is not necessarily the best form of contact! This poses for us at the same time a problem of great responsibility which is difficult to master on the individual scale and the scale of a generation, and which probably is a judgment against our time. In this sense, we are the direct heirs of the conquistadors and the slave traders. What we export is very ambiguous: I see a proof of this in the form of frequently violent political rejection. As a consequence of the national revolts we brought forth as a reaction, the nations may not accept what they really need.

Here is my question: How will our century and the following one be able to ensure, in the plurality of cultures and the emergence of new entities to contend with, this confrontation between revelation and the pagan nations when the by-products have already invaded and transformed everything? The cultures are faced with the by-products, while the source is not even perceived.

You have spoken, in the matter of access to faith, about a liberation of reason. But is belief only in the order of reason? Paraphrasing Pascal, is not belief also in the order of the heart? How do you understand the phrase "God is love"?

I started my lecture with a prayer that I wanted to be personal, with the reading of a text of Saint Gregory Nazianzen. The way to the discovery of God is necessarily through that of prayer in which one is loved as well as loving. For one is loved first before knowing how to love. It is necessary to remember that the fundamental summary of the commandments God gave us is: "You shall love. You shall love God and you shall love your neighbor."

This commandment to love is disconcerting, for we do not see love as the object of an order. We put love in the category of desire, which by definition is limited, limiting, and capricious. We think that freedom is expressed in the freedom of an often blind desire. On the contrary, the supreme light gives us love as a commandment: "You shall love" is an order. How can love be ordered, and how can it then be a source of freedom?

This supposes that the human person discovers a love which is greater than the one he or she is capable of feeling; discovers the one who is beyond all things: God is not at the end of desire or of reason; God comes as a stranger who reveals himself to those who did not know him. In the desert the people were led to hear a word they had not heard before, a food they could not have imagined. In the same way, in the mystery of Christ people discover a depth of which they had no inkling. And the dizzying and at the same time vivifying abyss of God the Father is given to us only if we allow ourselves to be begotten like children, like sons and daughters. I did not dare go too far on this way. And what I am saying now goes beyond the limits of this type of lecture. You would have to go through the experience yourselves, embark on a personal exodus.

You referred to Buddhism and atheism. Do you consider that the various religions are ways to God, or that Christianity alone has the truth?

The Christian religion does not "have the truth." Human beings are always seeking the divine as one of the categories of the universe: the sacred is part of the universe. But God, when he names himself, is manifest beyond anything human beings can imagine and grasp. Go back to the text of Saint Gregory Nazianzen, to the revelation of the divine name on Mount Sinai, and to the saying of Jesus: "No one knows the Father but the Son, and no one knows the Son but the Father and he to whom he reveals him." This is also expressed in the Prologue to John's Gospel that simply sums up the entire tradition we adhere to: "No one has ever seen God" (John 1:18). To see God is offered as a hope and can only be the ultimate grace.

The Bible is not presented as a truth homogeneous to other opinions, of which one would say that they are errors—in the sense of being confronted with a problem that has one right solution and several erroneous ones. Revelation is that which gives access to one who is other, different from anything human beings can imagine. For only God is God. The word *God* leads to confusion. We made up this word in our Western languages as a generic term: the god "who," the god "of" . . . We make a genus of it: the god of the Hindus, the god of archaic civilizations, the god of the Moslems; thus one could put labels on the various species of gods just as one sticks labels on the various species of one genus. But what is proper to biblical revelation is the affirmation that there is only one God, that he does not belong to a genus, that he cannot be put into a class. He can only name himself, and his very name is mystery. In the struggle of Jacob with the angel, Jacob asks for his name: "Who are you?" The answer: "Why do you ask? My name is mystery."

To say that the biblical tradition and Christianity have the truth is too narrow a formula. For God erupts into history, gives himself, and delivers us from ambiguities and uncertainties, by placing us deep into a yet greater adventure. Vatican Council II issued a decree about non-Christian religions: this beautiful and short text names all the great organized religions of our time and shows how Christian faith recognizes in each one of them elements which are part of the common patrimony of all believers. Not in order to say that we are superior to these religions, but that our viewpoint is an original one. The total truth is not the sum of partial truths, but it is something else that appears; it is another who has come. Herein lies the originality of the Jewish and Christian traditions. The one of whom it speaks is not counted with anything, anybody, not even with the most general and fundamental categories of the human mind.

This presupposes exceptional processes. One doesn't attain the absolute, depth of being, or contemplation with the same process as one needs to discover the living God. The way to discover God is determined not by ingenuity and experiences in this domain (I can use the experiences of the East, those of the gurus, those of Buddhism—which is quite a reasonable project), but by God himself. The characteristic of the experience of faith is to accept that the processes of this experience be determined by the one whom we do not yet know.

Can the problem of ethics be viewed only within a religious context? Is human reason capable of tackling ethical problems?

Yes, it is capable of doing so, and even must do it. I said that biblical tradition was a resource for reason. I truly believe that these ethical problems belong to the domain of human reason, deal with

humanity; but the stake of our civilization is this: where to find an-
chors that would be solid enough so that humanity not be lost in an
enterprise launched by itself? We are really compelled to ask the
question of the basis of ethics, the basis of law. Where to find
guideposts that would be firm and solid enough so that reason itself
could determine what belongs to its own competence? I am not
claiming in any way that in order to pose the ethical problem one
must be a believer, a believer in the biblical meaning of the word.
For everyone has been given this capacity to discern good from evil.
But everyone also feels how weak is this capacity: one can lose the
guideposts. For his or her part, the believer can, using reason, through
the resource of faith, help to put human reason back on its feet. "Can
help": this does not mean that a similar enlightenment, a similar rational stance is not given to one who might not be a believer.

What explains the "relevance" of Christianity is that Christianity
and the biblical tradition tell in the name of faith truths which are
simply human. This is the meaning of the disconcerting validity of
what would otherwise seem to be a string of banalities.

*You spoke about the Polish people, of drunkenness, cohabitation outside
of wedlock, and abortion. What relation can be seen between these three
elements?*

I only named the evils I had spoken about a year ago when I met
Lech Walesa in Paris: we talked for three to four hours. I knew that
these problems affected Polish society for some time. I therefore asked
him this question concerning demoralization, destructuration, risks:
a country living in misery is quite susceptible to temptation. Ask
your elders about France during the German occupation and the
phenomena of denouncement, black market, and so on, all the evils
that a more or less balanced society sprouts when it is pushed into
misery and despair. And in general I think it is what happens in a
society when the degree of oppression and misery is strong enough
for the fact of being simply honest to become a heroic deed. A people with its back to such a wall of tragedy runs the risk of demoralization. Therefore I asked Walesa: "Are you not afraid that you will
not resist? That your youth itself will be carried away by such despair
and such corruption that you will lose what has been your strength?"
This is indeed the great risk for them. He answered: "I don't think
so. We overcame that risk a few years ago. Now we are capable, I
hope, to hold for twenty years."

But nobody knows, nobody can predict. . . .

FRANCE AND HER BAPTISM

✳

Beyond the Immediate Ruptures

W hat do we see? First the priests, but also Christians of all ages see with astonishment that the ground is slipping away from under their feet. Young people are not as sensitive to this because it is not their ground. They do not have the same guideposts, they do not measure changes the way we do. But such is the characteristic feeling of those who are over forty or fifty years old. They see a change in the position of Christianity with respect to all mores, the cultural world, society.

This is not to say that society is becoming less Christian: today it is as little Christian as it was twenty, thirty, forty, or one hundred years ago. French culture does after all carry indelible marks of Christianity. As to the good folk who explain that paganism is the basis of Western and French culture, they are rather interesting, they are amusing even. But they should be advised to go and see what is happening in countries of truly pagan culture, for instance, Buddhist or Shintoist ones, in a universe where Christianity is totally absent. The West was born to itself from its encounter with Christ. We are in a country where culture, language. . . .

And also political speeches. . . .

Yes, also political speeches; at times we have the impression of listening to the sermon of a pastor . . . sometimes a bad sermon, but a sermon nonetheless. . . .

The way in which religious language, the language of the Bible, of

Interview by Robert Serrou in *Paris-Match* [illustrated Parisian weekly magazine], 4 April 1981.

127

the church, has penetrated culture, economics, politics proves that we live on a certain Christian cultural basis. It is therefore difficult for me to talk about "dechristianization." You know, by the way, that the French Revolution coined the term: in 1793 they wanted to suppress all Christian references in the mores, the usages, the ways of telling time, and so on. They wanted to "dechristianize" French culture. It failed since Christianity is woven in the very depths of our culture, the French culture.

This does not mean that faith is omnipresent or that religious observance is a habit of the majority. That's quite another story! For it is indisputable that a certain coherence between faith, mores, ideals of life, generosity, Christian vision of the world is less and less accepted by the majority of the French people. Fifty or a hundred years ago any man of good sense was a Christian without even being aware of it. Some supplementary religious truths rounded out the Christian faith, but Christianity was identified with good sense. Today this is not at all the case.

How can we live in such a situation? Most of our contemporaries have a difficult time at it. The young people invented marginality and use it as a political tool of protest. They are also less bound to situations of uniformity. Now we are people used to social consensus, to unanimity, to a steady society or, at the most, one that is divided into two or three camps. It is difficult for us to see a society which escapes or seems to escape us. This nostalgia for unanimity is felt by all people. First by the Christians. We ask ourselves how it is possible not to feel that Christianity is falling back or is unlivable, when it is not praised by the opinion of the majority. How can one hold a minority viewpoint? How can one resist the hammering of cultural or ideological advertising? How, through Christian fidelity, can one decide not to do like anybody else, without however leaving for the mountains to raise goats? How can one bear the lack of approval? How can one live as a dissident in ordinary circumstances, in the name of a conviction received from God? How can one not accept prevalent opinion as a criterion of truth, good, and right?

This is a crucial problem in all our societies. It is said that archaic societies were closed. But our modern societies are far more terrifying: they are tremendously spellbinding and uniformizing. What is astonishing is not only that Orwell was absolutely right and that the Gulag and the Nazis came before 1984; it is the fact that we are going to reach 1984 without having really understood totalitarianism. The spell is so powerful that all these good folk don't see anything anymore.

We are therefore in a contradictory situation: on the one hand, people expect something from us Christians—without knowing exactly what. But on the other, as soon as we propose something, it seems to be ridiculous or unacceptable because it is upsetting. Perhaps we should not be surprised by such a contradiction. For the church is, like Christ, a sign of contradiction.

And then?

The second point: the church of France is paying a heavy price to French history itself. Let me explain: a diocese is theoretically, in the vision of the church, a local church, a particular church. At the same time, it is a human and Christian community with which there is a kind of historical, concrete, and affective identification. People identify with a given group: this is my church; I belong to the church of such a country, of such a place. This also has a very strong spiritual significance as well as a carnal one—in the meaning Peguy gave to the word—a human and solid significance.

Now in France there is no such thing as a particular church. There are departments.[1] I found that out in Orleans. Here is a department, the Loiret. It is made up of several parts that have no real connection except that of having been determined by the administrative will of the French Revolution, so that the prefect might, by breaking up local particularities, ensure a specific administrative management and control of the central authority. Thus the department of the Loiret became the diocese of Orleans. And the departmental model is a function of maintenance of order and administrative management of a certain Jacobin vision of state and country. When I used to say "the diocese of Orleans," the Gatinais people would retort: "We are not from Orleans!"[2] Never will there be an effective, human, and historical identification of a whole third of the department with the old church of Orleans. Which means that the bishop is compelled, since the days of the Constituent Assembly, to take the prefect as his model. What we have to rediscover is that the bishop is not a prefect, because a particular church is not a department.

When we compare our dioceses with those of Italy—which are far

1. An administrative division instituted by the French Revolution. There are 95 departments in metropolitan (European) France. (Translator's note)
2. Gatinais is an old region of France predating the department of Loiret. (Translator's note)

smaller—or with the German provinces whose sizes vary so widely, we become aware that the church identified with a whole culture, the history of an entire people. Our model in France was that of the Jacobins.[3] This is the price we have to pay, the price of French history.

But to make up for it, there is a church of Paris?

Yes, because even though it might seem paradoxical, in Paris there is an effective identification with the big city. One is from Paris, even if one came from the provinces and it is a very fortunate thing.

Third discovery?

The effects of the past fifteen years on social life and Christianity, for the countryside was emptied and turned upside down during those years. It led to tremendous changes in mores.

During the last century, every little French boy or girl learned the catechism. The results were criticized, which brought about successive and fortunate reforms because they matched the evolution of thought, pedagogy, and so on. But for the past three years there has been a rupture in catechesis and this is not because priests gave up or because catechical methods are failing; there are objective reasons to be found in the countryside: school busing, a week without a break[4] where it is already in force, more leisure, sport associations, majorettes, football, and *pétanque*[5] events.

With all this, children are not being taught catechism any more. A rupture is happening. The results will be felt in fifteen, twenty years from now. A major crack is opening in the continuity of the generations.

What can the church do?

I don't know. This is truly a serious issue. Not only does the church have to react in her hierarchy, but the whole French fabric of parents, educators, members of the city councils must do so. This is especially felt in towns where school busing has countless consequences. You see little children get up at 6 A.M., come back home at 7 P.M., and their village is a bus! I did not know that when I arrived

3. The most powerful party of the French Revolution, synonymous with the French revolutionary mentality. (Translator's note)

4. Since the law of separation between church and state of 1905, the school week was interrupted by a day off on Thursday so that parents, if they so wished, could give their children the religious education of their choice. But a new law, under the Fifth Republic has abolished this custom and is progressively enforced so that school is now held on the regular week-day schedule in almost all of France. (Translator's note)

5. A French form of bowling. (Translator's note)

in Orleans; I discovered it. I had read articles in the newspapers, yet I had not paid attention to the issue.

This is an important factor. It is as bad as making people live in concrete. People protest against projects and housing complexes. But this daily uprooting of the children will, in my view, have equally serious consequences on future generations, on their balance, the human environment that is theirs, the adults with whom they talk.

Lastly, I discovered the priests. I knew priests, but I did not know *the* priests. A priest only knows those with whom he works on a daily basis: those closest to him, his friends. As bishop of Orleans, I had to know all the priests of the diocese.

A diocese where there were upheavals. . . .

That too, but it is of no importance. All the priests of a single diocese, and that is quite a difference!

By accepting this responsibility, that is, of responding to them and on their behalf, I was led to reflect in a new way about what a priest is, about my own sacerdotal condition . . . I then learned many things. Nobody can imagine the fantastic amount of generosity they represent. How can there be at the same time such a heavy weight of misery and generosity? This is a magnificent story, but it is practically impossible to tell it.

Is it possible today to demand that a priest make a vow of quasi-poverty? Is poverty a modern virtue? And what does it mean? I am thinking about the condition of the priest.

I will answer in two slightly different ways.

First of all, the clergy I belong to and whose admiring witness I am has no successors, and will probably not have any in the state it has reached. There will be no more country priests such as I have known. Because circumstances have changed. Everything has changed. Therefore it is impossible to pose the problem of a return to what was. It is not possible, and in any event, it is all over. We do not have to make any decision: this is the way things happened.

In fact, who are the priests of the future? Those who are now in the seminaries or those who will enter, which brings us to 1990, 1995 . . . When we realize who they are and how many they are, we have to admit that we are in a situation of tremendous rupture. You know the figures. The present rupture (be it chronological or numerical) in the French clergy has already gone beyond—in scope and duration—the rupture that took place during the French Revolution.

The consequences of such a rupture in the tradition cannot be imagined at this point in time. Look at the nineteenth century since the restoration of the monarchy, from the religious viewpoint. The consequences for the life of the church, the movement of ideas, all can be explained in part by a break in tradition that existed within Catholicism. Because there had been a total disappearance of all religious facilities as well as of the capacity of transmission, one had to reinvent the Gothic neo-Catholicism of the nineteenth century. It had to be reinvented because nothing had been left. There were no more universities, no more libraries. One had to reinvent the Dominicans, the Jesuits, the Benedictines, liturgy, piety, and even theology, just as Viollet-le-Duc reinvented Gothic architecture!

A tremendous rupture took place at the end of the eighteenth century. The nineteenth century was very poor from the religious viewpoint. The great stars of the time were eminent men, but they represented an impoverishment of religious content in comparison with men of the same caliber in the previous century. Neither Germany nor England had to go through such a rupture.

Today we live through a cultural and historical rupture of the same magnitude. The number of priestly vocations fell down so low for fifteen years that a return to the previous level cannot occur as if nothing had happened. This then is an important problem: How are we going to handle this rupture? People of our age do not all realize the importance of this break. They live as best as they can through it. Though some people feel it instinctively and they suffer. They experience it as remoteness, abandonment and rejection. Others dream about a restoration such as the one that took place in the nineteenth century. Whatever the case may be, this is now a fact, the rupture is inscribed in our history. How are we going to survive if we do not have the intellectual equipment? One does not manufacture a university professor or a professor of theology in three years; fifteen or twenty years are needed. Even if God sends us great gifts, saints, there is a need for a ground, an accumulation of various talents to have masters of novices, spiritual fathers. This is one of the urgent problems we have to address today.

As to the pope, he has a tremendous merit: he perceives the problems and he poses them beyond these historical limits. He calls to a national consciousness going beyond short-term problems. The question: "France, what have you done with your baptism?" is a splendid and disconcerting one. No one today has ever thought about the baptism of France. But we are thus compelled to relocate our own continuity beyond the immediate ruptures.

Do you have an answer in the face of this rupture or are you asking the question yourself?

This is a question I am asking myself. It is a key issue. I will give you an example: there are now priestly vocations, but they are of another kind than those of the past, if not on the spiritual plane, at least on the human one. Today mature men, who already have professional experience, are called by God. Their approach is obviously not the same that was linked in the past with family, adolescence, schooling—I am thinking about minor seminaries which are fewer and not surprisingly so. Let us not forbid the Spirit to bring about much more numerous vocations. But the kind of men God is calling today is different from those of the past, and the priests they will become will be different.

There have always been late vocations. But in the past they were much rarer. The candidates had to be accepted, pave their own way, because their very experience marginalized them. Today there are many men of this kind and the clergy who will thus be formed will not be the same. The stereotypes, conformities, and habits will be different.

I am meeting the men who are going to be ordained in Paris this year. They tell me how difficult it was for them, who had an occupation, earned a living, had an autonomous life, to enter into a system of constraints such as the one they had to undergo in order to become priests. They do not earn money anymore; they are subjected to a school system; they lead a collective life in which they have to render accounts to others; they have to subject their rhythms of prayer and their spiritual life to a spiritual director, to someone, to a community. This is a problem for them. In the past the people who entered a major seminary were often prepared since childhood, and they encountered no difficulties. Today the major seminary is experienced as a spiritual trial.

How can one connect this new clergy with the old one? There will not be two churches, this is impossible. Here is an example of the way we have to experience this rupture which, by the way, covers many other things.

Such as?

It would be difficult for me to describe them precisely. Because of my personal experience, I was somehow marginal. I met unbelievers, I had to go from the outside to the inside. As people said about me:

"He is a convert, he is discovering." I have the impression today that my experience has become common among the young. It is in a way as if I had joined the rest of the unit! To be sure, there are gaps of generation and language, but such is in fact the kind of quasi-spontaneous problem of the Christian younger generations.

Will the church of the year 2000 be like that?

I think so, because the church of the year 2000 will be that of the people who are now twenty or twenty-five years old.

Do you think about this?

Yes, that church is here!

You were talking about the poverty of priests.

Wretched means seem absurd to me. The poor priest engaged in pious industries to find a few pennies is still with us, unfortunately! Some are compelled to do these things. But today, with young people, we are dealing with men such as I described them before: they were preparing for a career when they made their decision. To be sure, the prospects can change because we are entering a period of unemployment. . . .

Would it be a remedy to become a priest?

I should hope not! This kind of men, when they join the clergy, renounce money. By vocation they not only give up marriage, but a profession. Therefore they will disqualify themselves very quickly by putting an end to their professional training. Then the engineers and civil servants will not find jobs any more. They are compelled to take risks. They do not tackle things the way their elders did, and they have to have very good reasons to do what they do.

The problem of money is posed today in a different manner than it was in the past. Then it was clear: one espoused a relatively poor church in which one lived in a wretched way. I have seen terrible examples of this in Orleans! It may have been a manifestation of generosity, a tremendous detachment. But many lived in such a way because they had no choice. Today the opposite is prevalent: the question is posed inversely.

Lack of Priests
and Spiritual Poverty

To be a Christian in France today is to be unlike others. It is even to be the opposite of everybody else. Fifty years ago one could say at times that to be a Christian was clearly to be "right-minded" (Remember the great angers of Bernanos?). Now the Christian is not "right-minded" anymore. I call "right-minded" those who think like anybody else. The tragedy of Christians is that they can no longer obey the modern form of "right-mindedness" which is advertising.

The existence of the church entails sacramentality, and therefore priesthood. One of your first initiatives in Orleans was to reopen a seminary. What do you think about the future of the priesthood?

The problem of priests is totally dependent on the existence of the church herself. To give you an example: the seminary of the diocese of Dakar was founded a century ago. A century was needed for the emergence of a minimum of Christian community in certain ethnic groups in order for vocations and African priests to be possible. Vocations depend on the state of a people, and not the other way around. The problem of vocations in France is not that of priests in the first place, but that of the French people and the Christian people in France. If there are Christian communities that are believing and fervent, they will receive vocations either in the known forms of religious life or in new forms of consecration or in the priesthood . . . There will even be more than needed. A great spiritual generosity calls for a fruitfulness that matches it.

Interview by Gérard Leclerc in *Le Quotidien* [right-wing daily], 10–11 April 1982.

Besides which, what does it mean: a need for priests? I have yet to meet a sociologist who could tell me the optimum rate of priests for the population. According to what criterion? In response to what need?

The problem must be posed the other way around. When there is a Christian people, there arises such a spiritual demand that the mediation of the priest is all the more enriching and that sacramental life becomes itself a source of enrichment. One of the tragedies of the French clergy was that it came from a relatively narrow social sector of the population so as to serve people who were more interested in a certain religious conformity than in the awakening of a strong and fervent faith. French priests experienced a feeling of usefulness which was tragic at times (see the *Diary of a Country Priest*). But not everybody is a country priest. In reverse circumstances, during very fruitful and spiritual times there is a superabundance of generosity which is channeled in other directions. Thus from certain parts of rural France in the nineteenth century came men and women who offered themselves for service in Africa and other areas. This is happening again today in other parts of the world—Africa, for instance.

We are entering an era in France of a great lack of priests, in comparison with the recent past. The next years will be terrible. This comes from the spiritual poverty of our own nation. The real problem is to reawaken Christian fidelity among believers. Then the necessary vocations will arise.

Renewal Cannot Be Programmed

*F*rench society is often depicted as completely secularized: a case perhaps unique among the countries of Catholic tradition. Do you agree with this opinion?

On the whole I agree, though one must clarify certain points. If you really want to use this term, you must not forget that France has been a "secularized" country for a long time. France is the only country in Western Europe—or to put it better, in Christian Europe—where there has not been a complete identification between Christianity, culture, and the nation. For you, in Italy, the work of Dante established the language and the culture; and his work is deeply Christian. In Germany the creative event of the national language was the translation of the Bible by Luther.[1] There was in France a somewhat similar event starting with the Renaissance, but the inspiration came from pagan antiquity. Since the beginning of the sixteenth century, that is, since the beginning of modern times, two very different currents can be distinguished within French culture: the Christian tradition and the secular and libertarian movement. In those days the country folk were not quite christianized. They were brought into Christianity through two successive periods: the first one after the Council of Trent (giving us what we call today areas of Christian tradition, Brittany, for instance) and the second one after the French Revolution, during the restoration of the monarchy. Sec-

Interview by Luigi Geninazzi in *Il Sabato* [Italian weekly], 3 July 1982.
1. See also, on this matter, the earlier interview, "Christianity Is Indissolubly Linked to Judaism."

137

ularization does not therefore appear in France as a recent phenomenon, but as a sign of inner rupture within the culture of our country. The conflict between the two currents was manifested in the form of an antireligious struggle: during the Enlightenment, atheism was far more virulent in France than elsewhere; and it was in France that the secular revolutions of the past two centuries took place which gave birth to the great attack of anticlericalism. On the other hand, French Catholicism brought forth a very specific clericalism: since it could not identify with the totality of the culture, it claimed for itself a central place in the nation by taking a shortcut through politics. It seemed several times that political power would be the decisive locus of the unity and presence of the Christians: a temptation for the church, but also a temptation for politicians to use the church. Thus the secular party was led to conclude that there could be no political freedom unless the church were destroyed. And this finally explains why, in France, the conflict between the secular party and Christians always looked like a war.

I must add something very important though: in France the religious movement of spiritual renewal does not coincide with this struggle between the Catholic and secular parties. There are several levels that one must carefully distinguish in the history of French Catholicism: for instance, in the seventeenth century there was a great popular renewal at the very moment the Catholic party was about to lose power. This explains how the church was always able to resist the trial of the Revolution: the high clergy collapsed, just like the fidelity of the ruling classes, but the faith of the people perdured.

How did this permanent challenge that secularization means to the Catholic church manifest itself these past years?

You can say that until twenty years ago there was a relatively consistent Catholic world that had been able to resist within the divided society that I have just described. Today this world has been swept away. There remains however a given: French culture, in the broadest sense of the term, is widely imbued with Christianity, even if this exists only in a very diffuse way. I mean to say that even in its secular and secularized expressions the historical consciousness of the French nation retains, in its roots, a remnant of Christianity. In other words, all the speeches that have been made up to our time about secularization must not lead us to conclude that French culture is a pagan one, one never touched by Christianity. In this respect, the question that John Paul II asked during his visit in France is a fundamental one: "France, what have you done with your baptism?" In this question is an implicit and essential affirmation: France was baptized. A new evangelization cannot disregard this fact.

What should France do to become aware again of this baptism? Or to put it better: What, in your opinion, is the duty of the church in such a crisis situation?

We have to manage with what we have: we receive from the past values inscribed in a culture, but no ritual or social consistency. Therefore we have to give back to Christian life its integrity, reevangelize and rebuild the church, bring about its rebirth. We cannot rely on the determinism of education or on a tradition of social behavior. It is enough to observe what is happening in the new generations: ritual gestures that punctuate Christian existence are less and less carried out. If we do not react effectively, we will soon find ourselves in a situation that would be similar to what obtains in the Lutheranism of East Germany or in Sweden, where Christianity has lost its social significance.

How then can you define the basic problem that Christianity has to face in France today?

It is not a problem of pastoral methodology, strategy, or of making an administrative chart. The key issue is different: What spiritual content do we find today among Christians in France? If there is only a vacuum, we will surely be swept away. We are living now a historical moment: our back is to the wall and we are able to see clearly that Christianity cannot be received any more as a cultural given, or conceived as a sociopolitical given, or transferred as an educational given; Christianity is a response to a call, to an accepted grace. In a word, we cannot harbor the delusion that we will be able to retain something of our Christianity without having to receive it anew. If you reread the great modern witnesses to Christianity who were given to France—Leon Bloy, Peguy, Maritain, Bernanos—you will realize that these genuine prophets had described already many years ahead of time what actually did happen. With great lucidity they understood that we were going astray. Leon Bloy wrote: "This Christian people does not live off its inheritance."

This is in fact a call to conversion, and it was made, not without reason by great converts. . . .

Exactly. I hope that all that Leon Bloy perceived a century ago with much suffering will become for Christians of my time a motive of hope. You see, when I, as archbishop of Paris, put myself in such a perspective, it gives me great serenity and great inner freedom.

You have just named some of the great Christian authors who have made French Catholicism a model for the other countries of Europe. I am thinking in particular about the fascination it exerted on Italian Catholics in the fifties and sixties. French Catholicism was an example of unity between an intense life of faith, a cultural development adapted to the times, and a consistent political commitment. What came out of all this in the end?

What you recall is an ideal which was only very partially achieved in France. I am going to tell you a little story which is of major importance to me and which is a good illustration of the role French Catholicism had vis-à-vis other nations. In 1950 (I was then a young seminarian) I found myself in Berlin during my military service. During a *Katholikentag,* I had the opportunity to talk with a priest of a German workers' parish.[2] Convinced of the superiority of the French, I started to explain to him with a passion what he should do in his parish. He interrupted me by saying: "You French people are masters in the art of creating models, and we Germans, in the art of mass production. When you reach the stage of mass production, then we will know whether your model is workable."

All that you spoke of, intense faith, cultural and political commitment, was a hope for us too, but it did not materialize. In the fifties and the sixties we spoke of reforming the parish in the direction of community; but the experiments did not measure up to our ambitions. We did produce models of liturgical reform, but later on, who knows how, we found ourselves in a dramatic situation when we had to implement the liturgical reforms decreed by the Council. We rediscovered the diaconate and proposed it to the Council; but we are the country where the ratio of deacons to the population is the lowest. During the Council, our bishops developed new forms of participation of laypeople in the apostolate; but due to a persistent clericalism, we have in fact little others can envy. In brief, we were able to provide images and models, but the project was not accepted by the people.

Is this the fault of a too obtuse people or of a too intellectual project?
It is impossible to say. . . .

2. *Katholikentag,* Catholic (Church) Day, a convention of German Roman Catholics occurring every other year.

I am afraid that the second hypothesis is the true one. But you have to answer me.

I will limit myself to this reflection. A project, no matter how intelligent and interesting, if it does not have in itself the conditions for its implementation, is a chimera. In the history of the church there have been many projects for reform. It is enough to think about the beginning of the thirteenth century. But a Saint Francis of Assisi was needed for the initiative to bear fruit and transform the heart of the church. Our time needs witnesses. And every morning and every evening I pray the Lord to be able to recognize them. Perhaps they are already here, but we have not recognized them.

Talking these past days with French Catholics, I gathered this notion that the church in your country has disintegrated. In fact, there are communities, but they do not know one another and, moreover, there is a strong polarization between right and left, between conservatives and progressives. What do you think about this?

The fact is that both are exactly alike: all of them deem faith to be a given fact, a sort of patrimony. The church exists for them and therefore they take the liberty of judging her. They behave like people living in an old house inherited from their parents, and they attempt to make it more comfortable: some propose to repaint the walls, others, on the contrary, want to change the furniture . . . the house is still there, but nobody thinks about it. Until one day the whole thing will collapse, the foundations will crumble, and the walls will crack. Thus some people of my generation realized with astonishment that their children no longer had this richness of faith that they had received and which enabled them to become conservatives or progressives. What they deem to be an immutable given is now questioned: the house does not exist any more.

This viewpoint stresses that the threat is not directed so much against the institution as it is against our faith, which is judged. The church is not disintegrating; the fidelity of men and women is being tested. But not everybody is ready to understand this.

Let us talk now about the workings of this church of France: the parishes, the movements, the institutions. I noticed that you are very appreciated among young people and intellectuals, even secular ones. But among certain priests of the ecclesiatical structure there is a distrust and almost a challenge directed against you. How do you explain this? How do you analyze the situation?

You will forgive me for not wanting to answer your first question.

As to the analysis of the situation, it is undoubtedly very difficult. All of us, clerics and laypeople, have had to undergo harsh trials during the past few years. We had great apostolic ambitions; they foundered. We dreamed about great reforms; they did not materialize. We hoped for a renewal of the faith. The reverse is true. Those who lived through the fifties and the Council are wounded today, as it were. They are still there, on the battlefield; God certainly loves them for their fidelity; but they have no descendants. This is a terrible trial of sterility and death. I often meet worker-priests and they all ask me why I don't send young men to them. Do you understand this? As if it depended on me, the bishop. As if it were a problem of organization. But if we are lacking priests, if the old ones go away without replacement, this means that the crisis is a deep one. This is the trial this church of today has to undergo. And when it is threatened in such a way, there is a temptation to accuse people in their own environment, to find culprits at any cost, to become divided. But we have to accept this trial of death without giving way to the fear that death is all powerful. We need a great act of faith to believe that through this cross God is calling us to life and fruitfulness.

Outside of the Catholic church, I think that there is a current of rediscovery of Christianity, even among agnostic people. . . .

Many unbelieving French people received through the intermediary of culture a portion of the Christian inheritance. Thinking back about my own experience, I have to admit that I discovered Catholicism through the culture I received in a state lycée, a secular one. I read Pascal eagerly; I was interested in Corneille and Racine; all the authors we studied in school. We live now in a time when fundamental questions are surfacing again, with the intuition that Christianity might have a vital importance for society. In this perspective, I think that we are facing tremendous possibilities for new evangelization. This does not mean that they will agree with us when we talk to them, but they will, in any case, pay attention.

What will be the future of the church in France?

If you really compel me to play the prophet, I will say that it is possible that the renewal of the church will go through a new evangelization. We find ourselves in a very strange situation: never did Christianity seem so new, at the core of culture and civilization; but at the same time, Christians appear to be old, tired, and worn out by their inner disputes. It is as if there were a difference of potential; in such a case, there occurs a shock; a current is created. I think that something of the kind should happen. Thirty years ago there were great Christians, but very few people paid attention to them. Today people come back to ask fundamental questions. Will we still have great Christians?

What Dechristianization?

C *ontrary to what happens in other religions, the Catholic church*
grants a prominent place to the clergy, the corollary being a certain
passivity on the part of the faithful. Does this seem to be a good thing to
you?

Twenty years ago the Second Vatican Council forcefully brought
back to light this truth that the church is the totality of believers. Let
all Christians effectively become responsible for the objectives and
the life of the church; this is a priority goal. Theoretically, the ori-
entation is clear; practically, the implementation remains difficult, because it goes against the constant drift of social life. But this is part
of the ordinary paradox of the church. She is periodically shaken up
from the inside by forces dwelling in her—for believers, this is the
Spirit of God—and she then becomes in very different societies a
ferment of renewal by reforming herself. She arouses hope and hos-
tility at the same time. Some suspect us of being hypocrites, others
accuse us of fostering utopias. This being said, and in order to answer your question, a privileged place given to the clergy can lead to
abuse and cause passivity among the faithful. But who is to be blamed
for this drift? Clerics? Laypeople? Generally speaking, our society,
for comfort's sake or in the name of efficiency, tends to rely more
and more on "specialists." For their health, sick people turn to physicians. In the same way, parents drop in the lap of teachers their
educational function. . . .

Is not the primary task of a leader of the Catholic church in France to

Interview by Gérard Dupuy and Luc Rosenzweig in *Libération* [left-wing Paris daily], 27
September 1983.

144

struggle against the dechristianization that affects entire sectors of society?

What is the nature and the significance of this "dechristianization"? It seems that French society was "christianized" because social rituals were identified with those of the Catholic religion. In the great majority, those who were born were baptized, those who reached puberty received their first Holy Communion, and those who married and those who died went through the church. All of this covered in fact very diverse situations of beliefs and convictions. Do you really think that the nineteenth century was a period of unanimous faith? As to the Voltairean bourgeoisie of the eighteenth century and the idle aristocracy of the end of the seventeenth century, how could you say that they were christianized? Even during the periods when religion was prevalent one could have doubts about the christianization of society. At the beginning of the seventeenth century, Father Marsenne, a philosopher and mathematician, a friend of Pascal, bemoaned the fact that there were twenty-five thousand atheists in Paris. Was he really exaggerating?

But today we have figures and sociological studies. . . .

Of course. But still, one has to know how to judge the figures, to interpret them correctly. I just read a study about the catechization of the children of Marseilles. If you look at the numbers of the children who went through the entire catechism during their schooling, it is true that the number has tremendously declined during the past twenty years. But at the same time, the ways of catechizing have evolved since five years of catechism are now required instead of three, while the population has become more mobile. If you consider the children who had one or two years of catechism, their percentage has remained more or less stable. The figures stress a different problem but not a collapse. In the same way, we notice a tremendous drop in the number of people attending Sunday Mass, the famous "Mass goers" of the sociologists. Yet surveys show that Catholics who consider themselves observant are quite more numerous than the figures given for the Catholics attending every Sunday. Why? Some of those who used to come to Mass almost every Sunday kept in fact the same social behavior when they went only from time to time. It is the concept of "regular practice" that has changed its meaning for some people. It is a change in behavior but not necessarily in convictions. It is certain, however, that there is a tremendous crisis. But it is not certain that this crisis led to a modification of the faith lived by the French people for several decades.

Could you be more specific?

French society, like perhaps all Western societies, is losing ground in religion, but also in morality and demography. The bloodlettings and moral and spiritual failures of the last century left us with open wounds which are far from healed. I am not sure that we got over the perverted hope of the Soviet revolution or the vertigo of Nazism and the annihilation it fostered, or the great slaughters of the two world wars. I am not sure that the old world did not die somewhere, secretly. Our countries are materially wealthy, but where are our inner resources, our intellectual, moral, and spiritual resources? I want to join all the men and women who hope with all their strength that they will bring them back to life.

The Church: Interpreter of the Ethical Demand

L et us talk anyhow, if you agree, about the school issue. It has had deep repercussions through the movements it brought forth. Didn't the latter show that the image of the church in French society had changed?

I think so. But the change came before the happenings of these past weeks. Quite often, in the history of France, the mutations—which are in fact slow mutations—do not surface except by fits and starts, and each time we play to ourselves the movie of a revolution. In the school issue we are faced with something of an average or long duration. Public demonstrations are nothing but a symptom.

Which means?

You may recall the first words of my speech in Versailles: "Who are you?"

Why this question?

To help us all to reflect. No one could have told offhand who was present. The left wing would have been pleased if there had been only right-wing people. The right wing would have liked the sole presence of the political opposition. The "hawks" of the "secular" clique would have preferred the "sectarian" activists in favor of the parochial schools, and so on. Now it is impossible to understand what happened if we refer to the usual categories whose simplistic motivating interpretation is that Catholics are conservatives, that they vote for the right wing and that they are bourgeois. Such an image is boosted by some electoral surveys which, however, do not take

Interview by Olivier Chevrillon, Jacques Duquesne, and Georges Suffert in *Le Point* [weekly magazine of centrist tendencies], 23 April 1984.

147

into account the stable and deep elements of any religious convictions. Observers have convinced themselves that beliefs do not exist any more, because they don't see them, but when such events show up on the little screen, the picture becomes too complicated.

This simplistic and summary image of Catholics has changed anyway?

Of course. But let us turn back to the past, if you agree. We just experienced thirty years of expansion. These thirty "glorious" years have anesthetized the moral conscience of our people. Anesthetized the way speeding can make one feel "high," or the sun can stupefy. All at once, France took a step that other nations had taken before and more slowly.

After the terrible ideological, political, and national tragedies that took place from the start of the century until the end of World War II, all of a sudden, France, which was a country with a rural tradition, entered the world of plastic, highways, mechanization. Add to this rising incomes; add the permissivity of mores in a society which until then had been naughty but prudish. This society inverted its system of values when it had the feeling of entering modernity.

But while everybody was thinking in terms of growth and wealth, ideology, morality, and even political rifts did not "follow." May 1968 was, from the ideological viewpoint, a real revolution, while politically speaking it was only a pantomime; the revolution was to become aware that reality could not be grasped with the help of obsolete words. At that time, when I heard Daniel Cohn-Bendit declare at the Place de la Sorbonne that Aragon was a "Stalinist scoundrel," I understood as the students did that an era was coming to an end. Youth had just broken away from the conformity it had inherited from the past century.[1]

Let's sum it up. Expansion, brutal exposure to modernity, and, at the same time, death of the ideologies. . . .

Especially the ethical and religious order as a whole that appeared as ruined from the inside, obsolete, disqualified offhand by rationalizing ambition and the technical mastery of nature, and especially of society. The unavoidable consequence is to do without God. Not only not to believe in Him anymore, but not to believe anymore that one could conceive God. Thus dechristianization was translating on the sociological plane a cultural fact that was already well established. Thus the temptation to make of the "death of God" a theology and of "secularization" a pastoral program.

1. Daniel-Cohn Bendit was a student leader and fiery orator during the little "revolution" of May 1968.

But what vanished was not, it seems to me, what people thought it was. The religious phenomenon had regressed if one measured it by the quantifying indices of religious sociography (all that is involved in religious practice and can be measured). We were facing indications reflecting changes in behavior connected with the modernization of French society as a whole. The believing minority was included in the great evolutions. But the religious phenomenon is not linked solely, in a country like France, to behaviors that can be measured by empirical sociology. In essence it is a symbolic patrimony and a semantic memory, repressed at times, but never destroyed. Now—and here I come back to your first question—we are witnessing today a certain resurgence. Not the rebirth of what was dead, but the return to light of what had been hidden underground, an awakening from anesthesia, the return of what Maurice Clavel called "the great repressed One," God.

What exactly do you mean when you say: "symbolic patrimony"?

Social reality concerns symbolism, the humanity of man and ethical problems, therefore the most fundamental realities. There is today, in various sectors of social life, a gap between the institutions and their ethical basis. This is the consequence of the aging of these institutions and the aging of our civilization. But while people claimed to have stifled them, the fundamental problems of human persons are back with us: ourselves in the face of our conscience, ourselves in society.

When I was twenty years old, we first had to justify our being Christians: though we are Christians, we used to say, we are human. This was a parody of Saint Paul's formula: "They also, and I even more." They are inclined to science, and I even more; they are political, and I even more, and so on. All this vanished twenty years ago. This suspicion is no longer in the collective consciousness of the new French generations.

We have gotten quite far away from the demonstrations on the school issue. . . .

No. The crowd in Versailles may be one of the signs of a returning memory.[2] Awakening from the amnesia of recent decades brings people to the rediscovery of the church as the honest interpreter, the honest symbol of these ethical questionings. The church is not the oppressor

2. A mass demonstration of about a million people took place in Versailles in April 1984 to protest a law through which the socialist government attempted to clamp down on the few liberties left to the schools of the Catholic system. Cardinal Lustiger spoke at that rally, though he did not take part in the march itself. The success was such that the law was repealed and the Minister of Education had to resign. (Translator's note)

of humankind, the enemy to destroy, the foe of enlightenment, the opiate of the people, and so on. But really and honestly, it is speaking legitimately—because it is disinterested—for human beings claiming their own humanity.

You do not believe that this is an accidental encounter, because, after all, the school issue. . . .

As far as I am concerned, it is not accidental. The occasion was accidental: Versailles. But the place of Christianity in this issue does not seem accidental to me.

Is not your application somewhat limited? First of all in space: the phenomena you describe are not all peculiar to France. And the crisis has earlier origins: it comes from the ideology of the nineteenth century. . . .

That ideology did not realize that it was robbing an inheritance which did not belong to it: the Christian patrimony. It behaved like a prodigal son, generous but irresponsible.

As it happens, Catholicism is now and on this point (family, education, freedom) the popular vector. But we could well find ourselves in a reverse situation concerning other problems. For instance, all that pertains to the mastery of the body and biology. In its sexuality and genetics, the body is becoming the object of a technical and industrial domination whose ethical justifications and technological limits we cannot see. All this is erupting today, but it had been in preparation for decades, and had been a goal for a much longer time. I am not too sure about the popular feelings on this issue. If one wanted to make a survey, the worst madness might be approved by quite a significant percentage of the people. The mad physicians of Auschwitz were perhaps nothing but forerunners, and the bloody eugenics of the thirties in Germany find at times a white-gloved justification in the hospitals of 1984. I am not sure that, in the face of such a problem, the same Christians and the same bishops are not going to find themselves alone.

Would there be other cases in which the church would find herself alone?

Racism. In its strictest definition which must not be confused with the immigration problems. As far as the latter are concerned, political society has already given up. The Communist party, which always had the advantage of its avant-garde, was the first to send out its bulldozers. Then other parties, seeing how unpopular the issue was, prudently gave up. And I predict—or, to say the least, dread—the time when we Christians, we the church, will find ourselves alone, in midstream, openly asking public opinion to look at a crucial problem even if it does not want to see it, even if electoral calculations suggest its camouflage or outright rejection. In these disputes, the church, even though she has the same role in the matter as in the school issue, runs the risk of finding herself removed from the sociological majority of the French people.

On these three points: (1) school and youth; (2) biology and morality; (3) immigrants and racism, there is a gap between the ethical problems of society and the capacity of the public institutions to take them into account. This gap is dangerous for French society. It betrays powerlessness in response to what is essential, that is, to the demands of ethics.

In fact, I would like to see statesmen rise from the political sector and I would like them to understand that politics can be a noble thing when it knows how to take these ethical problems into account, that the highest form of reason is submission to morality. Politics, when it is guided only by electoral indices, appears to me as a terrible danger: it subordinates the choices of reason—therefore of human freedom and of morality—to mere fluctuations of desire.

But people will retort: "What morality?" A pluralistic society can accept various moralities.

At least one must try to pose moral problems. They are posed brutally for a generation that does not know quite where it stands. For instance, the reactions of young couples with regard to sexuality. Perhaps they are aware that the body is not an object, that affectivity is not merely desire: this concerns human dignity and happiness, the respect one owes to oneself.

You think that this is the attitude of the majority? The opposite seems to prevail.

No doubt about it. But I am not sure that the sense of responsibility, therefore of access to a real moral plane, is not in the process of making a comeback. Not as a mass movement, but perhaps a current daring to express itself. Some reactions, at times marginal, testify to this phenomenon. They can be marginal or excessive to the point of pure nihilism: look at the pessimism of some movies or novels. Negative radicalism, disillusion can be symptoms of a question that is posed but has no answer. For instance: the strange mixture of eroticism and mysticism of Philippe Sollers.

THE CHURCH
AND THE
EUCHARIST

Here Is the Church

Matt. 16:13–28

H ere is the church, here she is as Jesus prophesied: "On this
Rock I will build my church." The future tense of Jesus is
our present. As the apostle said, we are the building where "every
structure is aligned on him, all grow into one holy temple in the
Lord" (Eph. 2:21). At this point in time, Jesus himself is building
his church. And here is this church.

These words of the Lord make us see where the unity of our church
resides. The unity is not the product of our mutual consent; it is not
the result of our concessions, our agreements; it is not based on our
mutual understanding. The unity of the church is Christ himself, he
who comes before us. The unity of the church is achieved when
everyone of us listens and hears this word: "If anyone wants to be a
follower of mine, let him renounce himself and take up his cross
everyday and follow me" (Luke 9:23). The unity of the church is
given to us as a way. A trying way which uproots us, poor disciples,
from our refusals and avoidances, so that we can follow the Lord
where he wants to lead us.

The unity of the church is a work of redemption freeing us from
our sins. Peter protests and this is not a passing incomprehension.
Peter is opposed to the Passion of the Lord, and this is not a tem-
porary misunderstanding. Peter expresses all that withdraws and refuses, all that resists and opposes the way of Christ in us, for unity
is before us. Yes, brothers and sisters, two popes, Paul VI and John

Homily at Notre-Dame of Paris, 27 February 1981.

Paul II, have wanted the crozier of Peter to be a cross. In my turn, I decided that the cross had to go before us and guide us. Entering this cathedral, I place before my eyes and I show in front of me this living wood of the cross, as the sign of the Lord who is before us. He is the one who makes us a people purified by the blood of his cross. He is really the way, the one who gives us access to the Father. He asks us to enter by his own way and gathers us in unity when he makes us share in his Passion. The way of the cross is the only way of unity for Christians. Whoever refuses unity is an obstacle to Christ. Whoever refuses to follow Christ hurts unity.

If we follow Christ on his way, then Jesus enables us to know the truth, and also to be delivered from our lie. Indeed, here are astonishing words in the mouth of Peter: "You are the Christ, the Son of the living God" (Matt. 16:17). Jesus recognizes in them the voice of the Father in heaven: "Simon, son of Jonah, you are a happy man! Because it was not flesh and blood that revealed this to you, but my Father in heaven" (Matt. 16:18). And yet, this revelation of the Father remains obscure to us, even though our lips repeat it together with Peter. When Christ announces his Passion to us, together with Peter we object and we escape, we become divided and we are torn: "Heaven preserve you, Lord," he said, "this must not happen to you" (Matt. 16:23). Jesus recognizes in these words his trial and the temptor: "Get behind me, Satan! You are an obstacle in my path because the way you think is not God's way but man's" (Matt. 16:23).

Only Christ who goes before us, our master and our Lord, can know and recognize what spirit dwells in us and speaks through our mouth, the heavenly Father or the temptor. For he is not only the Way, but he is our Truth, the truth of the church. Not a truth of which the church would be the mistress or owner. For the church does not have power over the truth. But the Truth has power over the church, the concrete and historical truth, the eternal Word made flesh who comes to dwell among us and gives himself to the church. He is the truth that was before us and marches in front of us. Christ is the only one who can judge the truth of our words about him. He wants to give the grace of saying the word that the Father inspires in us by giving us his Spirit. He wants to give us the grace to be freed from our lie, our temptation, when he calls us to follow him. Yes, the truth is working in us. Whoever lets the Truth seize him, goes to the Light. And he becomes free.

Which is why, we the church of Christ, tell him: "You are the Son of the living God!" For Christ is Life. "For anyone who wants to save his life will lose it; but anyone who loses his life for my sake will find it" (Matt. 16:25). The task of the church is thus clearly indicated to us. The enemy is pointed out.

Who is the enemy? Death. Death has a thousand names. The name of hatred, the name of fratricidal murder, the name of refusal of God. It can also be called Hiroshima. . . . Death has a thousand names. It has the smirking face of the devil, of Satan. It springs from the heart of man when man dares not to love life.

But since Life has risen inside us and among us, since Life opens the way for us, since Life offers itself as the truth that judges us and enables us to talk, then we can believe in life and welcome life. And we dare to confront our enemy, death, not as a foregone conclusion before which we should crumple, but as an adversary that we can vanquish. Yes, death is not the last word, the ultimate significance of human existence. We believe in the Lord of life. This is why we love life. This is why we give life.

"What then, will a man gain if he wins the whole world and ruins his life?" (Matt. 16:26). This question of the Lord is addressed to us and received by us, not as a reproach but as a hope. Today human beings are in the process of gaining the whole world. What good is it to them if they do so only at the cost of the death of men and women? Which is why we have to dare ask this question of the world, in the name of Christ, and in our own name.

And we must also receive and hear the second question of Jesus: "What has man to offer in exchange for his life?" (Matt. 16:26). And we must dare tell it. For we have welcomed the Lord of life. Which is why we can, in this indescribably beautiful though fascinatingly cruel world, dare to confront any threat from death and open the door to hope. For according to the promise of Christ, the power of death cannot prevail against his church.

Thus we are preceded by our Lord, our master, our Christ, he who gathers us in unity by making us share his Passion, he who reveals our Truth and the truth of humanity by surrendering his life for us and delivering us from lie, he who is Life given for the world to have a superabundance of life. Yes, here we are with Christ. Yes, here is the church built by Christ. Here is the church.

Very dear and beloved brothers and sisters, we are here at this focus of communion in which the Lord gives himself to us in this ecclesial mystery gathering men and women of multiple origins, diverse backgrounds. We are not all in the same communion, and yet, through faith, there is already this unity and this love that the Lord wants to make present to men and women.

Now I call on you to respond to the Lord. For when we profess the faith of the church, we recognize him who dwells in us and to whom we surrender our life.

But I would like you to tolerate a parenthesis on my part, a quasi-fantasy. And for you to allow this, I must first tell you a story. It is in the Gospel. Jesus and his disciples go to Capernaum. Arriving at home, Jesus questions them and asks: "What were you arguing about on the road? (Mark 9:34). The disciples remain silent for they were arguing along the way about who was the greatest among them. Then Jesus tells them: "If anyone wants to be the first, he must make himself last of all and servant of all." Then he takes a little child, stands him among them, kisses him and says: "Anyone who welcomes one of these little children in my name, welcomes me; and anyone who welcomes me welcomes not me but the one who sent me" (Mark 9:36–37).

I would like the children who are present to come forward and stand around me. They are a reminder for me as well as for you of the mission entrusted to us. They are the image of Christ, he who is "the greatest" of the church and made himself the servant of all. They are our future. In them we recognize the Lord of life. Come, children. . . .

As Peter Followed Jesus

Wis. of Sol. 6:12–16
1 Thess. 4:13–18
Matt. 25:1–3

C hrist invites the church to watch during the night of history because this parable announces both the absence of the bridegroom who has gone away and his prompt return. And in this night of history we must carry in our frail hands the light that pierces the darkness, the light entrusted us by God.

We are gathered this evening to pray for Pope John Paul II on the anniversary of his installation. It seems to me that these words of the Scriptures, meditated on today by the whole church, are very fitting: this is really what God wants to tell us today. There may be among you people who are not familiar with the Christian faith and who do not understand why we gather to pray on such an anniversary. It is not as you might think—I am talking to those who are perhaps farthest from our customs, and least familiar with our way of feeling— it is not to celebrate an anniversary in a solely human way, in honor of someone who has an important office.

The church recognizes in human events signs coming from God. She recognizes in this apostolic ministry we all share, bishops and priests, a sign that God gives to the church, even through our weakness and our sin. And how much more in the ministry of the pope! For the election of a pope is an act of the church through which the church must recognize the language God addresses to her. Thus at all times, in all centuries, through the human faces God gave the church as shepherds, we have been given at the same time, the ability

Homily at Notre-Dame of Paris on the occasion of the third anniversary of the installation of Pope John Paul II, 8 November 1981.

to recognize in them the shape of our way, even in the weaknesses of every servant, pope though he be. In such a way, the language of mercy and that of the greatness of God are revealed to believers. In such a way, God gives to the church the sign of the power of his word and his presence.

Tonight our prayer is made of affection, respect, confidence in the person of John Paul II but also, and in a fundamental way, of this thanksgiving in which we, as the church, do not cease recognizing what God does for us, seeing in the ministers who are given to us, and especially in the ministry of the pope the sign of Christ our servant, who opens for us the way to which he call us.

Through these past three years, are we able to try to discern the light of our time, the specific light of our time? I think so, and I will attempt to do it, in faith, with you.

We live in a fantastic time of grace and hope. The church has experienced a tremendous spiritual event: the Council. To see this event only as an act of government, with decisions that were discussed and made, accepted joyfully by some, and diffidently obeyed by others, would be to view things in a totally pagan manner. The Council was a spiritual event because the entire church put herself in a state of availability and obedience to the gift of the Holy Spirit through her own weaknesses and her own limitations. Here is a truly collective event, a spiritual and collective one, which is rather unique in human history—when an entire church relied visibly on the power of God to ensure her own life and open the way to her obedience. The successive faces of the men who were given to her as ministers in this spiritual event were John XXIII, Paul VI, and John Paul I, each one according to his grace. When God gave us Pope John Paul II, to exercise the ministry of Peter as bishop of Rome, it seems to me that the sign God wanted to give us, and one that was immediately manifested in his ministry, is the fruitfulness and youth of the church. Remember, we experienced the Council as a tremendous hope. And now, open your eyes: see how the church herself arises, new, multiple, young with new faces that we, old Christians, may have been unaware of. The spiritual event of the Council, with the arrival of this pope coming from a Europe which is not the same as our own, who witnesses for other nations than our own, shows to our wondering eyes the surge of the Spirit in whom the church gathers in the joy of recognition.

Remember: when the pope went around the world, like Paul the pilgrim of the churches, wanting to communicate to them the gifts of God and to receive from them the gift of God, the church herself was revealed on the way of the pope. We did not see the pope in South America: the pope brought to the eyes of the world the church that is in South America. We did not see the pope in Africa: the pope, through his visit, brought to our eyes the church being born in Africa. We did not come to see the pope here: when the pope came here he awakened our church that may have been asleep. Thus what was contained as a seed, as a spiritual power in this hope of the Council, begins to unfold as an immense and measurable wealth for the joy of God.

And then, as is logical, as is normal, since she is the sign of Christ, our church shares in the Passion of Christ. We know it; the Lord Jesus Christ told us; she does not cease to repeat it every day, every Sunday. And God has permitted it to be visible to our eyes, that the violence of the world brought forth from the sin of humankind be also borne by the pope. Perhaps we have been wounded in our hearts, torn, scandalized that nothing sacred exists anymore in this world; but after all, it is normal for him who follows the Lord Jesus Christ, as Peter followed Jesus Christ, to bear in himself the marks of the Passion, to bear in his flesh and in his spirit the weight of violence and hatred in order to bring mercy and pardon. We see what our destiny is: our destiny, as a church, is to take part in the Passion of Christ, and thus we become signs of Christ. In this Christ himself utters the Beatitudes upon us.

Lastly, we have retained this formula that has become strange and that, abruptly, becomes more visible in our time. We remembered that a man rose in this world, who has no human power except that of our love and our faith. And he says: "Humankind must be respected. Humankind is loved by God. Humanity is at the center of the world because God put it there." These truths that are so simply and forever betrayed, we too, as a church, have to bear them, not as a program, not as a declaration, not as a conviction, but as a gift that God gave us. Who then is this man who can overcome all outrages? What then is this dignity of humanity that can go beyond all contempt? What then is this freedom of humanity that is capable of overcoming every prison? What then is this voice of humanity that is heard, even in the silence of the annihilations? It is that of the risen Christ who wants to make of us witnesses to his resurrected life. The tremendous force of the affirmation of our dignity and of our rights is nurtured in the secret of our faith by the presence of the resurrected one in whom the true dignity of humanity is finally given. Which is why we can, we too, we of the church, and we must follow this way which is the way of our time: the resurrected Lord himself asks this of us.

Brothers and sisters, I do not want to extend this meditation, but when I told you at the beginning how our time seems to me rich and beautiful in the night through which we must watch and wait, it is because our time is rich and beautiful from the call that God addresses to us so that we can be his witnesses: it is a rich and beautiful time when love is called to give its proofs, *its proof*: Christ, the redeemer of humankind.

The Challenge of Christ

There is a paradox that we are hard put to bear in the face of public opinion. Especially amidst the clang of weapons, in the face of explosive propaganda, under the flood of preconceived images, and the anxieties manipulated in our hearts: it is the paradox of what the pope wanted to do by going first to England as had been scheduled, and then to Argentina.

We guess that this is a strange, unclassifiable step, one that cannot be compared to the shuttle of intermediaries, the negotiators, the mediators, the men of appeasement and reason. But it is almost impossible to clearly define his role, the mission he wants to accomplish for those who do not exactly share our faith and the way it is expressed: in the British Isles and in Argentina, in the midst of two warring nations, he celebrates the Eucharist. He who does not understand Christianity from the inside sees only, after all, a banal and repeatable rite, the central rite of Catholics: in the last analysis, the thing they can do best!

If this were a prayer like any human prayer, a rite such as any civilization (and any religion) has been capable of inventing, a rite like any other rite, this celebration of the Eucharist would have been, in fact, something ludicrous, tragically ludicrous, while, perhaps at the very moment it is taking place, men fall in battle and war rages. This manner of praying seems to have no influence on the implacable march of events.

Homily at Notre-Dame of Paris on the feast of Corpus Christi, 12 June 1982.

And in fact, a mere chronicler of the present time, the passing time, sees all along the weeks, months, years, and centuries the cruel logic of might, fear, hatred, delusion, and of generosity perverted into ambition. Good causes, equally distributed, contradictory rights leave on our earth their bloody trails. To the extent that one cannot help but ask: In this endlessly renewed contradiction, what cynical and cruel logic is hidden, logic of interests, ambitions, cruelty?

Will these steps taken by the pope fall into forgetfulness, like the supplications which always mark the calamities of the world? These gestures, surprising at first, but banal in their ineffectiveness, are they only the barely comprehensible awakening of an innocent religious conscience, of a powerless moral velleity confronting the merciless logic of power relationships?

And here we are, thinking more or less what everybody else does . . . Here we are, more or less afraid of telling ourselves what we have been told, in the name of the Gospel, to say or to condemn. When, in the name of the Gospel, we would like to free this world from the misery that comes from the hearts and hands of human beings and is constantly harming them. Let us not be surprised by such a judgment that we suppose is in the mind of those who do not share our faith. Let us not be surprised by this judgment that part of us is voicing. It reminds me of the sentence that Saint Luke wrote about Christ on his cross; three times, as the evangelist relates, all the powers of the world, the priests, the Roman soldiers, and the people, and also those who were crucified with him, tell Christ: "He saved others, let him save himself! Get down from your cross, if you are the Savior!" This suspicion and this thought that we carry in ourselves, Christ bears in the humanly useless and humanly futile solitude of his cross. This suspicion that we carry in ourselves in the unbearable challenge of the Christian mystery. This suspicion that we carry in ourselves measures the step we have to take to be, in our turn, disciples of the crucified, in order to be in this world the witnesses of the resurrected.

And if the pope, in the presence of two warring peoples, celebrates the Eucharist, he not only performs a religious rite which is identical here and there, and, given human conflict, therefore contradictory to hostile hearts, to what seems to be a determinism of history, or to economic stakes or powers. He bears, in his own hands and in his own flesh, and also in the flesh of the Christians who receive the body of Christ, the presence of the crucified, made present in his body. He distributes, through this eucharistic act, the challenge of the cross. And this madness of the cross is the affirmation that the last earthly word is not within the logic of the world: that the weakness of the innocent, the Son of God made human, is stronger than the strength of the powerful, that it acts continuously as a challenge and ceaselessly provokes those in whom it acts.

One does not say Mass the way one concludes a cease-fire and one does not sign a treaty the way one sings a Te Deum. To celebrate the Eucharist commits a people, with its weaknesses, to the act of the offering of Christ, to the unbearable challenge which from then on has crossed history: from then on, in the human condition, which might appear as a desperate one, absolute hope is present. From then on, present in humankind is the strength of the Spirit that gives the courage to forgive, to love, and to persevere in this work of pardon and salvation. "Salvation for many," "blood shed for the salvation of many," blood of Christ, life of Christians offered in Christ: endlessly renewed task, laborious task, experienced as a long night, when the disciple of Christ questions himself or herself, asks when the night will be over, when the light of God will come, long night which tries faith, which tries fidelity, which tries love. But in spite of the darkness, Christians are given the strength to watch!

The Eucharist is the act through which the deliverance of the world, the Redemption of the world, pardon, are at work, associating Christians with Christ's offering for humankind to be delivered from its own weaknesses, its own sins, its own demons! It is a challenge, the challenge of a God who becomes a man, and who makes of these men and these women the members of the body of his Son, torn, pierced by the faults of men and women—simultaneously sinners and forgiven. Thus this is not a ludicrous manifestation of an impossible unanimity, but the sacrament of the Passion, given to suffering people so that they may be able to stand and fight with the weapons of Christ and of pardon.

I give you a last point for your meditation: the celebration of the Eucharist makes present the salvation of the world, working in the members of Christ. It manifests the hidden, buried presence of Christ in this world. This is the body, this is the blood: "Real Presence." Real Presence of Christ in his Eucharist. Real presence of Christ in his ecclesial body. Real presence of Christ in the whole of history. Presence that is buried to prepare the harvest.

Thus my brothers and sisters, let us not be surprised that we must pray ceaselessly so that hope and love may live ceaselessly. Let us thank God for the grace we receive in celebrating the Eucharist of Christ. Such grace is not exhausted in the few minutes we are spending here together. It is the soul of the world, the breath of the world, the salvation of the world. Since the Spirit makes us available, we will be able, if need be, to hear the challenge received by God himself: "Get down from the cross!" And we will be able to answer with Christ: "Into your hands, Lord, I commend my spirit." And with Christ we will be able to utter the words of pardon. And with the risen Christ we will be able to announce the peace whose source is the Spirit, the one who gives life.

Body and Spirit

In the church and in humankind, the gift of the Spirit is not something belonging particularly to a group or a movement: it is the Gospel itself. For here is the Good News that Jesus has come to announce: the times have come when God is going to pour out his Holy Spirit abundantly on those he has called. So that they will accomplish the work that the Father in heaven has entrusted to man: to live in the holiness whose only source is God himself. The entire promise of the Old Testament that Jesus has come to fulfill concerns not only the advent of the Messiah, the savior-Christ, but also his work: the gift of the Holy Spirit to the people he has gathered, to the new people thus created. For the Spirit is the one who raises the dead, forgives sins, creates a new people—the church of God, the church of Christ—for the salvation of the whole world. Nearing the hour of his Passion, Jesus tells his disciples: "It is good for you that I am going."

We must strive to understand the meaning of the event in which we are immersed, this unique and singular event, the unique Pentecost in Jerusalem, in the cenacle. Then the apostles, the twelve pillars of the spiritual temple made of Christ himself and the adumbration of the people to come, promised to Christ and begotten in Christ, the apostles thus receive the promise of the Father, accomplished by Christ. This is precisely the work of salvation, the Good News.

And here is the Good News: God has come to save men from

Pentecost homily at Notre-Dame of Paris for an assembly of charismatic groups, 10 June 1984.

perdition. That is, ultimately from death whose most intimate, most secret face, whose real substance is not nothingness but sin. In the death of human beings and the horror it provokes, sin is revealed: denial of love, denial of life. And God who is life—the living one through whom we live—gives back to us, his creatures, sanctity and life, thus delivering us from sin, tearing us away from death, returning to us the freedom that is ours as children of God.

God gives his very own life from the time of his first call to sinful humankind hiding in the garden, in the darkness after its rejection: "Adam, where are you?" He does so at that very moment through the seed-promise of deliverance that will be granted to the descendants of Adam and Eve. He does so in opening at one and the same time the hard road of sinful humankind and the hope of humankind loved and delivered. He does so when he calls our father Abraham and miraculously gives him in superabundance of love the unhoped-for son, token of the even more incredible face-to-face promise when Abraham himself is called "friend of God." He does so when he opens to him the prospect of a countless people of cosmic dimension, a people "more numerous than the sand of the sea or the stars in the sky." And this people, born of the Covenant and in love, is destined to be a priestly people, the share chosen by God, thanks to whom the whole universe is given back to the Father, creator of all things, in praise and power of life. And God gives his very life when he already calls this people "my son, my beloved." He does so when he entrusts to this people his commandments, commandments of life, through which they are called to act as God acts, to live in holiness with the very holiness of God: "Be holy for I am holy." He thus shows in a practical way what the life of humankind must be when it is totally held by God who loves it.

But human beings, called by God, cannot stop measuring the abyss of their own powerlessness, the absurdity of their refusal, the inconsistency of their withdrawal. Human beings, tempted to get hold of God to make themselves into "God," are endlessly measuring their sin by the very process. They should surrender to grace and let God act in them, let God grasp them rather than want to grasp God, let God use them rather than want to utilize God, recognize that they are the people gathered by God rather than the people boasting of the grace given to them. People whose holiness, demanded by God, can only be the fruit of a grace given by God. People whose love can be the rule of life if they let themselves be touched by him who is love and who gives life.

Thus, my friends, in the very gift that God makes of his own life through his commandments, the people feel that God alone, coming to dwell in their heart can enable them to answer the call of God: "I shall give you a new heart and put a new spirit in you; I shall remove the heart of stone from your bodies and give you a heart of flesh instead. I shall put my spirit in you and make you keep my laws and sincerely respect my observances" (Ezek. 26:36). You will not have to teach one another anymore, but the Spirit himself living in your hearts (Jer. 31:33–34) will give you "the knowledge of God filling the country as the waters swell the sea" (Isa. 11:9). And the peace that comes from God will cover the entire surface of the earth.

The reconciled world is the world divinized by the heart of humankind in which dwells the Holy Spirit. And here is the promise of God: he will give his Holy Spirit so that humankind can live by the very power of divine life. How could this be? (As you can notice, I am using the words asked by the Virgin Mary of the angel.) By the gift of the Son, the only Son of God, of him in whom the fullness of the Spirit dwells, eternal Word made flesh in whom our nature belongs fully to God, held by the Son who unites it to his divine nature. And divine nature—thus coexisting and united with human nature in the person of the Son—receives and gives, from Father to Son, the gift of love of the Spirit which satiates the humanity of Jesus. As to him, he fulfills perfectly all the commandments of the Father, he accomplishes perfectly the promise, for he is the one through whom and in whom the perfection of holiness and love, the perfection of the vocation of humankind reconciled with God the Father and living in communion with the holy will of God the Father, achieves the Redemption of humankind, the priestly task to which it has been called.

Jesus is not a dream we have about a perfect man, but humanity according to God's will, the new humanity, the humanity born again of a new birth, who is not anymore mere creature, but the Son living the life of the eternal Son of God, and in whom dwells the fullness of the gift of the Spirit. If he entered in the passion of his death to redeem us from our sins, if, by the strength of the Holy Spirit, the almighty God, Father in heaven, has raised him from the dead, it is so that through the gift he made to us, the Spirit be given to the brothers and sisters of Christ.

Jesus resurrected, in his visible condition, let the Twelve touch him. Ascended into heaven, he is now hidden in the glory of God, in the secret of God, until the fullness of time. Then comes the event of Pentecost, fulfillment of the promise. The event of Pentecost, sign of this historical time, is as unique and singular as the moment when the angel announced to Mary the Good News of the Kingdom, as the birth of Jesus in Bethlehem of Judaea. It is as unique and singular as the act of Redemption, as the death of Christ and his Resurrection. And this unique and singular event of Pentecost is accomplished once and forever and definitely. For it is the work of the Father in heaven who is thus founding his church: the church of God the Father who is at the same time the church of Jesus Christ through the gift of the Spirit to the apostles. Pentecost and the church are one and the same thing. Just as there is only one Pentecost, there is only one church.

There are divided Christians, sinful Christians, separated Christians, unfaithful Christians. But there is one church because there is one Christ, because there is one Spirit, because there is one Father in heaven. A body, the body of Christ, made by God and not by us. There is a division from the moment we claim to take hold of the gift of God to make it ours. Each time we tear away something from God, we divide the gift he made to us; each time we consent to God, we are gathered by him and reestablished in the unity and love of his body. Each time we sin, we are separated, we are divided; each time we are forgiven, we are reconciled and brought back to this communion. Each time we are merciful, we work toward this unity.

Thus through the same act the Lord will give his Spirit as he had promised, and build the church of his Son by calling men and women of all races, all tongues, to share in the condition of Christ. The Holy Spirit seizes and gathers in a single body that is the body of Christ all the men and women who make up the church. So that there is no Spirit without the body, and no body without the Spirit. There is a Spirit only in the body, and there is a body only in the Spirit. This is a mystery of unity, of redemption, of mercy, of compassion, of suffering, and pardon; it is a mystery of faith and resurrection which gives us life.

The riches and the plenitude of this event of Pentecost are manifest in the mystery of the church. The first event related by Luke in the Acts of the Apostles is the symmetrical scene of Babel which means that from now on the only Word of God is pronounced in the particularity of history. The apostles are Galileans, as is Jesus, and this particularity remains forever unique. Yet through the gift of the Spirit their particular language becomes universal, and the testimony of the Twelve, who like Peter are Galileans (he had been recognized in the courtyard of the high priest by the servant girl: "You too are from Galilee like Jesus. I recognize you, you have the same accent."), becomes universal. Their word is heard beyond the frontiers which were created by the ambition of human beings and divides them, ever since they had wanted to grasp the divine power and take its place through the blasphemous challenge of the tower of Babel.

Their language is understood because the Spirit itself is heard in their mouth when they speak, the Spirit itself touches the hearts of all, wherever they are. The miracle is not a phenomenon of simultaneous translation: the miracle is that God speaks to all human beings even when they do not get along. The language of God is spoken to everyone in spite of all differences, all divergences, all oppositions. The language of God is able to reach the heart of one who rejects his call, able to make a sinner, one who has become deaf, hear the news of salvation, able to make one who has become dumb because of his or her rejection, sing the praises of God.

From then on, the force of the Gospel, the force of this Good News constituted in a body, cannot be stopped anymore by all the barriers that the sin of human beings has erected in this world. The real barriers are not those of power, money, fame, human means. For a long time the People of God have known that such appearances are nothing, pitiful idols in the face of God's greatness. The real obstacles to the Gospel are sin keeping humankind in prison, its rejection, its downfall, its hardened heart.

And here is the Good News: the Holy Spirit unites with our spirit to make us aware of the goodness of God who comes to dwell in us. And humankind is from then on called by the church to become, in the church, the temple of God, the dwelling of God. This people receives the desire, the will, and power to act according to the divine power that is now in it, the power of the Holy Spirit: "Be perfect as your Father in heaven is perfect." This people can live in the fullness of the commandments by becoming one with Jesus. When we love, Jesus loves in us and we love in Jesus through the gift of the Spirit. When our sin is forgiven, Christ takes us in his Passion, and we, in our contrition, share in the Passion of Christ through the gift of the

Spirit. When we believe, Christ gives us the strength to exorcise doubt in us by making us surrender our life united to his into the hands of our Father in heaven through the gift of the Spirit. When we give our life, Christ shares in our death, as in his Passion, and we share in the death of Christ on the cross through the gift of the Spirit. When we foresee today a reconciled world we already taste the hidden glory of the risen Jesus and Jesus already makes glory shine in us, the glory he will give to all men and women at the end of the world, through the gift of the Spirit. When we proclaim the Good News, Jesus speaks through our mouth and we let the Spirit "speak" Christ himself.

Thus this body, the only body, is the locus where the Spirit is manifested. The Spirit never divides, it always unites since it makes up the body of Christ. The Spirit always manifests the church in her reality and reveals her beauty, the very beauty of the bride "adorned for her bridegroom," prepared for Christ. Through the Spirit we accept Christians as our brothers and sisters, such as they are and where they are, in spite of the feelings they inspire in us. Such and such Christians, some community or other, some part of the church may seem to us to be the opposite of what we are, the opposite of our convictions, our opinions, our ideal of holiness. Yet they are loved by God and they are the church, the same, the only church. There are not two churches, there are not several churches. There is one church, the only body of Christ, and no other one. She is the one God loves, the one he gives us to love. Even if my brother or sister hurts me, he or she is the one God gave me. I did not choose this one or the other, God chose him or her as he chose me. And I too am given to him or her. There are not two churches: there is not a present and a future church, an assembled church and a hoped-for church. There is no ideal and chimerical church according to our dreams and a real and contemptible church composed only of people like us, sinners. There is only one church.

The church of God is the fruit of the grace God gives us when he takes sinners like us to make this sanctified body. This gift of sanctity coincides with the church in her diversity. This gift of sanctity given to these gathered sinners is continually new, brimming with strength, ceaselessly bearing new fruits.

In concluding this meditation, I would like to remember the place where the church herself receives this surge of God's gift, the Holy Spirit. The church receives the surge of the Holy Spirit when she baptizes, identifying a man or a woman—created in the likeness of God—child or adult, with the dead and risen Christ. The church receives the surge of the Holy Spirit when, through confirmation, she lets the baptized person take part in the gift of Pentecost. The church receives the surge of the Holy Spirit when—and I am going to do it now, uniting in my ministry all the priests who are gathered here—we celebrate the Eucharist of Christ.

Indeed, we are going to utter the words of Jesus: "Take and eat, all of you, this is my Body given for your sake. Take and drink, all of you, this is my Blood, the Blood of the new and eternal Covenant." But before, having stretched our hands over the offerings, over the bread and the wine presented for the sacrifice, we ask in the name of the church the gift of the Spirit so that the Spirit, in this Eucharist, make this bread and wine into the body and blood of Christ, the one body where the living reality of the church is manifest and the drink given to her. In this moment, in this act, speaking through the mouth of those who have been ordained and who act in the person of Christ, head of his body, Christ himself gives his body and blood as food and drink to his gathered people, so that this people living the divine life of the risen one, may be filled with the holiness that comes from God. Such is the first invocation of the Spirit.

And the second one, after the Consecration: when the celebrant, speaking in the person of Christ, head of his body, asks God the Father to grant that his ecclesial body which will receive the eucharistic body of Christ be filled by the Holy Spirit so as to become thus one body and one Spirit in Christ. The sending of the Spirit is ordained at the manifestation of Christ and the constitution of his body. And the supreme gift, the unique gift, is vouchsafed to us in the Eucharist, which is never achieved except through the ministry of the apostles and their successors. For there—and only there—we see the fullness of the body of Christ: Christ himself is made present through the ministry of the priest acting *in persona Christi capitis,* in the name of Christ the head, so that the whole church may recognize herself as the body of Christ and one with him.

It is therefore an incredible splendor of grace and a boundless hope that are thus given to us. For, in this way, we are given the joy to act in union with Christ, so that all holiness, all power of salvation existing in Jesus now may be fulfilled in the countless multitudes of men and women forgiven and saved who make up this body. Until the fullness of time, when all humankind, gathered, blessed, reconciled, will discover through our faces, unveiled at last, the face of their only savior, when tears will be wiped away from our eyes, when there will come the ultimate victory of the risen one over death and sin, when at last the immaculate bride of Christ will appear in all her beauty, where there will be no other temple than that city where God is dwelling.

THE
BAPTIZED

The Mission of Christians

2 Cor. 9:6–8
Luke 14:12–14

W hat does Jesus expect from us when he utters these words? Does he want to open our selfish hearts to a little more equity? Does he want us to share some of our happiness, our wealth, with those who are wounded, unhappy, poor? Or else, does he want us to come out of the narrow circle of our friends, our family, those we consider and who consider us as estimable people, to invite to our banquet the excluded, the humiliated, the banished, the marginals? Or else, does he want us to compensate the irremedial miseries of men and women, with a bit of tenderness the sadness of those who, for the rest of their life, have become handicapped, lame, and blind?

Of course we must answer yes to each one of these three questions, because Christ asks all of this from us, but not *only* this. He asks much more. And what he asks touches the vital core of our existence and that of all humankind: this core is love, such as it comes from God. This core is the generosity of the gift we receive from Christ. Yes, the Lord Jesus proposes to us here an incredible demand. But to give us courage and hope, he utters a new beatitude for those he is calling to such a love: ". . . That they cannot pay you back means that you are fortunate, because repayment will be made to you when the virtuous rise again" (Luke 14:14). This blessing reveals to us the reality of the love to which we are called: to give without expecting a return, to love even with the risk of not being loved.

Homily in Vienna, 10 September 1983.

Let us look at the hypothesis in which reciprocity is possible. "When you give a lunch or a dinner," the Lord tells us, "do not ask your friends, brothers, relations or rich neighbors, for fear they repay your courtesy by inviting you in return" (Luke 14:12). In such an invitation, we exchange something that can be measured. We are in the realm of contracts, in the normal system of social life: there is always a "debit" and a "credit," there are always accounts that can be balanced, there is always a balance between given and received, there are always debtors and creditors. This is not love but business. And men are always tempted to turn love into a business.

Let us look at the other hypothesis: "Now when you have a party, invite the poor, the crippled, the lame, the blind" (Luke 14:13). One who gives does not only give something that one will be able to get back: a meal, a share in the feast, some honor. By giving without expectations of reciprocity, one gives from himself or herself, a person gives *himself or herself,* not as one gives an object.

People imagine at times that love means making an object of oneself for the pleasure of another. This is not the gift of self, this is no love: this is selling oneself without receiving payment. It is also reducing love to business. Here, on the contrary, we are confronted with the mystery of love springing from the vivifying paradox of the gift of freedom, given and received. Let us attempt to enter into the comprehension of his life-giving love.

This love is expressed here by its negative consequences: "that they cannot pay you back means that you are fortunate" (Luke 14:14a). What does this mean, positively speaking? Does it mean that the gift, the love, must be unconditional, without any kind of expectation of reciprocity? Should we love then without any hope of return? Is it humanly possible? If we do not want to be deluded, we have to reply earnestly: "No, it is not possible."

An unrequited love is a dream, a chimera. He who would run such a risk, would end up experiencing death. To love in such a way is to go to one's destruction. Love is getting out of oneself for the other, not for nothingness. And this difficulty is not ignored by the Lord Jesus Christ, since he does add: "You are fortunate, because repayment will be made to you when the virtuous rise again" (Luke 14:14b).

The blessing of Christ is given to us in the Resurrection. It applies therefore to those who have undergone the trial of death. It is thus a love that goes beyond the strength and the limitations of human reason, a love whose generosity is absolute, a love whose logic goes in this world to the trial of the cross.

I have just said that such a love was humanly impossible. Yes, because, in truth, it is a love to the measure not of the creature but of the creator. It is a love to which we are called, but first it belongs to God. This is truly the way God loves. It is truly the way he loves *us*.

The love that is God is revealed to us in the inconceivable mystery of the Holy Trinity: Father, Son, and Holy Spirit. This mystery is proposed to our faith. It unveils for us the unfathomable abyss of a love which is gift without reservation. He who gives does not annihilate himself but manifests himself eternally in his gift, even though he gives everything he has. He who receives, receives himself from this love that he returns in full with the same generosity. From this mutual gift springs the confounding and inconceivable love that is the Spirit. The words of Jesus related by Saint John the Apostle give us a glimpse of the beauty of this love and make it familiar to us at the very same time its greatness remains incomprehensible.

The fullness of this love that is God is also manifest in the generosity of our creator. The Father gives us life, to us and to the whole universe, in the image of his Son by the power of the Spirit. Giving us life, he gives us the power to love. Yes, we were not, we were nothing. And the sovereign love loves us to the extent of creating us in order to love him and to love one another as he loves us. Our life takes on its full meaning which we discover in the mirror of the revealed mystery of God's love.

This mirror is given to us when we look at the glorious face of Christ, our redeemer. The human experience of the wounded and lost person is called to be transfigured in the divine experience of the children of God who must love as the Son loves. They must love divinely in their human condition. This is their salvation.

Christ blesses us if we love our brothers and sisters as he loves them, with the same divine power of love. This blessing enables us first to face the greatness—that is tragic for us—of such a call to love for all persons, the challenge of our own loss, our own death. This blessing invites us to follow Jesus Christ in his Passion.

But the blessing of Jesus invites us to a still greater act of faith in the hope of resurrection. Yes, we are asked, we, lost and wounded persons, sinners with narrow and hard hearts, to share the fate of Christ and to take part, through grace, in his divinity. The blessing of Jesus promises that the love which is thus given will be returned to us when the virtuous will rise. We will receive the grace to commune in the joy of the virtuous, the communion of saints, the men and the women who are gathered in God because God brought them together in him.

We receive the historical mission to love divinely because, in history, we are given as a blessing the hope of being taken and transfigured in the mystery of God. We thus become the permanent proof of the divine greatness of humanity in its vocation. We thus become the token of the divine hope that must guide the actions of humanity.

The divine force of loving by giving everything, without reciprocity, without expecting a return, which transforms the human experience of love, witnesses to the presence of the risen one in us and nurtures our hope of the resurrection. This is the eucharistic experience of the church. Being in communion with the body of Christ, she is in communion with this power of love. Christ himself becomes our food on this way which is steep and frightening for our fear and smallness. Christ gives himself to us; at the same time, he gives us the Spirit who is love and enables us to face such a trial.

As you see, you have to go much further than just sharing. You will have to do much more than give a little of your surplus or even of your needs. You will have to do much more than give in order to compensate for the injustices of this world. All this is part of the desire and ambition of all men and women, and it is our common nobility. But in baptism we Christians have received from God a call, a mission, and a duty that are greater yet: to be a sign and a sacrament in this world of the very love of Christ and of its boundlessness, to be the bearers in the world of God's design which goes beyond all the dreams of humankind.

To reconcile everything in Christ and to make of everyone a child of God and a temple of the Spirit: this is the design of God; this is not given to the world as a surplus one could do without. It is necessary for us to be saved from our personal loss as well as our collective perdition, that the power of Christ's love seize us and transfigure us.

We are entrusted with the beatitude of the eucharistic feast. Here the body of Christ is given to lost men and women, to the poor, the handicapped, the lame, the blind. They receive the riches of God so that they can run on the way of the commandments, so that they can stand up like risen ones, so that their eyes can see light. This feast of the eucharistic body can only be distributed in this world by the ecclesial body of Christ: you all belong to it, my friends. Invite to the feast "those who cannot repay you." Give with the generosity of God. Love with the love of Christ (2 Cor. 9:7–8). Then you will know how much you are loved and you will know joy, since "God loves a cheerful giver" (2 Cor. 9:7).

The Salt of the Earth

Jer. 1:4–9
Rom. 10:9–13
Matt. 5:13–16

"You are the salt of the earth, you are the light of the world." You are the salt of the earth, like the salt of the Covenant, the instrument of reconciliation with God of a world that is lost without God. You are called to take part in the offering and the work of the Son, which he exerts sovereignly and which has been entrusted to us in the world. You are the light of the world. Jesus said: "I am the light of the world." You are the light of the world to the extent that, in Christ and through Christ, your good works manifest the Father in heaven. What work manifests the goodness of the Father in heaven? That in which God himself is revealed by making everyone his child in the beloved Son. Our vocation is to enter into this assimilation with the Son of God; we are called to participate through faith in the Passion of Christ who saves the world. Such is the happiness of the disciple according to the Sermon on the Mount. Such is Christian presence, Christian action in the world.

The sociopolitical field, like all other domains of life, is a locus of Christ's Redemption. There sin is unveiled, but also the struggle for salvation which does not only concern our social and political action. The action of human persons in society is itself the object of another judgment, the work of another struggle, that of death and life. In every person who seeks justice, there is injustice; in every person who seeks the common good, there is desire for one's own good. This is why the hope of human justice does not bear fruit; society

Homily at the Katholikentag, Düsseldorf, 4 September 1982.

182

has to be saved by other means than those which are commonly given to human persons in order to act for the good of all.

Only the mercy of God, given in the crucified Christ, pulls human persons away from this injustice and gives them freedom to be and become just, to work for justice and for peace. The mission of Christians, your mission, is a share of Christ's mission.

This mission implies an affirmation: there is a right, there is a good. There is for us an objective and absolute determination of good and evil, of what is obedience to the will of God and what goes against it. In spite of evident relativisms due to history and cultures, Christian faith maintains and brings into this world the affirmation of an absolute: that of the dignity of the human person and respect for individual rights. The eminent dignity of the human person is based on the act through which life is given by God to humankind, together with the conditions of this free life: the Ten Commandments.

But in our world of injustice and violence, to be witness of such an absolute affirmation, to be the salt of the earth and the light of the world, is to reveal this absolute by becoming a representative and brother or sister of the Son who came in our flesh to call all sinners. For the savior Christ manifests the glory of God and unveils to us our genuine dignity: as creature, he is the image and likeness of God and the revelation of the only Son. To affirm the absolute of our personal dignity is to reveal the glory of God "rich in mercy, Creator and Redeemer of man."

Christians can witness by acting in Christ and through Christ, as long as they have faith and the sacrament of faith, baptism, which gives us a share in the Passion of the servant. Whoever would be the presence in history of the absolute right of human beings, of their personal dignity, of the right of God, receives today a vocation which is like that of the crucified. Such a person chooses to become the instrument of forgiveness and re-creation: "You are the salt of the earth, you are the light of the world": receive through the strength of the risen one who is light, the capacity to live his redeeming offering, becoming the salt of his sacrifice.

Such is, in history and in the realm of human societies, the work of faith. To believe is to let God act and is to become cooperators with God. It is, in the patience of history, to enter into the Passion and the work of Jesus Christ. Salt of the earth, light of the world, Christians have the mission of witnessing to the absoluteness of God and to human dignity; they also have to deliver human beings from their delusions about false justice.

The first delusion is to believe that we can conceive justice without being wrong and achieve it without faltering. This is not possible for our intelligence or will. Another delusion offers the achievement of full justice as an immediate possible historical goal.

The Christian, through faith in Christ, delivers men and women from these delusions. For faith reveals in justified and forgiven men and women the sinners who are incapable of continuing their work of justice without God. For faith manifests to human persons all the dimensions of justice. There is in this world a state of achieved justice. Human persons are not fulfilled in justice and holiness: they remain pilgrims in history. If they imagine that they can achieve justice in this world, if they want to attain an ideal of justice on earth, they reduce it to the measure of their desires and ideas: this is the source of totalitarianism. Justice cannot be fully achieved except through God's action which is ceaselessly curing persons of their injustice and sin, which justifies them and helps them to work with justice, and saves them from Hades and death until the day of the resurrection.

Outside of faith in the justice and salvific action of God, the ideal of a civilization of love and justice is invariably betrayed by the experience and cynicism of history. By fighting for the rights of humankind and against the delusions of justice, faith sustains the hope of a civilization of love, not as a social utopia but as a gift of God that is ceaselessly given, forever received anew in the church, for the world. This is true realism: to believe that love is possible because of hope. Christian hope in Christ enables us to work ceaselessly in spite of its negation by hatred, war, destruction, injustice.

Indeed, every generation discovers the limitations of what the previous generation imagined to be an ideal of justice. Does not all the work of elucidation that societies do on their own conditions often appear to be the work of disillusion? But is it not often in order to propose a new and even worse delusion? The pacifist ideal that followed World War I seems a delusion after World War II. Today this game of disillusion and reinterpretation causes doubt, suspicion, disappointment and despair.

But Christian faith is never disappointed. Hope does not disappoint. Sin does not prevent one from believing in mercy; the injustice of men and women does not prevent one from believing in the justice of God; and hatred does not always forbid belief, again and again, in love. Such is the strength of hope: it perdures and is renewed in patience, in communion with the redeeming work of the crucified Messiah, in expectation and recognition of our deliverance in Christ.

"You are the salt of the earth, you are the light of the world." You are the presence and sacrament of Christ in the world, buried in the ground like salt, exposed like light, humiliated and exalted like the crucified. You are the bearers of the Christian paradox, hoping against all hope, loving your enemies, forgiving all, living on mercy.

Fight for justice while confessing in faith that your political and social action will not bear fruit, except through the work of God. Believe in the God of mercy, who gives grace and makes you just, capable of working with him in the measure of his hope. Love human society in its earthly achievements, but remember that none will be accomplished until the heavens and the earth are renewed by mercy, in the heavenly Jerusalem, at the end of time. There we are led, where the immolated lamb whose sacrifice we are now commemorating awaits us.

Christian Vocations

Luke 2:22–40

I n this episode related by Luke, we see gathered in the temple, in God's house, as they had been prophesied beforehand, almost all possible forms of holiness and call from God. There are those who stay discreetly in the shadows and some whose names are not even given to us: the old man Simeon, and Anna, the elderly widow and prophetess; and Mary and Joseph. They are gathered, all of them called by God, to greet the child Jesus, Christ the Messiah.

Jesus

In order to understand these very different vocations, we therefore have to look with faith on the child Jesus before anybody else. For it is in him that any possible vocation is fulfilled. It is from him that any possible vocation receives its origin.

Can we talk about his vocation in the sense we commonly use this term for ourselves today? In our language and within general experience, outside of the Christian understanding of things, what does the word signify? It indicates an inner drive leading us more or less irresistibly to chose a certain calling, to follow a certain path. In brief, it expresses the most secret desire of a person, at times hidden and buried, his personal and deep will which will be revealed irrepressibly in the end. It must not therefore be confused with the changing impulses of childhood or youth. For a mature vocation to

Homily at Saint-Sulpice, Paris, during a vigil of prayer and adoration for priestly and religious vocations, 2 February 1984.

exist, there has to be awareness, self-control so that one can decide what to be according to one's own will.

What then is the vocation of Jesus in the strongest sense of the word? Psalm 2 tells us: "You are my Son, today I have begotten you." Again, at the time of baptism and Transfiguration, God personally reiterates the many prophecies: "This is my Son, the Beloved, my favor rests on him" (Matt. 3:17).

The vocation of Jesus, while he does not yet have the use of words—he who is the Word made flesh—the vocation of Jesus from the very moment he is carried in the womb of his mother, is first of all and fundamentally the loving choice made by God the Father through which he gives flesh to his eternal Word. Jesus, Son of Mary, receives his vocation through his very begetting. Like the prophet, and far more yet, he has been called from the womb of his mother.

Vocation is this fundamental act of the Father in heaven through his eternal Word and the power of the Spirit. The Father avails himself of the holy humanity of Christ, Word made flesh, to reveal to the world the infinite and fathomless love with which he loves us. Tremendous design of God the savior who, in order to offer salvation to all, calls and chooses Jesus, the chosen one. Simeon says that he is: "A light to enlighten the pagans and the glory of your people Israel" (Luke 2:32). For the vocation of Jesus condenses in a flash, in an incredible way, what was already contained as a promise in the vocation of Israel. The glory of God coming to dwell in the human condition is manifested in Christ.

Vocation as we receive it from the child Jesus, vocation in the strongest sense of the word, is nothing but the immensity of God's love given to the creature so that it can live and be saved. A gesture of God who wants, by this call, to give to the world the token of love, to give to the world the life of love.

Reiterating a verse from a psalm—at least such as it is quoted in the Epistle to the Hebrews (Heb. 10:7; Ps. 40), in the passage we read at Midnight Mass—the Word said: "God, here I am, I am coming to do your will." The will of God is not an arbitrary order to which he would submit himself in a passive way but the very revelation of God's design: his salvific love, manifested in the sovereign freedom of Christ who obeys as a Son.

Mary

Let us now look at the vocation of the Virgin Mary. She too is included, through her act of faith, in this election, this choice, in the vocation of her Son. Catholic instinct made us recognize that *her* vocation was made of the holiness granted to her from the moment she was conceived for the salvation of all. In the faithful silence of Mary what is accomplished is the design God had in choosing and calling her. This child, born of God by the power of the Holy Spirit in the weakness of virginity, this child, promised work of the Most High, is now presented in the temple according to the Law. Not in order to redeem him or take him back in any way, but to surrender him totally, as the entire holy people and as Mary herself, to the one she belongs to and whose glory dwells in the temple.

This presentation of the child in the temple, as Hannah (whose song is repeated by the Virgin Mary in the Magnificat) did for her son Samuel (1 Sam. 1:24), anticipates the surrender of the Son offered in his flesh on the cross and the gift that Jesus himself will make of the disciple to *the* mother and of the mother to the disciple. We cannot be unaware of this thanksgiving action which is already a sacrificial act.

Vocation and vocations

What are Christian vocations? They are part of the very vocation of Christ; they share in the call he received and transmitted to us, to cooperate in the work through which he came to do his Father's will and save the world. A Christian vocation is not a way of life or of being, neither is it an inherent need in human societies, nor even a necessity for the good of Christian people. It is not anything that we could measure, prefigure, or decide beforehand. As a manifestation of the fullness of God's love, it is fully inscribed in this act of salvation through which God reveals his mystery in time in order to save the men and women he loves.

All who are baptized participate in this vocation: to be like Christ, to share in the offering he makes of himself and of us to his Father, becoming thus associated in the messianic work of deliverance and salvation, being consoled by the consoler so as to become his witnesses, receiving the strength of the Spirit, sharing this glory of the children of God which brings to the pagan nations, in the darkness and the shadow of death, the joy and light of life; communicating to the world the law of holiness given in Christ to transfigure the human condition.

Vocation to holiness: prophets of the coming Kingdom

The powerful demand of holiness is manifested in the diversity of vocations. Each one of them is a precious treasure entrusted to the church for her joy, for the joy of the Father in heaven who sees, in this world outraged by sin and human tears, these shining gems of holiness that are now irrevocably embedded in the human condition. These are precious pearls lost and found again, hidden splendors—visible to God's eyes—from now on surely anchored in history, punctuating its course, so that the believer knows the world is not lost since it is ceaselessly saved by this work of holiness manifested in it.

The holiness of the baptized is brought about by the singular vocation that God awakens among them: vocations of men and women who answer the call of Christ to the point of anticipating in the present time the glory and transfiguration that will be ours in the future. While we are still in the condition of men and women, while we are still in the succession of time and generations, they live in the renunciation of human love in its fruitfulness and also its joy, so as to be, in the here and now, the sign of God's absolute sharing among those who love him, the absoluteness of life.

In this apparent death of a dimension of human existence, they become signs given by God of the resurrection of the dead; they accept this apparent death of their human power so that the fruitfulness and the power of love coming from God be visibly resplendent. In these days of relativism, they are witnessing to the absolute. In these days of begetting and death, they are witnessing to the resurrection. They are given to their brothers to be the signs of what they are called to live.

Christ puts into their hearts such a love for God that no riches of this world could ever content them since God is their only riches and all is given by God. In their voluntary and chosen poverty, they testify that in Christ, who became poor for us, the whole universe is given to the charity of human persons and not to the unjust greed of their possessive instincts. This gift is made for them to commune in brotherhood and not for them to tear one another in willful homicide.

In the oblivion of their own life, in humble, poor, and chaste obedience, they show the sovereign freedom of the children of God who, renouncing the limitations of their own will, commune sovereignly with the will of the Father in heaven who wants to save the world. Thus, in their lives marked by limitations, even by sin, they anticipate and manifest the mystery of the cross and of the resurrected one.

These vocations to the consecrated life are the treasures that God gives to the church for the salvation of the world. We must pray that he grant them to us, but we must especially pray for those to whom such vocations are given. Those who are called to this form of holiness are not called for themselves but for their brothers and sisters; they can only be carried by the holiness of the church, who must thank them and give thanks to God for the precious gift that is bestowed on them.

Sacerdotal vocations, bishops, priests, deacons: ministers of Christ the servant

Lastly, my brothers and sisters, this ministry which is mine—apostolic and episcopal ministry shared by the brothers, priests, and deacons who are around me today—this ministry received from the apostles is the sign that he who speaks in the ecclesial body is truly Christ. It means that the church is not a widow but a bride fulfilled by the hidden bridegroom; it means that the church is truly the body of Christ. We do not ourselves baptize, Christ himself baptizes through the ministry of those who have to witness to the power and the presence of Christ. We do not commune with ourselves, but Christ gives himself to us when he shares among us the Eucharist, bread and wine. We do not forgive our own sins, excusing or absolving ourselves, but Christ himself, through our ministry, grants the pardon of his Father. Through our ministry, he becomes the servant of his body, witness to the merciful love which is ceaselessly given and surrendered to us.

Christ does not abandon his church; he gives her life. The Father does not abandon the disciples he has given his Son; he gives them his Son. What more can he do? This is why I have always thought that this priestly ministry would never fail the church if believers respond to the call of God. For God, who sent Christ into the world to save it, cannot fail to call or choose those through whom the presence of his Son is manifested to the body he gave them in his church.

Therefore the most fundamental point in this call is holiness, which is for all and allows particular forms of holiness—the diversity of lay, religious, and priestly vocations—to arise as a fruit of this body of Christ to whom we belong by his grace.

To pray for vocations is not to ask God—like disoriented supplicants—to give us the grace to send a "good thing" that "God would refuse us" (Matt. 7:11). We do not pray for vocations the way we supplicate for bread in times of famine.

To pray for vocations is to say, one and all: "Lord, here I am to do your will, to respond to the call to holiness you address to me, to us all." Then, and only then, from his sanctified body, God will bring about, even from the present stones, men and women whom the church needs to be signs of the holiness and absoluteness of God, servants of the servants of God, ministers through whom Christ himself will be present in his body.

When Christ said: "Ask the Lord of the harvest to send laborers to his harvest" (Matt. 9:38), he does not indicate a prayer which would lead us to believe that God is deaf, but a prayer about the very people called by God himself.

May we, my brothers and sisters, on this day and at this time of secret thanksgiving for the salvation of all peoples, offer ourselves to God, sharing with Mary the heartbreaking prophecy that God made to her: "You see this child: he is destined for the fall and for the rising of many in Israel, destined to be a sign that is rejected—and a sword will pierce your own soul too" (Luke 2:34–35). And may we gratefully thank God for his Son given to us. "The salvation which you have prepared for all the nations to see, a light to enlighten the pagans, and the glory of your people Israel" (Luke 2:30–32).

SHEPHERDS

✳

Shepherds after My Own Heart

Jer. 3:15

W hat is the relation between celibacy and the priesthood such as it exists in the Latin church? This is the issue I would attempt to address today, trying to go back to the roots—both the spiritual and the ecclesial ones—of such a question. What I will say is the cause of many questions, which would call for a much more rigorous study from the historical as well as from the theological viewpoint. I am fully aware of this. I do not have here the means or the competence to meet such demands. Do not be surprised therefore if I proceed with affirmations and references rather than with demonstrations.

However, it seems to me that the viewpoint I am going to present answers a need of spiritual coherence, the coherence of choices made by free men acting under the sway of the Holy Spirit in the church for the service of the People of God. This coherence is put by God in the life of his church and in the freedom of his children. God does not wait until the experts have agreed to date a text or develop a theory in order to enable people to live in faith and hope in the service of love.

The episcopate and the monastic vocation

First, let us note a universal ecclesial practice: in the Eastern as well as in the Western church the episcopate is always given to men

Lecture in Rome on 25 March 1981, published in *Communio* [Catholic periodical], vol. 6, no. 6 (November–December 1981).

195

who have first of all been called by God to the celibate vocation. In fact, to be more precise, we should say: "the monastic vocation." Here is a small but significant testimony to this fact: in the Maronite church (and perhaps in other Oriental churches) when a nonmarried priest is appointed bishop, the ritual prescribes that he first receive the monastic cowl before being ordained, since his condition as celibate priest finds its significance and scope only through this relatively fictional affiliation to the monastic condition.

In this practice, which is common to the churches of the West and the East, we can clearly read the spiritual logic binding together what can be called a state of life and a way of consecration, with a ministerial and priestly function. Let us look at it in some details since it will be an important point in our reflections.

To be brief, let us say that the church chooses her bishops from among its monks. What does the word *monk* mean in this case? To take this word literally, a monk is a man who belongs to an organized way of life, which is the actual monachism in its different kinds. To account for the practice, it seems to me that the word must be understood in a more general and fundamental meaning. The church chooses her bishops among those who have the monastic vocation, for example, among those who—while not necessarily belonging to a visible and organized body of monks or to the world of the monasteries—have been recognized by the church as possessing a confirmed call from God in poverty, celibacy, and obedience. Here is for us, Latins and Westerners, something rather disconcerting, for we put in this definition only the "religious" in the canonical sense of the term. And the first difficulty is to understand how "seculars" can live with demands which are canonically reserved for religious. Yet this is a fact. We are therefore compelled to admit that the demand to leave everything in order to follow Christ is a spiritual demand, one given by the Holy Spirit to every Christian—and this demand is that of renouncing all the powers of the world to follow, here and now, Christ in his Passion, thus becoming in anticipation, for the church, witnesses to the coming of the Kingdom given by God to his resurrected Son.

Such a vocation can, in fact, be fulfilled by affiliation to an organized body that can be called "the monks" with their rules that the church has codified. But before belonging to such a body, it is first of all a call from God which belongs to the pure freedom of God and of the church, and that the church can ratify if God grants her the grace and if it is necessary for the common ecclesial good. For there can be vocations that remain hidden from our eyes and lived in the anonymity of ordinary life. God does not have to account for his grace to the canonists.

But in order to give the sacrament of the episcopate, the apostolic ministry, the sacrament of orders in its "capital" function (presence of Christ the head in his body), the church places her choice under the divine initiative which has been the first to awaken in the heart of certain men such a call and, at the same time, the grace to respond to it.

It does not follow that every "monk" thus defined must necessarily be called to the priesthood. For monks can be men or women, educated or ignorant people, people called to responsibility or solitaries. The church must therefore use judgment through the means she defines in order to appoint those who will have to fulfill this episcopal ministry with its specific demands and particular graces. But the church first must assume this divine vocation such as we just outlined.

We must now ask ourselves this question: Why, in such a unanimous way, in the West and in the East, did the church accept such a practice, reserving for episcopal ordination men who had first been called by God to consecrated celibacy? I will leave it to you to answer the question. One could talk about convention rather than necessity. It all depends on the mode of reasoning. But in a spiritual logic, we have to spell out very clearly and conjointly the ecclesial ministry in its highest form and the gifts of the Spirit such as God instigates them in human freedom.

Indeed, we should now define, at least summarily so, what this episcopal ministry is, priesthood par excellence, in order to answer the question that I have just posed. Here too, I can only give a general outline and refer you to a deeper study allowed by the wealth of tradition. The texts of Vatican II and the rite of ordination give us a key. The bishop, exercising in the church the priestly ministry is given to the church-body of Christ as a sign of Christ the head. Thus the whole church can exercise the priestly act of Christ described in the first Epistle of Peter by receiving in the sacramental grace given in the episcopal ministry the assurance that the word which is spoken in her is truly the word that Christ utters in his church, and that faith brought about by the Holy Spirit is truly the common faith of the whole church. This guarantees that the holiness given by the Father to his church comes indeed from Christ himself who acts in the sacraments, and so that unity in brotherly love which must always gather the members of the church in mercy and pardon is truly that which is accomplished and operated by Christ himself in his body. Through the priestly ordination of the bishop, the church is assured that she receives herself from Christ, priest, prophet, and king. A formula recently quoted by John Paul II condenses the significance of the sacrament of orders through his priestly ministerial act, the bishop (the priest) acts in *persona Christi* before the body of Christ, for example, the church.

I come back now to my question: Why this strong bond between a divine vocation to consecrated celibacy included in the "monastic vocation" and the duty of the episcopal ministry? This bond compels us to use criteria of discernment which are fundamentally ecclesial and which are intertwined like the arms of the cross: on the one hand, the free gifts of the Spirit poured out in hearts, always for the good of the whole church, the order of holiness hidden from human eyes; and on the other, the objective, ecclesial, and social aspect of the ministry, a service in which the apostle will necessarily be identified with the suffering servant: "The servant is no greater than his Master."

The episcopate and the other ordained ministries

Paradoxically, the Second Vatican Council was needed to define clearly the sacramentality of the episcopate. It remains true however that the two other forms of ordained ministry (the priesthood which was, in earlier times, qualified as being of "second rank," that of priests who are cooperating with the bishop, and the diaconate) form together with the episcopate the totality of ordained ministries.

In a way, what I described very sketchily for the episcopate applies also to priests and the deacons. They both participate in a way in the episcopal ministry according to specifications whose constant features have not been altered by the variations of history. Priests and deacons take part in the priestly ministry of the bishop that the liturgy, for all of them, divides according to the same classical triple form: ministry of the word, ministry of the sacraments, ministry of communion. To limit myself to priests, we must say that they exert jointly and in collegiality the episcopal ministry. Since properly defined priesthood is linked to the existence of a church, and the specific church, the local church as we say, is the diocese, the bishop is the priest of this particular church; the priests are his collaborators who enable him to confront in time and in space the divisions and extent of a diocese, reserving to him a unity of communion which is the particular and historical form the universal church has in its functions. The bishop himself is the guarantee of this communion by remaining in communion with the churches scattered throughout the world, while the bishop of Rome, successor of Peter, has charge of guaranteeing the unity in faith and communion. Through the ministry of the bishop every particular church is thus, thanks to communion with "the bishop of Rome" as John Paul II likes to call himself, the guarantee and the sign that this particular church is the concrete realization in this place and time of the universal Catholic church.[1]

As to the deacons, they serve the church and their brothers by helping the bishop in his episcopal ministry according to the modalities of the diaconate, of the service, always in the three visible fields of priestly ministry.

From the outset the church has had many other forms of ministry to which the Latin church gave recently the name of instituted ministries. These are ministries defined for certain specific functions exerted in connection with the hierarchical ministries. They do not have the same sacramental and symbolic scope. It is therefore very important to see that they are not defined according to the same criteria; ordained ministers are defined, not in terms of their usefulness or the needs of the community, but first of all in terms of the sacramental structure of the church. Their purpose is essentially to manifest the sign of Christ giving himself to the church, to manifest what Christ does for his church (ministerial priesthood) so that the whole church may fulfill her vocation which is to offer herself in Christ to God, thus accomplishing the received mission (royal priesthood of the faithful). In this it is truly the unique priesthood of Christ that is exercised. Ordained priesthood is truly at the service of the universal priesthood of the faithful through which Jesus unites everyone of his brothers and sisters and the communion of his brothers and sisters in his offering. Thus he achieves the work of salvation through history.

1. I use these two adjectives, *universal* and *Catholic,* on purpose since they do not have exactly the same meaning nor the same theological bearing. It would be too long to explain this here.

Married priests and deacons

The Eastern church has the constant practice of ordaining mostly married priests and deacons. What representation of ordained priesthood can be manifested in this bond between vocation to marriage and ordained priesthood?

Seen as God's design, marriage is an integral part of the story of creation, and is present as early as the first commandments when humankind receives its most fundamental vocation. The sacrament of marriage shows human beings exercising in holiness the sovereignty of God himself over the world. Marriage also fulfills their vocation to bear "the image and likeness of God." We must note that in the second story of creation in Genesis the singularity of the man is marked by the insufficiency of the animal condition to explain the couple and the fecundity of man and woman: to singularize man, God himself must offer him a woman companion, who is both like and unlike him. Man has a divine vocation: he is not situated only in creation but in the work of the creator; he has a divine function. In marriage, coming before the history of salvation, there is thus a very radical vocation calling man and woman to live in holiness, in communion with God, in order to be the instrument of God's Kingdom on this earth. Thus in the work of Redemption, Christ—the new Adam, as Saint Paul says, and this is quoted in the wedding liturgy—brings back to light what sin and the stigma of death had hidden in the human condition. He returns redeemed man to his original splendor.

To give back to marriage its full and entire dignity is one of the fruits of Christ's priesthood. When the priestly ministry and the diaconate—both ordained ministries—are given to those God had first called to marriage, there is a new image of the work of salvation which appears, for the service of the faithful, in participation in the redemptive act of Christ. It is certain that in the Latin church, this new composition of Catholic priesthood has a significance that we are not usually able to understand.

However, one must pay careful attention to considerations that, even though they are of a canonical order, remain of utmost importance. It is in fact a constant usage in the Eastern church to follow a strict chronology between the moments and levels of vocation and commitment. The choice of state of life is absolutely first in time: either marriage or the monastic life (as I defined it earlier). It is only then that the bishop can, if he deems it useful, ordain either an already married man or a monk. But then, once he has received the ministry of the church, the ordained man cannot go back on his decision or change his initial state of life. For instance, a monk who would have received the diaconate or priesthood cannot marry anymore: his service to the church binds him to his vocation in life. Since he was chosen within a vocation (gift of the Spirit) for a service to the church—that of manifesting to the faithful the presence and the ministry of Christ who gathers them together—the ordained man sees his initial choice sealed by the irrevocable seriousness of the cross, and the mission is thus received to become a sign of Christ. The personal vocation to a state of life, which was first chosen freely in a purely personal way, is from then on marked with an eternal seal. In this respect, the purely charismatic aspect of the monastic or married vocation and the properly ecclesial aspect of a ministry willed by God are mutually reinforced to give a definitive image of what could still have appeared earlier as reversible in extreme cases. Another impressive point is a confirmation of this first one: in the Eastern church, if a married priest is widowed, he is not allowed to remarry, because the discipline of marriage, to which he committed himself in his priesthood, receives a new and radical significance. Priesthood and especially the priesthood of the bishop are conceived in the figure of Christ, bridegroom of the church who is the only and eternal bride. So that the vocation of marriage becomes for the priest like a prophetic sign of the total ecclesial mystery: it is thus, even in widowhood, absolutely irrevocable.

I am pointing this out, too rapidly, only to stress how much in the practice of the Eastern church the fact of ordaining a married man or a single man is not a neutral, indifferent, or disciplinary decision. It is, in fact, a new spiritual image of the priesthood, a new composition of the Catholic priesthood.

Before I go on, I have to stress two more details. First of all: to ordain a married man as deacon or priest implies an aspect which is generally passed over, though it is decisive. For if the ordination is given to a married man, when the church so decides, one must realize that his wife and his family are also involved. This involvement of the wife and the family in the ordination of a married man is not simply a matter of interference (which exists) between a specific calling and married life: thus, in the case of the sailor whose work compels him to have strange schedules, to be away from home, to take risks, and so on, so that the choice of the trade directly concerns his wife. Here we are not talking about such an involvement. In the case of a deacon or priest's ordination, things are quite different. Not only does the wife have to give her explicit consent, but the two sacraments support and sustain each other. Indeed, if the priestly or diaconal ministry aims at the edification of the church, the sacrament of marriage aims at the edification of a family which, as Paul VI stressed it, must be seen as an *ecclesiola,* a little church; it is already part of the fabric of the church, as the first cell emanating from the design of the creator, shining with the splendor of a new creation, privileged locus where the riches of restored love are manifested in privileged relationships between husband and wife, sons and daughters to parents, brothers and sisters among themselves. This fabric of love when lived in a Christian way is the very flesh of the sacrament of marriage and also its fruit. The sacrament of orders fully includes it. One can thus see that there is a strong correlation even in the form of the ministry between the priestly task such as it could be lived by a married priest or deacon and a community which is called in its majority to live in the same sacramental system of marriage.

Thus to become the wife of a deacon is of great import to a woman, though the ordination is that of her husband and she can in no way take his place. It would be perfectly unthinkable for the church not to take into consideration a sacramental reality (marriage) when it is included in another sacramental reality (ordination). Marriage as a sacrament and state of life must be perceived in its spiritual correlation with the sacrament of ordination just as much as the state of consecrated celibacy.

I have spoken of what is called "secondary" priesthood and the diaconate as if it were one and the same thing. In fact, there are two distinct forms of vocation, as I had the opportunity of saying previously. In this vein, the appropriateness of the diaconate to marriage would have to be studied and elucidated in greater depth—I cannot do it now—in order to show how the diaconate is manifested in two different ways when it is given to a married man or to a monk. In exactly the same way, there is a particular image of the priestly ministry when it is that of a monk, and another one when it is that of a married man.

We can thus clearly see that in the tradition of the church another way of priesthood is possible which includes a previous vocation, that of marriage.

The discipline of the Latin church

Throughout the meanderings of history, a choice and a will are clear as early as the high Middle Ages firmly to link priestly ordination and a vocation of a monastic type. I am perfectly aware that historians are of various opinions on this issue. One could show very mixed and doubtful motivations among those that, in practice, led the medieval Councils to impose celibacy on simple priests, collaborators of the bishops. Some have stressed the economical implications (maintenance of the ecclesial patrimony), while others highlighted the more or less gnostic influences (the Cathars, and so on). In brief, all the reductionist arguments were used. I will not enter into historical argumentation. What can be legitimately affirmed in all cases is that there is a very strong and ancient spiritual tradition, which dates at least before the thirteenth century, to situate the relation between celibacy and the priesthood at the level of a spiritual coherence such as I first introduced under the heading on the episcopate—a field where there is, moreover, the common tradition of the Western and Eastern churches.

In this particular case, the proper dimension of the decision made by the Western church in linking priesthood to monastic celibacy seems to be related, without excluding other levels of analysis, to a *spiritual choice*—I stress these two words. In fact, the choice aims at tightly binding ecclesial practice concerning the priesthood with ecclesial practice concerning the episcopate. It is meant to extend the constant spiritual choice of bishops to all priests who, by definition, work together with the bishop. The same vocation of life is thus generalized because this is the same sacrament. In such a case, in order to understand this spiritual choice, one has to refer to its first source which was described for the bishop. Why this choice? How can we avoid incoherence? What is clear and highlighted? It highlights and stresses what Vatican II forcefully repeated: the sacrament of the priesthood is a magnificent coherent and inseparable whole, no matter what its diverse forms are. Thus the ministerial priesthood of priests really participates in the plenary priesthood of the bishop vis-à-vis his church. This major point might have been somewhat obscure during the previous centuries. People even came to question the sacramentality of the episcopate (which is rather strange from a historical viewpoint) as if the weight of the priesthood was first bearing on the "secondary" priests while, to the contrary, it fully qualifies the episcopate. But this paradox does show what high dignity the "secondary" priesthood had reached in the spiritual consciousness of the West, since the total sacramental and spiritual force was invested in it to the extent that—and Easterners could only admit it with difficulty or fail to understand it—the episcopate did seem to some historians a mere confirmation, an addition of juridical authority, and not a properly sacramental character.

One consequence can be inferred from this historical finding: the West invested in the priesthood of the "secondary" priests the whole spiritual content which, in the ancient and universal tradition of the church, was concentrated on the episcopal ministry. Of course we are talking here about a spiritual choice, and not at all about a chance happening or a mistake. For he who makes a spiritual choice surrenders his freedom to God. By freely choosing to obey the Holy Spirit, he lets a path be opened for him and accepts a demand. And if he does it when God suggests it, it is in order to identify himself with the crucified Christ.

For a spiritual choice is not only an option among other possible options, according to a logical or technical rationality, for a greater effectiveness in history. No, a spiritual choice is achieved when an individual, a group, or a church chooses to respond to the call of God, thus entering in a way of holiness and spiritual fruitfulness. What matters most at that moment is in no way the expected effectiveness nor the rational coherence of objectives with means, but the fulfillment of a divine will calling for an act of self-oblivion, self-surrender to the power of God. When Joan of Arc went to the stake, she made a spiritual choice and not a choice of political coherence or diplomatic effectiveness. When Saint Vincent de Paul threw himself totally into the love of the poorest, he might certainly have answered economical needs, but in fact he responded to a spiritual choice. When the Western church made this spiritual choice, she was aware of obeying a call from God, and it is truly in such a way that all the reformers, the popes, the men of God, the spiritual people and popular consensus perceived priestly celibacy—as a demand of holiness, first of all and essentially a demand of holiness, whatever taboos or complexes might have been mixed with it.

Two different spiritual and ecclesial logics

At the beginning of the century there was a great dispute about the nature of vocation and the criteria of its discernment which prefigured somehow present discussions. Among the involved parties, Canon Lahitton supported an extremely functionalist doctrine that based the priestly vocation solely on the call of the bishop and the judgment of the church. On the opposite side, Father Branchereau, C.S.Sp., advocated a definition of the call rooted solely in the inner vocation. This dispute was settled in the subsequent practice of the church in favor of a middle way which takes both tendencies into consideration. In fact, that dispute, which was very important at that time, dealt with two very different spiritual logics corresponding to two quite distinctive types of situations. One can indeed legitimately support a functionalist conception of the priesthood, on the basis of an existent community and the need it has to obtain a shepherd made for it, to celebrate the Eucharist—otherwise it cannot become a Christian community. And such is the logic we can see at work in the Eastern church.

This is what a Lebanese friend told me: when a Maronite bishop finds out that the priest in a mountain village has died and the community is deprived of the eucharistic celebration, he goes up to the village, gathers all the Christians, and tells them that he will not leave the village until a man has been pointed out to him: a good Christian, a good father, trusted and a friend to all so that he, the bishop, can then examine him to decide whether he can be ordained. In this peasant and Christian tradition a long time in the seminary is not indispensable. Finally, the only thing the postulant will go to study in Beirut before his ordination is the ritual of the celebration (which he already knows by heart anyway for having followed it every Sunday since he was a child).

In a civilization where Christianity is supported by the entire culture and is perfectly integrated in concrete life, the functionalist definition of the priest has a legitimate application, without any vocational twisting. The bishop only imposes on the community the necessity—which is already felt—of accepting a priestly ministry which will enable it to live on. By ordaining one of its members, the bishop gives to the community the criterion of its belonging to the universal church. Indeed, the community could receive the priest, as if from the outside and like a special gift of unity, while here the choice is made on the spot. In fact, the difference is not that clear cut: the community supplies a man, but receives the ordination itself as a gift from the church. The fact that the ordained man is already known does not change the essential. Thus we see here the true functionalist model of the priestly vocation.

Yet if the preceding analyses are taken into account, it appears clearly that for the bishops of the Eastern church as for the bishops and priests of the Western church the logic that is chosen is not exactly such as described. Why this? Because, faced with a community, a bishop cannot demand that it choose a man to become a priest; a community can lawfully choose for itself a chief, appoint a representative, elect a mayor, and so on; but it does not have the means to choose and give a priest meant for celibacy. For if the condition for choosing a priest is nothing less than the call of God to devote one's entire life to the Passion of Christ so that the man may manifest the power of the Resurrection—what we have defined as being the monastic vocation—then no one on earth can substitute himself for a properly divine initiative since God calls or does not call. Neither the church nor anybody can impose celibacy: God calls a man to it, and through the voice of the bishop the church helps to discern and authenticate the vocation of man to consecrated celibacy for the sake of the Kingdom. No Catholic priest of the Latin church should be in a position to say that he was constrained by the church to celibacy so as to be ordained. Yet this spiritual anteriority of God's call to the gift of his entire life for the Kingdom does not necessarily mean a chronological anteriority. A man can be seized at first by the apostolic call, the call of the mission or the service of his brothers before he clearly thinks about celibacy, giving up power and possessions. To ordain him as a priest, the Latin church will have to help him discover if God is effectively calling him to such a gift and to confirm him in his choice. This is moreover an objective and subjective criterion which is of infinitely precious discernment as a source of certainty and faithfulness for the one who receives it. In such a case, the functionalist theory does not apply, for the bishop and the church have, as it were, tied their own hands, by subjecting practical (and even spiritually practical) needs to the sovereign freedom of the charisms and grace.

This then is *a spiritual gamble for the church*. How indeed are such charisms born? One could truly say that they come from the intertwining of human and divine freedom, but one can also say without falling into contradiction that they arise from the fervor inspired by faith, hope, and charity of a community, which thus becomes the ground for the charisms. In this view, we will say that the church bets that God does not cease to call men to make the spiritual offering of their whole life. And it will therefore be among these men, called by God to the "monastic vocation"[2] that the bishop will look, later for those who might have the required disposition for the priestly ministry. Religious vocation to celibacy is a God-given vocation; it can be authenticated in the church; it finds there its proper role; but it is not the same as the priestly vocation, remains anterior to it, and in any event is not sufficient to fulfill it. However, the church subjects her own choice—in the call to the priestly vocation—to previous evidence of the vocation by God in certain men who will devote themselves totally in a form of holiness.

This has a practical consequence in the management of the church itself. In the Western church, I cannot as a bishop say that for the good of my diocese, which has a certain number of communities and a certain population, I need a certain number of priests and that this need is a demand. Such reasoning would be a challenge to God. I can, in the best of cases, say this: there are many communities and it would be good if we had that many priests. But I could not tell young men or a community that I demand so many priests. I can only pray with them that God awaken in the community enough generosity so that some will fully devote themselves to follow Christ. Then, and only then, I will choose among those who have chosen a specific vocation those who have the proper dispositions for a priestly vocation. In such a concept of things, the introduction in the West of what is called the permanent diaconate, that is, the ordination of married men who will remain deacons for the rest of their life, constitutes a major source of riches, and undoubtedly was greatly misunderstood until now. This spiritual capital includes the reintroduction in the Western church of this particular form of holiness offered by marriage linked to an ordained ministry. And, in fact, without presuming God's gifts for once, I can tell a community: "I will not leave until you point out a candidate for the diaconate." By ordaining him, I do not take him away from his vocation to marriage or from his trade in the world; thus I do not prejudge divine grace. This concerns a service to the community, and ordination transforms it into a sacramental ministry. The reintroduction of the diaconate might therefore modify very favorably our global vision of the ministries.

On the other hand, when it comes to priestly ministry, if one takes

---

2. In order to avoid any ambiguity, I want to stress that the adjective *monastic* here, as understood in context, qualifies the attitude of total surrender to God for the sake of the Kingdom and not the decision to live within the limits of a cenobitic or eremitic rule.

into account the spiritual choice made and kept for centuries by the Western church, we cannot discern any valid motive—I mean any sign from God—that would authorize us to change it. It is in no way a surprise that such a spiritual choice be presently experienced with conflicts and difficulties. For a spiritual choice always seeks to respond to a demand on the part of God, which unavoidably implies a sacrifice. Thus the present difficulties do not suffice in any way to question our spiritual choice. To do so, one would have to have evident signs of God's will. Even if we cannot exclude the possibility that God may ask us to make another spiritual choice, it is not at all evident today that he gives us signs pointing to another choice.

A spiritual choice can be questioned only for spiritual reasons, and never on grounds of organization, administration, and sociology, even when such grounds are legitimate ones. Such reasoning would be a twisted one. I would not give up charity on grounds of usefulness. I would not renounce faith on grounds of efficiency. I would not renounce hope for my own pleasure. One has to remain on the same plane, which is a spiritual one. And to change the spiritual choice of the Western church, what are precisely lacking today are spiritual reasons.

I will add an important comment. In history we find that there is no fixed ratio between the effective number of priestly vocations and needs that could be tallied. The functionalist theory cannot explain these discrepancies because its reasoning is Malthusian: it would tend to calculate the number of priests on the basis of the number of people, towns, or Catholics. But it cannot account for a distortion due to excess, while it wants to remedy a distortion due to shortage.

Now the lessons of history show—supposing that history can show anything—that at certain times God has called a profusion of vocations whose superabundant generosity was expressed either in the religious life (both men and women) or in the priesthood, and this way beyond the tallied needs of communities. This surplus of spiritual riches was, in all of history, a treasure that God gave to the church as a whole. Irish monks reevangelized medieval Europe. The people discovered between the fifteenth and the nineteenth centuries received the riches of the Gospel due to a surplus of generosity in vocations from Europe: from the attempts of Saint Francis Xavier to the missionary congregations of the nineteenth century. In France itself, as Canon Boullard had already well shown, certain dioceses, certain areas have, through their absolutely gratuitous superabundance of Christian fervor, given birth to priestly vocations that went to other areas and other local churches less rich in response.

The spiritual choice of the Western church is thus not to link the priestly ordination with mere pastoral needs that could be tallied and projected by statistics. Which enables us, paradoxically, to give way to a logic of gratuitousness, that is, of grace—since God does not reason in a technocratic way—to transform the number of ordinations from an administrative decision into a gift of faith. When Pius XII wrote the encyclical *Fidei Donum* and created the organization allowing the transfer of a gracious surplus of vocations to other countries (for a long time France had too many priests for her own needs if one compared her situation with that of other countries however described as Christian such as Italy, Poland, and Spain); and he could only reason on the basis of the gratuity of grace.[3] For only those who had already accepted the monastic decision of detaching themselves from a rooted community through poverty, obedience, and chastity could achieve simply and totally the passage from their original country to another local church.

Since the decree of Vatican II on "Ministry and the Life of Priests" *(Presbyterorum Ordinis),* the stress has been placed, especially in France, on the "missionary" aspect of the priesthood, to the extent that this has at times become the decisive and essential element. And it is truly in such a way that many priests have received the call to the priesthood and want to live it by becoming witnesses to the Gospel for the men who do not know it, to those who are the most removed and the poorest, in brief, by becoming apostles of a missionary church. Such a perspective was able to arise only in the logic of priestly vocation based on the gratuitousness of spiritual consecration. Indeed, the functionalist vision deals first with the exclusive service of a community and not with a mission thus understood. The fact that the spiritual choice of the Latin church has allowed its emergence and growth is a grace given to the entire church, and the latter cannot refuse it.

This supposes also a certain manner of living one's celibacy. I for one am convinced that we were not always told all that celibacy entails. I belong to a generation that has repeated and heard constantly during our years of formation: "We are not religious." In a way, though priests are not canonically religious, the reverse must be said.

3. It was this very surplus of vocations that made possible the missionary spurt after the war and especially the worker-priests.

I challenge anybody to live in celibacy and the chastity it implies without deviations or mutilations, but as a coherent achievement, if there is nothing of what generally applies to the religious. Which means that one has to have adequate spiritual inspiration and therefore to avail oneself of the necessary prayerful means. It also means that the priestly ministry must be lived as a surrender of one's freedom to the service of the body of Christ, the most detaching and liberating obedience. The constant attempt of the Western church, at least since the Council of Trent, to ceaselessly reform the secular clergy, just as the permanent fascination with the Rule of Saint Augustine, cannot be explained otherwise. For the permanent danger of the Western clergy has always been to exempt itself from the "monastic" condition, to aim too high (forgetting its bases), and to become secularized either through wealth or without it, through naked power: the danger to turn ordained priesthood into a career, a kind of promotion in the world. And in spite of appearances we are still threatened by this danger.

Union and Otherness

W e celebrate this ordination by anticipating the feast of Corpus Christi. And in fact, the Eucharist is perhaps the time of our life when we can most clearly see and understand the relationship that Christ wants to have with us, the bond that the Father, the Son, and the Holy Spirit create between all the women and all the men he calls to become one with Jesus, his Son. Thanks to this feast, we might perhaps even see more clearly, at this moment and in this sacrament, the meaning of the priestly ministry of the baptized who receive the sacrament of orders for the service of the body of Christ.

Indeed, in the Eucharist as we feel instinctively, something happens which goes beyond a family feast. For the very boundaries of the family are those which give its members the joy of being gathered among themselves around the table: they are bound by their kinship and marriages, rich in familial memory where their recollections are anchored, and in them dwells the joy that they can receive from their meeting at the time they have chosen to gather; they are joyful for the dishes they have prepared and they are ready to confide in one another whatever will come to their mind.

When we gather together for the Eucharist, all these elements of the family feast are present again, but they are, as it were, swept away all of a sudden, overwhelmed by much more than we can understand. For the table we have prepared is not our own, it is that of Christ. For the assembly that we make up is not completed by us,

Homily at Notre-Dame of Paris on the occasion of the ordination of nine priests, 23 June 1984.

211

but each one of us is an unworthy guest. Called gratuitously, each one of us knows that others are waiting outside of the circle. We do not know their shape and their face, nor the sound of their voice, nor the color of their skin. And we might not even understand their language. But they too are invited.

We know that this table is open to the measure of God's arms, he who loves all the men and women created in his image and the likeness of his Son. And on this table, as we also know, there are not only things that we have prepared or brought. Often we would be content to offer our life, but in the Eucharist there is more than our life whose depth and thickness and form we hardly understand as long as it has not received from Christ its deliverance, fulfillment, and transfiguration. "What we are to be in the future has not yet been revealed" (1 John 3:2). We can see this: we offer more than our life. We offer the life of Christ in his body and in his blood.

And in the Christ we offer, in the Christ who offers himself, all those gathered around Christ become the same offering to the Father in heaven. Through the love of Christ, the sacramental bond unites in him all those who visibly share in his mission. The power of the Resurrection even goes to seek in the depths of death those who, in our eyes, have vanished forever. The power of forgiveness coming from him goes to find those who were lost, to give life to those who were prisoners of the death of sin. All participate invisibly in this visible celebration of the Eucharist.

The memory which gathers us around this Eucharist is far greater than what each one of us remembers. It is the memory brought to life in us by the Spirit. Jesus tells us in the Gospel of John (14:26) that his Spirit will remind us of all he said. Our memory thus given back to us in the Eucharist is the memory of the People of God. Not only the memory of the church in the diversity of its forms of holiness, but the memory of the people of Israel from whom was born Jesus the Messiah. But the memory of all humankind receiving itself in this revelation as a child of God: humankind created by God and loved by God who wants salvation for all, humankind called by God to communion and peace, life and hope, happiness and holiness.

When we celebrate this banquet, we are seized by a greater love. This love already goes beyond the limits which, without wanting it, we might have wanted to set. This love, which is greater than our heart (1 John 3:2), widens the narrowness that we could have imposed on it without even being aware of it. For the measure of the

Eucharist is Christ, he who is always making himself present in his church according to his promise: "And know that I am with you always, yes to the end of time" (Matt. 28:20).

But in the Eucharist we also see the distance between us and Christ and we see that, in a way, we the church are not Christ. We cannot pretend that we are Christ: we belong to him, he gathers us, he gives himself to us. And at the same time we do understand that he is so distant we cannot make himself ours. We cannot grab him and tell him as the men on the road to Emmaus: ". . . they pressed him to stay with them. 'It is nearly evening they said' " (Luke 24:29). Unlike Mary Magdalene we cannot cling to him. "Do not cling to me" (John 20:17), Jesus told her. And to the disciples: "It is for your own good that I am going" (John 16:7). "Where I am going you cannot come" (John 13:33). He who makes us like unto him is other and remote, while he makes himself near and present in this Eucharist.

This is the same Jesus whose nearness and remoteness we thus measure. We do not see him with our bodily eyes, we do not touch him with our hands, we do not hear him with our ears. And yet faith shows this to us, experience testifies to it: in this Eucharist when we eat his body, we become his body. He makes us present to him and makes himself present to us, becoming only one being with us, uniting to him, giving us all, sharing all, making us like him in all things.

What does this union mean? A solitary mystical adventure in which a disciple could see his or her life singularly united to Christ? Yes, in a way. For in Christ, we receive the personal mark of our existence which we will never know in this world. But he unites by this very fact all of us as a body, beyond the visible limits. He unites us to all those we cannot identify and count, the living and the dead. He also unites us to the countless people who belong to Christ and are gathered in the communion of saints, another name for the church.

Thus in the Eucharist Christ who makes himself close makes us perceive how incomplete and strange our life is to ourselves in proportion to the distance between him and ourselves. In the Eucharist Christ unites us personally to him by his presence; at the same time, he ushers us into the communion of a love that is so tremendous and inconceivable that we effectively live it as an absence. Lastly, in the Eucharist which we celebrate in remembrance of him, we receive the nourishment meant for travelers on the way to fulfillment until Christ who is now hidden in the secret of the Father will come in all his glory. He is the head, we become his Body. He is the bridegroom, we belong to the bride. He is the shepherd, we are the flock.

Thus in the sacrament of the Eucharist we see the distance and the absence of Christ at the same time as his nearness and his presence.

Then the Christian vocation appears more clearly to us if we look at the face of Christ we discover in the Eucharist. Already at baptism the Christian vocation is signified by unction on the forehead of the baptized and the word of the priest who unites him or her to Christ. Priest, prophet, and king. Every baptized person and all baptized persons together, the entire church, are united in the priesthood of Christ the priest. We are united in the mission of Christ the prophet: to announce the word of God, to be the spokespersons of God. Every baptized person and all the baptized together are united in the mission of Christ the king: to gather in unity the scattered children of God, to manifest the power of God's holiness that can and must transfigure this world in all its dimensions, from the depth of the earth to the heights of the sky, transfigure human life in all its dimensions so that, through the holiness of God, the life of man may be healed, saved, delivered, forgiven and so that sin, which mars the face of humankind, which mars the life of men and women in their gatherings as well as in their solitudes, be dominated by the power of love dwelling in Christ.

Every baptized person and all the baptized together, the whole church, receive the mission to share the priestly and prophetic kingship of Jesus who accomplishes in deliverance and Redemption this mission entrusted to humankind when Adam, facing his creator, was enjoined to master all things.

This triple mission is entrusted to the entire church which exercises the priesthood of Christ, priest of the new creation. We are all called to this priesthood. Such is our mission as a church. This is why birth to this body, baptism, can be celebrated in case of emergency or necessity by any baptized person, any Christian, any person intending to do what the church does. However, confirmation, a link with the apostles, is reserved to the bishop and his priests, thus reminding us of the unity and the coherence of this body.

But while in the Eucharist Christ is offered by all of us to the Father and we are offered by Christ to his Father; while in the Eucharist his sacrifice becomes ours and our love becomes his; while we make up one body, the ordained minister, the priest who shares in the priesthood of the bishop, is the sign in the midst of the church of Christ the head, other and absent, identified and made present in his body, the church.

Among the baptized who take part together in the mission of Christ, priest, prophet, and king, through this sacrament of orders by priestly consecration and the continuation of the apostolic ministry, some receive the gift of Christ to his church from his presence and nearness, while maintaining by this very ministry his distance and his otherness. The church cannot claim to be Christ; she is always transformed by Christ who gives her grace and we are always witnesses to the gratuitousness of his love. We have nothing to boast about, but Christ who dwells in us (Gal. 6:14; Phil. 3:3). Through the sacrament of orders Christ, who is manifest in his church as irreducible to this church, can by this very act be united to his church and become present to her.

You will reflect on these thoughts in order to understand why you, Christian people, do instinctively feel that the priestly ministry not only poses a problem of organization in a society needing permanent or specialized workers. You are well aware of this: we are not dealing only with tasks to be done, competences to acquire. You are well aware of this: we are not dealing only with systems of social workings, sharing of power and authority. You are well aware that there is more and something else. To grasp what is involved, you must go to the heart of the mystery gathering all of us: Christ and us, we and Christ; Christ and his church, the church and Christ. Otherwise we do not understand anything.

And you, my brother priests and bishops, we are held together by a long memory of priests, thanks to you, my friends, who are going to receive the sacrament of orders. You will have, because you are baptized, to live this union with Christ in the offering he makes of your life to his Father. You will have to live poorly and humbly like any baptized brother, the ceaselessly renewed brotherhood of the humble confession of our faults and the received pardon, the endlessly renewed hope of our salvation, the joy of a love received and shared, faith ceaselessly confirmed in its struggle and tenacity. You will have to live the impossible heroism of fidelity to Christ which is made possible by God. You will have to live this obedience to the commandments of the Covenant which the reading from Deuteronomy reminded us of. You will have to receive, as all Christians do, the blessing of Christ in the Beatitudes.

But at the same time, you will have to do more than what you think you are able to do and say. You will have to accomplish the ministry of Christ in his ecclesial body. You, who are only poor baptized sinners, will have Christ say through your lips in a few moments: "This is my Body given up for you." In this act which cannot be compared to any psychological experience, those who are ordained speak in the first person, in the name of Jesus, head of the body.

You will thus have to be witnesses to a unity, the measure of which is not to be found in your tastes, your passions, or your ideas, but in what Christ wants for your brothers and sisters. You will have to utter words of God in the name of Christ, more than you can understand or explain, more perhaps than you believe. For Christ himself is addressing his people through your mouth. This is a mission, a ministry.

You will have to explain a word which goes beyond your own convictions, your own comprehension, even your subjective sincerity of the moment. You are depositaries of the fidelity to this word like workers, stewards, people who are accountable. The Lord uses these parables with respect to those he hires for his vineyard.

You will have—and we have—to be for all our brothers and sisters the sign of God's merciful compassion: ministers, servants of pardon, reconciliation, peace, universal love. We, who have the same faults and the same passions as any other person, will have to give what we ourselves have to receive, to give more than we have ourselves; to give what God the Father expects us to give on behalf of his Son, through the power of the Spirit: the forgiveness of sins.

In this world you will have to be reminders of the mission of proclaiming the Gospel, a mission entrusted to the entire People of God; reminders in the very measure of Christ who sends us because his Father sends him and makes us share in his own mission. You will have—you who are of a people, a place, a time—to open your heart to everyone in every place, to all cultures, to all times. You who have roots will have to accept being uprooted for the love of Christ when this love leads you where you do not want to go. In the mystery of the Passion and the Resurrection you will have to be for yourselves the signs of what you are accomplishing.

My friends, all those who are here can witness, each in his own way, even in failure and mediocrity: all that I have said is not an abstract ideal; it is a reality often experienced humbly, in the humiliation, poverty, struggle, and often in suffering and misunderstanding. But remember the sentences you must have heard often enough in the stream of criticism thrown at you. Some priests told me with a kind of aggressivity: "I for one am a happy priest." Forgive the aggressivity, but you must know that it is true. For the happiness promised by Christ reaches to the very depth of desolation and misery, the common lot of humankind.

You must know that the fidelity of God is the guarantee of our fidelity, that the church, whose servants you are when you are the servants of Christ, is worthy of your love, because she is the sacrament of love.

If God Calls You

During these past weeks, I have met several young men who told me "I am ready to give my life for God and the church. But how can I be sure that God is actually calling me?" The answer can seem to be simple when this question is posed to me, bishop, successor of the apostles. To be a priest is to share the mission of the apostles.

I could therefore have told those who questioned me: "The sign that God is calling you will be my ordaining you. In this way, you will fulfill for your part the mission that Christ entrusted to the Twelve and that they transmitted to their successors. With me you will have the charge of this people who does not belong to us because it belongs to Christ who received it from his Father. This people to which we belong, we must extend our hands over to give the blessing of the Father, the Son, and the Spirit; we must put in its mouth the very word of Jesus, put in its heart the love which is life, put in its existence pardon and mercy, put in its eyes the light of truth, put in its hands the strength of hope so that the world may be saved."

Thus the answer is clear: receiving the sacrament of orders, a man can go ahead with objective confidence. He was taken by the hand, consecrated by the successor of the apostles whom Christ had called. He thus received from Christ himself the call to become a witness to his word, to go forward with the mission that Jesus received from his Father. A doubt can remain: is this not a purely human affair? Can this not hide some error in the choice?

Homily at the seminary of Issy-les-Moulineaux for the Day of Vocations, 13 May 1984.

When a man receives the imposition of hands and hears the words of his priestly consecration, God grants in this very sacrament a singular inner certainty. Just as in baptism he grants faith. This man discovers that it is not only a human word, nor fortuitous circumstances that brought him to this moment, to this offering of his life. He knows this in his heart of hearts; it is actually the voice of God calling him to offer his life. In this event, in this reality, he can say: "You, you are the one who is calling me. My certitude does not come from myself only, not from those who know me and advise me. You are my certitude. For the mission is given to me by you through the bishop who ordains me."

Yes, God himself calls us in our heart of hearts. To those who question me, this is what I say today in this Eucharist.

If God calls you, you will recognize him. In this world in which we live, a world seared and petrified by misery and silence, a ravaged world from which God appears to be absent, in this world, in your heart will dwell the burning bush of God's fire and you will recognize his voice not only for ourselves but for your people. This presence will ring in the universal symphony: not a lost desert, a meaningless world, but a world full of beauty. You will see that the world speaks and sings the praises of God, the universe in its material and spiritual splendor, the multitude of men and peoples in their fascinating history. You will recognize in this world a secret symphony; and the one who plays it: God, the creator of all things, will ceaselessly associate you with his song. Your life will sing of joy and you will know how to pray; you will want to pray. To the extent that you will want to give your life for him, this gift of your existence will not appear to you as loss, but as the greatest happiness of your life. If God calls you, you will recognize the one who calls you.

If God calls you, you will not revolt bitterly when you see stupidity, hatred, disaster, or injustice that seem to be triumphant. You will not be crushed when you see persons killing one another. You will not be desperate when you see misery oppressing people. You will not stop your ears when you hear the cry of the rebels, the cry of the dying, the cry of the dying children. You will not hit yourself in rage when you perceive lie and insult. You will not say: "What's the use?" You will not feel like dying or leaving. Why?

If God calls you, you will recognize the face of Christ, full of compassion, love and goodness. You will recognize the infinite tenderness with which God takes upon himself, in this compassion of Christ, the lost one who is found again, the dead brought back to life, and you will want to follow the Lord Jesus Christ, the suffering Messiah, even in his dereliction, so that humankind not be abandoned.

If God calls you, the cross will appear to you as a splendor of life and not as the supreme failure of the world. The cross will appear to you as the tree of life and not as the gallows of death. The cross will appear to you as the mark and the key enabling you to understand this world. If God calls you, you will want to follow Christ, in his Passion, for the salvation of your brothers and sisters, and you will not be afraid.

If God calls you, do not fear. If God calls you, your own dumb lips will be able to bring forth the voice of Christ that people will recognize. If God calls you, your sins will be forgiven and you will dare to give the pardon of God while being aware that you are so unworthy. If God calls you, you will be the minister and the servant of this broken and delivered body, the bread of life, so that men and women may be nourished by it. If God calls you, you will receive insults; people will speak ill of you, you will not be understood, but you will know that you share the fate of Christ. When he was insulted, he did not insult in return but forgave. When he was despised, he blessed God. When he was abandoned, he reestablished the communion of the lost with the love of his Father and our Father. If God calls you, you will not be afraid to surrender your life, for a surrendered life is united to the life that Christ gave.

If God calls you, your heart will open up to a dimension of love that you did not even suspect. You will love this people. Not only in the comradeship that everyone seeks. Not only in fellowship where men and women are at last available to friendship so as to banish the solitude of a heart wandering endlessly, not knowing where to find the warmth of communion. No! You will love all men with a total love. For you will recognize in everyone a brother or sister, a new and unsuspected treasure. You will love this people that Christ himself gathers and for which you are the figure of the shepherd. You will love this people who will carry you; even if they strike you, they will support you and give you strength: this people, the entire church in her maternal function made of love and peace, praying, praising and blessing God, and this people through which salvation enters the world.

If God calls, do not fear: you will recognize his voice, follow him. If God calls you, do not fear: the Spirit is your life.

My friends, Christians, God puts the burden of love on us, of faith and hope. Since we are priests, the Lord has consecrated us to be the sign and the presence of God in this body of which he is head. Let us know how to pardon and love one another, we who are entrusted in this world with the mission of bringing blessing, love of life, reconciliation, hope, and lasting joy.

LIVES
FOR GOD
※

Consecrated Life and Marriage

2 Kings 4, 8–11, 14–16
Rom. 6:3–4, 8–11
Matt. 10: 37–42

S eeing you and recognizing certain faces, I thought that truly your
lives are a grace of God. And that you are necessary to the church.
And necessary in this time and this present moment. Through your
very call, even in its obscurity, through your life which is often hidden and buried, you show in faith, to the eyes of all, what the condition of the church is whose most fundamental features are in yourselves, in your call, in your consecration.

The sign of the woman

Through your presence and your call you remind us all that the
church is often called by the God's word itself the "woman," the
"bride," the "new Eve"; that the daughter of Zion, Mary, she who
received her fecundity from God, is the mirror given to the church
in which she may recognize herself; that such is the condition of the
entire church. To the entire church, indeed, men and women, the
Spirit has given the grace of identifying with this feminine figure:
the daughter of Zion, the Virgin Mary, the bride sanctified by the
holiness of God. And through your call, in the name of all women,
whatever their Christian condition—mothers, those consecrated to
the service of their brothers and sisters, others called to the consecration of religious life—you present to the eyes of all how faith, how

Homily at Notre-Dame of Paris for the meeting of women religious on the eve of the
Eucharistic Congress, 13 May 1981.

this grace must be received by the entire church and what is finally our common vocation, women and men in the only church.

To say this, you can imagine, is to say much that goes beyond each one of our lives and their too evident limitations, which are caused by our sins, our narrow-mindedness, our lack of understanding. But in this ecclesial figure of which your vocation is the sign, we are called to recognize mercy and pardon, the maternal tenderness of God himself. And we must also, in this historical moment for the church, ask God for the Marian grace of silent patience and long waitings in faith so that we can welcome in this darkness and recollection the word of God without whom the church is not the church. We must present to all, men and women, this supereminent feminine figure in whom humankind, in the light of faith, recognizes the church of believers.

To recognize in your lives such a sign value is not to be deluded by a game of mirrors or of facile comparisons. Here is a fundamental truth which reaches to the deepest roots of life. Here is one of the strongest spiritual experiences since, each one of us, in the face of God's gift, must first be aware that he or she is one who accepts in order to let God's power work in him or her. Since the whole church will not reach her perfection until she recognizes herself in the figure of that woman who comes down from heaven, adorned as a bride for her husband.

Let your lives be a call and a gift for all! Let your lives be like a hidden sacrament given to the church, of faith, pardon, and the tenderness of God!

The two forms of holiness

And then there are the words that you have just heard read, the reading for this thirteenth Sunday in ordinary time, Matthew 10:37–42: "Anyone who prefers father or mother to me is not worthy of me. Anyone who prefers son or daughter to me is not worthy of me. Anyone who does not take his cross and follow in my footsteps is not worthy of me. Anyone who finds his life will lose it; anyone who loses his life will find it. . . ."

These words describe the mystery of your specific vocation and our specific vocation, as consecrated to God in the offering of our whole life. And this time it is not a matter of woman and man, but another duality, another multiple treasure which is proposed to our faith, in these two vocations given to the church: marriage and consecrated life.

Here is the first: the vocation to which God calls men and women to live in this world, through the power of the Spirit, the sanctification of human fecundity and of work. The vocation through which God calls men and women, in sorrow and in joy, in heartbreak and in hope, in the fruitfulness and in the sterility of their homes, their work and their life, even in the acceptance of a celibacy which was not initially chosen, to be those to whom the world is given so that the power of the creator may be manifest in the human condition, broken by sin while there is already the hope of a new creation.

And here is the second: this other call answering and comforting the first as the first comforts and answers the second. It is the call of those men and women asked by the Spirit to join here and now, through the death of their powers, in witnessing to the world to come. Men and women are called by God through grace to live, by sharing the death of Christ in the world, the hope and the testimony that the work of the resurrected is already in this world; men and women who, in the trial of voluntary sterility, rely on God to give to the world and to the church the most beautiful fertility; men and women who, by marrying the cross, will be signs of the Resurrection.

These vocations are bound to each other and reveal the hidden mystery. These vocations contain the riches of God's grace given in its incredible depth and beauty. A splendor which is hidden from the eyes of the world, these lives thus echo each other and form in their intertwining the revelation of the glory of God.

You are called through your poverty, your obedience, your celibacy, and your chastity here and now to enter the mystery of the death of Christ so that the lives you offer may manifest the hope of a new creation. And for Christians who have received that other vocation from God, the call is to manifest in the work of their maternal and paternal fecundity, in their work of consecration of the world, that the fruitfulness of the creation God entrusted to them is open to this hope of the Kingdom for which we are given as signs. Thus given to one another, we weave the flesh, the fabric of the only church, her seamless garment. Thus is begotten by the power of God the only body of Christ.

Faith opening the future

Be therefore joyful in your offering since Christ is making it in you. Have the peace of your offered lives even if, where you share it, in your communities, your congregations, you have at times the feeling of living a kind of collective death, because you have no descendants, no future. Be at peace and be in faith, since this is how God wants your lives to be offered. He will know how to give in this way the fruitfulness he wants for the church. None of you has offered her life for herself or for the good of her own religious family, but for the church. Think about our countless brothers and sisters in the world who have lived this identification with the crucified Christ in the apparent destruction of any human hope and yet are sources of life and fruitfulness. Think about the Mother of God standing at the foot of the cross. Think that her faith could not imagine the fulfillment of the promise. Faith does not anticipate through imagination over achievement; it buries itself in the great mystery of the Passion and God does the rest, when he wants and how he wants.

May the Lord be blessed for your lives! May the Lord be especially blessed for those who think of themselves as the least useful, the most mutilated, the most futile, the oldest! May God be blessed for those who think of themselves as the least efficient! May God be blessed for this gratuitous offering, proof of a love poured out on our weaknesses! May God be blessed, he who gives life to the body he wants to raise! He who grants, according to the hope transmitted by the prophet in the first reading, the fulfillment of his word to the one who trusts God!

To Earn One's Life

Wisd. of Sol. 2:23; 3:1, 6–9
Rom. 14:7–9, 10b–12
Matt. 10:37–39

To pray for the dead is a difficult and necessary task because death stabs us all in the back: it is treachery; it is never fair. And for those who suffer it by losing a being who is dear and necessary to them, no reason can be a consolation. Death is never proportionate to life.

Brothers and sisters, you can legitimately, before the whole social body, before the hierarchy of your superiors, ponder and reflect the gravity and the usefulness of the risk you are taking and perhaps of the sacrifice that is required from you.

As a Christian, as a bishop, I have to speak another language to you. I have to tell you—and those who do not believe will certainly be hard put to understand this—I have to tell you other words echoing those I have just read and that are those of Christ himself. Any believer, any disciple of Christ is forever placed before the absolute risk of failing in his or her life or earning his or her life. To fail in life is to cease living as a son or daughter of God; it is to lose one's genuine and profound dignity. And one can lose his or her life while remaining alive in this world.

You know this, since you have this unique role in society which makes you witnesses of the worst and the best. You know it, you who are neither judges, priests, physicians, fathers, mothers—in the eyes of the other citizens—but police, gendarmes,[1] firefighters,

Homily at Notre-Dame of Paris for the deceased of the Police and Humanism association, 6 November 1981.

1. Contrary to American legend, a *gendarme* is not a Paris policeman, rather he is a trooper of sorts, mostly encountered in the countryside and not under the same authority as the police

guardians of the security and the public peace. You know it, you who have to represent the power of right, law, morality, good. And most of the time you are at this undefined borderline where persons, left to themselves, do not know exactly where is good or evil, where are the guilty, the innocents, where is truth and where is error.

Well, to lose one's life is to lose this deep reason which makes each one look into the mirror and say: "Your life is what it is. But you are worthy of respect because, in spite of your weaknesses, you can look at yourself with the very look of God." And for a Christian, to gain one's life is to take as a mirror the eyes of God, and I daresay, to see oneself in God's eyes. A life which is worthy of respect is earned, even if it is paid with the price of death. Thus we do hope that every person who turns to the Father in heaven can gain his or her life through the respect that God gives him or her, through the love that God gives him or her.

I told you. I have to give you the words of Christ himself. Christ tells us that God respects those whom he loves. He looks at us not as one who would crush or destroy us, but as the one who loves us and gives us life. And the act of faith that we are asked to make is to believe in the dignity of God's children that God wants to give us, to dare to believe in the promise he made us. Then we are capable of confronting death face to face instead of being stabbed in the back. Christ faced death, not with the courage of a hero, but with the surrender of a Son who believes in the love of the Father.

As to your occupation, you whose task is thus at the border of all human choices, a task in which you are confronted with contradictory and often unbearable demands for the sake of men and women who are like all the others, do not give in—in your inner life—to indifference, to panic, to disgust, or to discouragement. Do not run away in your soul from problems that are too difficult. There are ways to escape: by seeking oblivion, by losing one's dignity, by looking for compensations. Do not run away from a situation that is too difficult. You must know that what you can demand rightfully from others can be obtained only in one way: by first giving it to them. You want respect and you deserve it: give respect. You deserve the gratitude of men and women: you will have it; but be grateful to the men and women who surround you and whom you serve. You are

proper, though there is a very close cooperation between the police and the gendarmerie. The gendarmes—whose name comes from *gens d'armes* or men-at-arms—are under military authority. (Translator's note) entitled to the truth and the truth is due you: give truth. You are entitled to love for you are at the service of your brothers and sisters: give love.

I know that such language can make people smile. But tell me: Do you have another language to offer to enable men and women to do the job you do? Is there anybody here who has something else to say without locking in an impossible mission those who have to be the keepers of society's good and must not lose their souls but serve people?

I witnessed the formation of the Police and Humanism association that invites us this morning to pray for your dead. Circumstances then were paradoxical and almost incredible. As a chaplain to students, I was almost on the other side of the fence (as it were), and I was surprised at first, incredulous, then overwhelmed to see that it was possible to recognize the other in his or her difference as a being worthy of respect and love.

Well, since this is possible, by the grace of God, do it.

To Bear Fruit in Old Age

Very dear brothers and sisters, this moment of common prayer is very important to give us back courage. In your condition, old age, you have to make an act of faith which is particularly difficult because it compels you to be much more Christian that our time probably permits. Thus you have to shoulder a double weight (as it were), that of the trial of age with its riches and that of the trial of faith linked to it—though our society wants to give to all, and especially to those who are aging beyond the time of activity, the practical and honorable possibility to live or survive.

However, in our day and age, in the very way younger generations, your children perhaps or your grandchildren, see things, old age is (as it were) fundamentally devaluated, as if it were only a leftover from youth, a failure of youth. And it happens that some people do not easily accept aging. Not only because at times it is at the cost of physical misery, moral suffering, greater solitude but also because of the judgment itself of younger people—one does not wish to be so judged and, as it were, rejected, effaced, and made obsolete.

This was not the case always and in all cultures. There was a time when old age was considered as the time of life when, with the weight of years, there was an accumulation of the weight of wisdom and experience. Some of you may have seen this when they were children. But the model of life that is offered to us today is an ideal where there would be no old age, no sickness, no ugliness, no suf-

Homily at Notre-Dame of Paris for a meeting of Vie Montante [Rising Life, a nationwide, church-affiliated association of senior citizens], 6 May 1982.

fering, no death, no injustice. The model of life that our contemporaries dream about is the artificial spring of an eternally smiling youth. And all that gives the lie to this dream, all that seems to find it wrong has to be hidden or removed, for it is upsetting. And perhaps you yourselves are tempted to think that you aren't worth much anymore since you are not in conformity with this model. And perhaps you think that you are of no great use.

Must one resign oneself to such a state of affairs? Must one merely adjust to it by attempting to make the best of a bad situation? As disciples of Jesus, you must not adopt this view of things. This view of things, of yourselves, would be a provocation, a denial of the faith which dwells in us and of the love God has for us. Moreover, in the light of God, you do not only have to await peacefully or miserably the end of your life. You do not have to try and catch up with the train, day after day complaining of its growing lateness. In the light of God, you are children of God, called by him to live in his love. In the light of God, you have in your hands all the weight of human existence, its weight of suffering, its weight of injustice; its weight of misery to which you are yourselves tributaries, with which you are in solidarity in your body and heart. Children of God, you have to fight in yourselves the struggle through which Jesus delivers the world. You have reached the precise point where one ceases to dream in order to enter the mystery of salvation. You have reached the precise point where, brought back to yourselves by old age, you see what human life and its limitations are: suffering, the prospect of death. And you need, with the strength of the sons and daughters of God, to fight this fight of faith without which the world perishes.

The model I evoked earlier is a dream: suffering does exist, and you are perhaps suffering. Suffering revolts the young, this is natural. You, since you are of Christ, transform your suffering which is unjust and revolting like any suffering, into a sharing in the Passion of Christ so that the young may not despair, may not be scandalized. Youth does not always know that death exists. You have it before your eyes through your nostalgia for those who are gone and whom you still love, or perhaps through fear or through anxiety about a greater suffering that might come. You know that death is inscribed in our flesh. But since you already died in Christ and rose with him, may the Holy Spirit give you the courage to face this mystery which is anguish for us, with the peace that God gives to his children.

Youth thinks that only the world matters (and the world thinks that only what can be measured and proven useful matters). You already know that a humanly useless life can be filled with the most sublimely useless, gratuitous love, even when no one shows you any love. You are witnesses to the given love.

Confronted thus with the true weight of existence, you are asked by God to go courageously to the very end of your vocation for humankind; the church needs your love, your faith, your hope, your courage, your peace. Since you have received the treasures of God's riches, you have to bear fruit in your old age, to be at this crucial point of old age witnesses to the power dwelling in those who were born from above.

In saying this to you, I am aware that I am calling you to the purest and harshest act of faith, but I ask you on behalf of God himself. And I dare to ask you because as I believe and as I know the Holy Spirit dwells in you and gives you the strength to do it. And also because the history of the church is here to testify to the ultimate word I want to leave with you. There are now countries where the trial of faith has been a radical one—I am thinking especially about Russia—and where ignorant youth had to receive the light of Christ from the hands of their grandfathers and grandmothers. The trial of fidelity and the spiritual desert can become there, in obscure fidelity to what you have received, the locus of a new light, a new hope, a new fruitfulness. Before the generations of youth, be yourselves. That is: be such as God loves you; thus you will become witnesses to love.

The Greatest Saint
of Modern Times

Prophecy of youth, sign of hope

The first and overwhelming reality in the life of Saint Thérèse is her youth. Twenty-four years old! And, as she herself said, she walked the road of a giant.

Do you remember, you of the older generations, the years of Saint Thérèse's life and those that followed: you heard about them from your parents and grandparents. What happened to youth in this century? What did it do in our country, in the other countries of the West, in the whole world? If some among you were eighteen years old during the terrible years of World War I, you know and remember the conditions of life of the young, the children, when this world in which we live was erected in its pride, ambition, and conceit. The young were turned into fanatics, torn away from their very selves to serve lost causes. And now, what are we doing with our youth? It is presented to us as the chimera of humankind, as the dream of life. Youth is used as an argument in advertising . . . The result is already visible: the youth that goes before us has left us and has nothing; we do not understand it and it does not understand us; we have lost it and it is lost. Youth, victim of the ambitions, errors, and delusions of our century which is so rich in beauty and hope! Youth which does not exist outside of the rest of humankind and belongs to no one. Each one of us, at one point in his or her life had youth to himself or herself; we too have been young!

Homily at Lisieux on the feast of Saint Thérèse, 25 September 1983.

Thérèse was twenty-four years old when she reached the end of her giant road. This young girl, sick in her body and wounded in her sensitivity, fighting alone against herself and against all she foresaw, was at the dawn of this tremendous and terrible century, the hope of life, of tenderness, of pardon, and goodness that youth brings when it is totally given to God, for God. In a little Norman girl, locked up in the obscurity of a Carmelite convent, many men and women of all walks of life found a sign of hope.

God wanted to use this weakness of Thérèse, sign of the youth which was going to be the victim of our civilization, to make of her the stake and guarantee of the salvation he offers to us. The sufferings and trials of Thérèse were, ahead of time, the very ones that were going to befall the youth of this century. But far from being a sign of loss, the youth of Saint Thérèse was an open door to salvation. Far from being an absurd destruction, it was an offering of liberating love. Far from being a slaughter (like the great war), it was the free sacrifice of a freedom enabling human persons to become free in a love giving love. It shows us in her obscurity, in her humility, in this unknown life, the daring that can be ours and the hope that God wants to put in us. This particular youth invites us to recognize that we are born from God, children of God; it gives us back hope.

Young people, when you look at Saint Thérèse; when you see the very young face of Saint Thérèse whose photographs, thank God, we have kept; when you look at her smile, I would like you to recognize someone who is of your age, one of you, almost an elder sister. See what she did: you can do it. You are not separated from us: you are our hope because God gives you, young people, a daring that might be missing in us, an intensity of love we need. You have received life: your responsibility is to give to the world the hope of life. Young people, you think that you are rejected, despised, unknown, you think that we do not trust you. God trusts you, you are children of God and your youth is a grace. You think that you came into a world where there is nothing to do because all is kept away from you: work, studies . . . Look at Saint Thérèse: in the secret of a humble life, hidden from all, she opened the door of love, forgiveness, and freedom. Your youth is a gift from God: accept it joyfully, give it generously, do not waste it, make it a source of love and daring. God is asking this of you, you who are ceaselessly given to the church as the sign of new birth from above.

Thérèse, at the beginning of this century, was already showing that we have to be reconciled with ourselves in this incredible and daring figure of God's youth when he gives birth to his children.

Prophecy of holiness, our vocation

The life of Saint Thérèse prophesies another truth. She seems to me to be essential for the time in which we live. George Bernanos was right to say that Thérèse is "the greatest saint of modern times." In the secret of her cloister, not knowing and unable ever to know in this world how her poor words, written in a child's notebook, would echo through the whole world, Thérèse wants to convince us—in a way which is all the more eloquent that her voice is so weak, so frail, the voice of a poor little girl—that holiness is possible for all, is the vocation of all; that love is meant for all because God loves us all. All of us are begotten, brought to life as children of God, in the grace of baptism, by the Father in heaven who loves us, God whose fatherhood is higher, purer, greater, broader, than any paternity in this world.

If you are fathers and mothers and love your children, you know that you love all of them, that you want to love all of them, even the weakest, and especially the sick ones, even the hothead and especially the one who fails. When your children cry, fail, are sick, or believe themselves lost, if you are really fathers and mothers, you love them, you try to help them, to reassure them, to give them back strength and hope. If you are really a father and a mother, you do not choose among your children. Even the one who tells you: "I want to leave you." Even the one who tells you: "I don't understand you." You love him or her, you cannot help but loving and forgiving. You must love all of them with the same love, and even with a greater love for the one who seems to you the most lost, desperate, and wounded.

Our holiness, the holiness of the Christian people, is to be born from God, to become children of God. In these incredible words we perceive what it means that God loves us. God does not tell us: "'If you do this, if you do that, I will love you." God does not tell us: "On condition that you behave in such a way, I will love you." God tells us: "I love you; I make of you my child in my Son, and because I love you, you can act as a son or a daughter of God." God tells us: "I love you and I know your wound, I know your weakness, I know your sin. Do not fear. Because I love you, you can love me in spite of your sin, in spite of your wound, in spite of your weakness, with your sin, your wound, your weakness. Because I love you and you are a child of God, I will carry your sin, your wound, your weakness. Because you are my son and my daughter and I give you life to make you like my eternal Son, Jesus Christ, through the Holy Spirit that I put in you, I am going to forgive your sin, heal your wound and give you the strength to overcome your weakness." And holiness is made for the little ones, that is, for those who accept to be carried in God's arms. They discover in the love God shows them who they are: sons and daughters of God. Holiness is first of all to be forgiven sinners, wounded people that God wants to heal, weak people to whom God gives the strength to love. Holiness is what is given to sinners: Thérèse understood this, she wanted to sit at the table of sinners, she did not try to be brave. Yet she had the daring to say that she knew she was a saint, a very small saint.

Brothers and sisters, I would like each of you and all the Christian people to be able to say humbly, poorly, and even contritely: "I too am a saint." Why? Because God gives you his love. Because when you confess your sins in the secret of God and you receive from the priest who heard you the pardon and mercy given to the church, you are filled with the holiness of God and thus you allow the love of God to be the heart of the world, the heart of the church. Thus you enter into the will of our Father in heaven who wants to give life to the world through our lives. The saints we are destined to become are those who enable the world to live and who save it. Today the fabulous ambitions of human beings fascinate us and, at the same time, terrify us, for we see quite well that their accumulations of power can quickly turn into calamity, that the best can bring the worst, that the most beautiful achievements can bring about our perdition, that the most tremendous and remarkable improvements can destroy what is most precious in us: our dignity as children of God created in the image of the Father, made like the Son, and made into temples of the Spirit. Our dignity as human beings, our freedom, our capacity to love and to pardon, all this, we ourselves run the risk of putting in chains and annihilating. This is not an illusory threat but a sad reality in many countries and in many ways! And now we live in fear, bitterness, guilt, and despair during these last years of the twentieth century which started under the sign of insane hope.

Thérèse, the little girl, when showing us the way of the holiness that is meant for us, exorcises despair before it comes, chases fear away before it comes, opens the path on which we must bravely advance. We must be saints. We can be saints. Not as we imagine saints to be, but as God enables us to become. Holiness is meant for all; holiness is possible for all: it is to be begotten by God, to be carried in his all powerful love—wounded, sinners, weak—to be healed, forgiven, strengthened.

Prophecy of the relevance of Redemption, invisible force of love

Prophecy of youth, prophecy of holiness, Thérèse says even more. She lives ignored by all in this house of Lisieux. No one knows her beyond her family circle. Her life is secluded: the garden is small; she has a short life; she does not know many things; she lives without radio or television, without newspapers. She is locked up in a world which, to the young people of today, might seem narrow and limited. Yet the life, the love, the daring of a young girl who was so isolated are at the service of the salvation of the entire world. She offers her life, her prayer, her suffering for famous men and women who are losing themselves, for the universal mission. What this little Carmelite experiences alone and in secret has an incredible weight on the scales of history, greater than that of so many economic, industrial, political forces, greater than that of so many intelligences and powers which created entire cities and destroyed human generations, built splendid things and heaped up disasters. Here is the secret that we carry in our heart, with all our faith, with the whole church: the secret of the meaning of our life.

We often have the impression that our life has no great significance, that it is a little speck of dust lost in a great whirlwind. Often we have the feeling that we can do nothing or almost nothing vital for ourselves, our relatives, parents, family, friends, those we love, but also and even more for the whole world. Most of the time we think that we do not have true freedom of choice or action. We think that the powerful of the world—heads of state, scientists, important people—can act, can really influence events, while we, ordinary folk, nobody listens to us, nobody hears or barely so! I meet important people: they ask me questions, they ask themselves questions. They too, like you, have the impression that they cannot do much. In the face of difficult and tragic situations they think: "We must do our duty, act for the good of all." But they are not sure of anything, they don't know what will happen. While they seem to us to be able to settle problems, they imagine that they have no grasp of anything and that reality escapes them as much as it does us.

To look closely at the course of events, we might believe that we are aboard a mad ship, without a pilot, and whose helm does not respond anymore. If one does not look too much at what is happening outside, one can feel secure as long as the ship is afloat and moving; but let a gale come and we do not know what to do and what to hang on to. Now we Christians—Thérèse reminds us of this—are hanging on to the helm. The force that moves the world is the love of God that Christ gives us and reveals to us in its immensity. A frail and unknown young girl of twenty-four can, from her convent, influence the destiny of the world through the secret power of her love.

Each one of our lives is useful. You may be poor, sick, old, ignored, lost, despised, but in Christ you have the great power of those God loves. God unites us to his Son to manifest the strength of his love. God who gave his Son to save us placed him in our hands, as he gives us the eucharistic body. He wants to associate us to this work, this task of redemption in which each one of us and each moment of our life matters. What matters is not what the newspapers print or what people see, it is the invisible and all powerful love which, little by little, builds the Kingdom of God until the day when he will wipe away all the tears from our eyes. He comes to dwell among us to make us like him, to save us and make us live, to share with us the joy of God, to make us discover the joy of being human and of accepting ourselves for he restores us to our true dignity as kings of creation, as beloved children of God. He gives us the joy of loving one another and of living in the communion of God, the very joy of Redemption in this paradoxical love of which the crucified is the sign: lost man, hanging on the cross, who by the power of the Resurrection is now a hope for all humankind.

Thérèse prophesies youth, Thérèse prophesies the holiness given to us all by the pardon that we, sinners, receive. Thérèse prophesies the incredible relevance of the Redemption in which we too participate and act in Christ.

Thérèse, this giant, "the greatest saint of modern times" because she is only a very ordinary young girl, hidden in the obscurity of a Carmelite convent in Normandy. Thérèse, little Thérèse, a real heroine because she is nothing but the sign of the power of love that God has for us all.

Thérèse, our little sister. What he did for her, God is doing for us too.